COMPILATION OF SELECTED
ECONOMIC DEVELOPMENT LAWS

As amended through the 118th Congress.

Prepared By M. TWINCHEK

2025

Forward

T his Compilation of Selected United States Economic Development Laws is a resource for those interested in U.S. laws governing economic development programs. This compilation includes laws governing the Economic Development Administration, the Appalachian Regional Commission, the Denali Commission, and other similar commissions and authorities.

The materials included comes from publicly available, open source information, prepared for the public by the Office of the Legislative Counsel of the U.S. House of Representatives and the Office of the Law Revision Counsel.

Items listed as a Statute Compilation do not appear in the U.S. Code or that have been classified to a title of the U.S. Code that has not been enacted into positive law. Each Statute Compilation incorporates the amendments made to the underlying statute since it was originally enacted and are current as of the date noted.

This compilation is not an official document and should not be cited as evidence of any law. The official version of Federal law is found in the United States Statutes at Large and in the U.S. Code, the legal effect of which is established in sections 112 and 204, respectively, of title 1, United States Code.

A special thanks is extended to the Office of Law Revision Counsel and the House Office of the Legislative Counsel for providing the U.S. Code and statute compilations; and to the Government Publications Office for hosting and making these available for use to the public. An additional thank you is offered to the staff of the House Committee who were gracious in responding to inquiries and providing background information on the legislation included. Questions and comments may be directed to:

M. Twinchek
Email: mtwinchek@outlook.com

Contents

Forward   i

Title 42 U.S.C., Chapter 28– Public Works and Economic Development   1
Economic Development Administration Reauthorization Act of 2004 - Sec. 605 .   57
Appalachian Regional Development   61
Regional Economic and Infrastructure Development 101
Denali Commission 133
Energy Policy Act of 2005–Sec. 356 151
Department of Transportation and Related Agencies Appropriations Act, 1999–Sec.
    329 155
Delta Regional Authority 159
Great Northern Plains Regional Authority 175
Federal Capital Investment Program Information Act of 1984 193
Title 31 U.S.C. Sec. 1105(e) 197
Delta Regional Authority Act of 2000 203
Economic Development Reauthorization Act of 2024 209

Public Works and Economic Development

Development

Title 42 U.S.C., Chapter 28

CHAPTER 38—PUBLIC WORKS AND ECONOMIC DEVELOPMENT

Sec.
3121. Findings and declarations.
3122. Definitions.
3123. Discrimination on basis of sex prohibited in federally assisted programs.

SUBCHAPTER I—ECONOMIC DEVELOPMENT PARTNERSHIPS COOPERATION AND COORDINATION.

3131. Establishment of economic development partnerships.
3132. Cooperation of Federal agencies.
3133. Coordination.

SUBCHAPTER II—GRANTS FOR PUBLIC WORKS AND ECONOMIC DEVELOPMENT.

3141. Grants for public works and economic development.
3142. Base closings and realignments.
3143. Grants for planning and grants for administrative expenses.
3144. Cost sharing.
3145. Supplementary grants.
3146. Regulations on relative needs and allocations.
3147. Grants for training, research, and technical assistance.
3148. Investment priorities.
3149. Grants for economic adjustment.
3150. Changed project circumstances.
3151. Use of funds in projects constructed under projected cost.
3152. Reports by recipients.
3153. Prohibition on use of funds for attorney's and consultant's fees.
3154. Special impact areas.
3154a. Performance awards.
3154b. Planning performance awards.
3154c. Direct expenditure or redistribution by recipient.
3154d. Renewable energy program.
3154e. Workforce training grants.
3154f. Congressional notification requirements.
3154g. High-speed broadband deployment initiative.
3154h. Critical Supply Chain Site Development grant program.

3

SUBCHAPTER III—ELIGIBILITY; COMPREHENSIVE ECONOMIC
DEVELOPMENT STRATEGIES.

3161.   Eligibility of areas.
3162.   Comprehensive economic development strategies.

SUBCHAPTER IV—ECONOMIC DEVELOPMENT DISTRICTS.

3171.   Designation of economic development districts.
3172.   Termination or modification of economic development districts.
3173.   Repealed.
3174.   Provision of comprehensive economic development strategies to Regional Commissions.
3175.   Assistance to parts of economic development districts not in eligible areas.

SUBCHAPTER V—ADMINISTRATION.

3191.   Assistant Secretary for Economic Development.
3192.   Economic development information clearinghouse.
3193.   Consultation with other persons and agencies.
3194.   Administration, operation, and maintenance.
3195.   Repealed.
3196.   Performance evaluations of grant recipients.
3197.   Notification of reorganization.
3198.   Office of Tribal Economic Development.
3199.   Office of Disaster Recovery and Resilience.
3200.   Technical Assistance Liaisons.

SUBCHAPTER VI—MISCELLANEOUS.

3211.   Powers of Secretary.
3212.   Maintenance of standards.
3213.   Annual report to Congress.
3214.   Delegation of functions and transfer of funds among Federal agencies.
3215.   Penalties.
3216.   Employment of expediters and administrative employees.
3217.   Maintenance and public inspection of list of approved applications for financial assistance.
3218.   Records and audits.
3219.   Relationship to assistance under other law.
3220.   Acceptance of certifications by applicants.
3221.   Brownfields redevelopment report.
3222.   Savings clause.

SUBCHAPTER VII—FUNDING.

3231.   General authorization of appropriations.
3232.   Authorization of appropriations for defense conversion activities.
3233.   Authorization of appropriations for disaster economic recovery

activities.
3234.   Repealed.

§3121. FINDINGS AND DECLARATIONS

(a) FINDINGS.—

Congress finds that—

(1) there continue to be areas of the United States experiencing chronic high unemployment, underemployment, outmigration, and low per capita incomes, as well as areas facing sudden and severe economic dislocations because of structural economic changes, changing trade patterns, certain Federal actions (including environmental requirements that result in the removal of economic activities from a locality), and natural disasters;

(2) economic growth in the States, cities, and rural areas of the United States is produced by expanding economic opportunities, expanding free enterprise through trade, developing and strengthening public infrastructure, and creating a climate for job creation and business development;

(3) the goal of Federal economic development programs is to raise the standard of living for all citizens and increase the wealth and overall rate of growth of the economy by encouraging communities to develop a more competitive and diversified economic base by—

(A) creating an environment that promotes economic activity by improving and expanding public infrastructure;

(B) promoting job creation through increased innovation, productivity, and entrepreneurship; and

(C) empowering local and regional communities experiencing chronic high unemployment and low per capita income to develop private sector business and attract increased private sector capital investment;

(4) while economic development is an inherently local process, the Federal Government should work in partnership with public and private State, regional, tribal, and local organizations to maximize the impact of existing resources and enable regions, communities, and citizens to participate more fully in the American dream and national prosperity;

(5) in order to avoid duplication of effort and achieve meaningful, long-lasting results, Federal, State, tribal, and local economic development activities should have a clear focus, improved coordination, a comprehensive approach, and simplified and consistent requirements; and

(6) Federal economic development efforts will be more effective if the efforts are coordinated with, and build upon, the trade, workforce investment, transportation, and technology programs of the United States.

(b) DECLARATIONS.—

In order to promote a strong and growing economy throughout the United States, Congress declares that—

(1) assistance under this chapter should be made available to both rural- and urban-distressed communities;

(2) local communities should work in partnership with neighboring communities,

the States, Indian tribes, and the Federal Government to increase the capacity of the local communities to develop and implement comprehensive economic development strategies to alleviate economic distress and enhance competitiveness in the global economy;

(3) whether suffering from long-term distress or a sudden dislocation, distressed communities should be encouraged to support entrepreneurship to take advantage of the development opportunities afforded by technological innovation and expanding newly opened global markets; and

(4) assistance under this chapter should be made available to promote the productive reuse of abandoned industrial facilities and the redevelopment of brownfields.

(Pub. L. 89–136, §2, as added Pub. L. 105–393, title I, §102(a), Nov. 13, 1998, 112 Stat. 3598; amended Pub. L. 108–373, title I, §101, Oct. 27, 2004, 118 Stat. 1757.)

§3122. DEFINITIONS

In this chapter:

(1) BLUE ECONOMY.—

The term "blue economy" means the sustainable use of marine, lake, or other aquatic resources in support of economic development objectives.

(2) CAPACITY BUILDING.—

The term "capacity building" includes all activities associated with early stage community-based project formation and conceptualization, prior to project predevelopment activity, including grants to local community organizations for planning participation, community outreach and engagement activities, research, and mentorship support to move projects from formation and conceptualization to project predevelopment.

(3) COMPREHENSIVE ECONOMIC DEVELOPMENT STRATEGY.—

The term "comprehensive economic development strategy" means a comprehensive economic development strategy approved by the Secretary under section 3162 of this title.

(4) DEPARTMENT.—

The term "Department" means the Department of Commerce.

(5) ECONOMIC DEVELOPMENT DISTRICT.—

(A) IN GENERAL.—

The term "economic development district" means any area in the United States that—

(i) is composed of areas described in section 3161(a) of this title and, to the extent determined appropriate by the Secretary, neighboring counties or communities; and

(ii) has been designated by the Secretary as an economic development district under section 3171 of this title.

(B) INCLUSION.—

The term "economic development district" includes any economic development district designated by the Secretary under section 3173 of this title (as in effect on the day before the effective date of the Economic Development Administration

Reform Act of 1998).

(6) ELIGIBLE RECIPIENT.—

(A) IN GENERAL.—

The term "eligible recipient" means—

(i) an economic development district;

(ii) an Indian tribe;

(iii) a State;

(iv) a city or other political subdivision of a State, including a special purpose unit of a State or local government engaged in economic or infrastructure development activities, or a consortium of political subdivisions;

(v) an institution of higher education or a consortium of institutions of higher education;

(vi) a public or private nonprofit organization or association acting in cooperation with officials of a political subdivision of a State;

(vii) an economic development organization; or

(viii) a public-private partnership for public infrastructure.

(B) TRAINING, RESEARCH, AND TECHNICAL ASSISTANCE GRANTS.—

In the case of grants under section 3147 of this title, the term "eligible recipient" also includes private individuals and for-profit organizations.

(7) FEDERAL AGENCY.—

The term "Federal agency" means a department, agency, or instrumentality of the United States.

(8) GRANT.—

The term "grant" includes a cooperative agreement (within the meaning of chapter 63 of title 31).

(9) INDIAN TRIBE.—

The term "Indian tribe" means any Indian tribe, band, nation, pueblo, or other organized group or community, including any Alaska Native village or Regional Corporation (as defined in or established under the Alaska Native Claims Settlement Act (43 U.S.C. 1601 et seq.)), that is recognized as eligible for the special programs and services provided by the United States to Indians because of their status as Indians.

(10) OUTDOOR RECREATION.—

The term "outdoor recreation" means all recreational activities, and the economic drivers of those activities, that occur in nature-based environments outdoors.

(11) PROJECT PREDEVELOPMENT.—

The term "project predevelopment" means a measure required to be completed before the initiation of a project, including—

(A) planning and community asset mapping;

(B) training;

(C) technical assistance and organizational development;

(D) feasibility and market studies;

(E) demonstration projects; and

(F) other predevelopment activities determined by the Secretary to be appropriate.

(12) REGIONAL COMMISSION.—

The term "Regional Commission" means any of the following:

(A) The Appalachian Regional Commission established by section 14301(a) of title 40.

(B) The Delta Regional Authority established by section 2009aa–1(a)(1) of title 7.

(C) The Denali Commission established by section 303(a) of the Denali Commission Act of 1998 (42 U.S.C. 3121 note; Public Law 105–277).

(D) The Great Lakes Authority established by section 15301(a)(4) of title 40.

(E) The Mid-Atlantic Regional Commission established by section 15301(a)(5) of title 40.

(F) The Northern Border Regional Commission established by section 15301(a)(3) of title 40.

(G) The Northern Great Plains Regional Authority established by section 2009bb–1(a)(1) of title 7.

(H) The Southeast Crescent Regional Commission established by section 15301(a)(1) of title 40.

(I) The Southern New England Regional Commission established by section 15301(a)(6) of title 40.

(J) The Southwest Border Regional Commission established by section 15301(a)(2) of title 40.

(13) SECRETARY.—

The term "Secretary" means the Secretary of Commerce.

(14) STATE.—

The term "State" means a State, the District of Columbia, the Commonwealth of Puerto Rico, the Virgin Islands, Guam, American Samoa, the Commonwealth of the Northern Mariana Islands, the Republic of the Marshall Islands, the Federated States of Micronesia, and the Republic of Palau.

(15) TRAVEL AND TOURISM.—

The term "travel and tourism" means any economic activity that primarily serves to encourage recreational or business travel in or to the United States, including activities relating to public or nonprofit entertainment venues in the United States.

(16) UNITED STATES.—

The term "United States" means all of the States.

(17) UNIVERSITY CENTER.—

The term "university center" means an institution of higher education or a consortium of institutions of higher education established under section 3147(c)(1) of this title.

(Pub. L. 89–136, §3, as added Pub. L. 105–393, title I, §102(a), Nov. 13, 1998, 112 Stat. 3599; amended Pub. L. 108–373, title I, §102, Oct. 27, 2004, 118 Stat. 1758; Pub. L. 118–272, div. B, title II, §2211(a), Jan. 4, 2025, 138 Stat. 3177.)

§3123. DISCRIMINATION ON BASIS OF SEX PROHIBITED IN FEDERALLY ASSISTED PROGRAMS

No person in the United States shall, on the ground of sex, be excluded from participation in, be denied the benefits of, or be subjected to discrimination under any program or activity receiving Federal financial assistance under the Public Works and Economic Development Act of 1965 [42 U.S.C. 3121 et seq.].

(Pub. L. 92–65, title I, §112, Aug. 5, 1971, 85 Stat. 168.)

SUBCHAPTER I—ECONOMIC DEVELOPMENT PARTNERSHIPS COOPERATION AND COORDINATION

§3131. ESTABLISHMENT OF ECONOMIC DEVELOPMENT PARTNERSHIPS

(a) IN GENERAL.—

In providing assistance under this subchapter, the Secretary shall cooperate with States and other entities to ensure that, consistent with national objectives, Federal programs are compatible with and further the objectives of State, regional, and local economic development plans and comprehensive economic development strategies.

(b) TECHNICAL ASSISTANCE.—

The Secretary may provide such technical assistance to States, political subdivisions of States, sub-State regional organizations (including organizations that cross State boundaries), multi-State regional organizations, and nonprofit organizations as the Secretary determines is appropriate to—

(1) alleviate economic distress;

(2) encourage and support public-private partnerships for the formation and improvement of economic development strategies that sustain and promote economic development across the United States; and

(3) promote investment in infrastructure and technological capacity to keep pace with the changing global economy.

(c) INTERGOVERNMENTAL REVIEW.—

The Secretary shall promulgate regulations to ensure that appropriate State and local government agencies have been given a reasonable opportunity to review and comment on proposed projects under this subchapter that the Secretary determines may have a significant direct impact on the economy of the area.

(d) COOPERATION AGREEMENTS.—

(1) IN GENERAL.—

The Secretary may enter into a cooperation agreement with any 2 or more States, or an organization of any 2 or more States, in support of effective economic development.

(2) PARTICIPATION.—

Each cooperation agreement shall provide for suitable participation by other governmental and nongovernmental entities that are representative of significant interests in and perspectives on economic development in an area.

(Pub. L. 89–136, title I, §101, as added Pub. L. 105–393, title I, §102(a), Nov. 13, 1998, 112 Stat. 3600; amended Pub. L. 108–373, title I, §103, Oct. 27, 2004, 118 Stat. 1759.)

§3132. COOPERATION OF FEDERAL AGENCIES

In accordance with applicable laws and subject to the availability of appropriations, each Federal agency shall exercise its powers, duties and functions, and shall cooperate with the Secretary, in such manner as will assist the Secretary in carrying out this subchapter.

(Pub. L. 89–136, title I, §102, as added Pub. L. 105–393, title I, §102(a), Nov. 13, 1998, 112 Stat. 3601.)

§3133. Coordination

(a) In general.—

The Secretary shall coordinate activities relating to the preparation and implementation of comprehensive economic development strategies under this chapter with Federal agencies carrying out other Federal programs, States, economic development districts, Indian tribes, and other appropriate planning and development organizations.

(b) Meetings.—

(1) In general.—

To carry out subsection (a), or for any other purpose relating to economic development activities, the Secretary may convene meetings with Federal agencies, State and local governments, economic development districts, Indian tribes, and other appropriate planning and development organizations.

(2) Regional commissions.—

(A) In general.—

In addition to meetings described in paragraph (1), not later than 1 year after January 4, 2025, and not less frequently than every 2 years thereafter, the Secretary shall convene a meeting with the Regional Commissions in furtherance of subsection (a).

(B) Attendees.—

The attendees for a meeting convened under this paragraph shall consist of—

(i) the Secretary, acting through the Assistant Secretary of Commerce for Economic Development, serving as Chair;

(ii) the Federal Cochairpersons of the Regional Commissions, or their designees; and

(iii) the State Cochairpersons of the Regional Commissions, or their designees.

(C) Purpose.—

The purposes of a meeting convened under this paragraph shall include—

(i) to enhance coordination between the Economic Development Administration and the Regional Commissions in carrying out economic development programs;

(ii) to reduce duplication of efforts by the Economic Development Administration and the Regional Commissions in carrying out economic development programs;

(iii) to develop best practices and strategies for fostering regional economic development; and

(iv) any other purposes as determined appropriate by the Secretary.

(D) Report.—

Where applicable and pursuant to subparagraph (C), not later than 1 year after a meeting under this paragraph, the Secretary shall prepare and make publicly available a report detailing, at a minimum—

    (i) the planned actions by the Economic Development Administration and the Regional Commissions to enhance coordination or reduce duplication of efforts and a timeline for implementing those actions; and

    (ii) any best practices and strategies developed.

(Pub. L. 89–136, title I, §103, as added Pub. L. 105–393, title I, §102(a), Nov. 13, 1998, 112 Stat. 3601; amended Pub. L. 108–373, title I, §104, Oct. 27, 2004, 118 Stat. 1759; Pub. L. 118–272, div. B, title II, §2212, Jan. 4, 2025, 138 Stat. 3178.)

SUBCHAPTER II—GRANTS FOR PUBLIC WORKS AND ECONOMIC DEVELOPMENT

§3141. GRANTS FOR PUBLIC WORKS AND ECONOMIC DEVELOPMENT

(a) IN GENERAL.—

On the application of an eligible recipient, the Secretary may make grants for—

    (1) acquisition or development of land and improvements for use for a public works, public service, or development facility or for the improvement of waste management and recycling systems; and

    (2) acquisition, design and engineering, construction, rehabilitation, alteration, expansion, increasing the resilience [1] or improvement of such a facility, including related machinery and equipment.

(b) CRITERIA FOR GRANT.—

The Secretary may make a grant under this section only if the Secretary determines that—

    (1) the project for which the grant is applied for will, directly or indirectly—

        (A) improve the opportunities, in the area where the project is or will be located, for the successful establishment, expansion, or retention,[2] of industrial or commercial plants or facilities;

        (B) assist in the creation of additional long-term employment opportunities in the area; or

        (C) primarily benefit the long-term unemployed and underemployed and members of low-income families;

    (2) the project for which the grant is applied for will fulfill a pressing need of the area, or a part of the area, in which the project is or will be located; and

    (3) the area for which the project is to be carried out has a comprehensive economic development strategy and the project is consistent with the strategy.

(c) ADDITIONAL CONSIDERATIONS.—

In awarding grants under subsection (a) and subject to the criteria in subsection (b), the Secretary may also consider the extent to which a project would—

    (1) lead to economic diversification in the area, or a part of the area, in which the project is or will be located;

    (2) address and mitigate economic impacts from extreme weather events, including development of resilient infrastructure, products, and processes;

    (3) benefit highly rural communities without adequate tax revenues to invest in long-term or costly infrastructure;

(4) increase access to high-speed broadband;

(5) support outdoor recreation to spur economic development, with a focus on rural communities;

(6) promote job creation or retention relative to the population of the impacted region with outsized significance;

(7) promote travel and tourism; or

(8) promote blue economy activities.

(d) MAXIMUM ASSISTANCE FOR EACH STATE.—

Not more than 15 percent of the amounts made available to carry out this section may be expended in any 1 State.

(Pub. L. 89–136, title II, §201, as added Pub. L. 105–393, title I, §102(a), Nov. 13, 1998, 112 Stat. 3601; amended Pub. L. 118–272, div. B, title II, §2213(a), Jan. 4, 2025, 138 Stat. 3179.)

[1] So in original. Probably should be followed by a comma.

[2] So in original. The comma probably should not appear.

§3142. BASE CLOSINGS AND REALIGNMENTS

Notwithstanding any other provision of law, the Secretary may provide to an eligible recipient any assistance available under this subchapter for a project to be carried out on a military or Department of Energy installation that is closed or scheduled for closure or realignment without requiring that the eligible recipient have title to the property or a leasehold interest in the property for any specified term.

(Pub. L. 89–136, title II, §202, as added Pub. L. 105–393, title I, §102(a), Nov. 13, 1998, 112 Stat. 3602.)

§3143. GRANTS FOR PLANNING AND GRANTS FOR ADMINISTRATIVE EXPENSES

(a) IN GENERAL.—

On the application of an eligible recipient, the Secretary may make grants to pay the costs of economic development planning and the administrative expenses of organizations that carry out the planning.

(b) PLANNING PROCESS.—

Planning assisted under this subchapter shall be a continuous process involving public officials and private citizens in—

(1) analyzing local economies;

(2) defining economic development goals;

(3) determining project opportunities; and

(4) formulating and implementing an economic development program that includes systematic efforts to reduce unemployment and increase incomes.

(c) USE OF PLANNING ASSISTANCE.—

Planning assistance under this subchapter shall be used in conjunction with any other available Federal planning assistance to ensure adequate and effective planning and economical use of funds.

(d) ADMINISTRATIVE EXPENSES.—

Administrative expenses that may be paid with a grant under this section include—

(1) expenses related to carrying out the planning process described in subsection (b);

(2) expenses related to project predevelopment;

(3) expenses related to updating economic development plans to align with other applicable State, regional, or local planning efforts; and

(4) expenses related to hiring professional staff to assist communities in—

(A) project predevelopment and implementing projects and priorities included in—

(i) a comprehensive economic development strategy; or

(ii) an economic development planning grant;

(B) identifying and using other Federal, State, and Tribal economic development programs;

(C) leveraging private and philanthropic investment;

(D) preparing economic recovery plans in response to disasters; and

(E) carrying out economic development and predevelopment activities in accordance with professional economic development best practices.

(e) STATE PLANS.—

(1) DEVELOPMENT.—

Any State plan developed with assistance under this section shall be developed, to the maximum extent practicable, cooperatively by the State, political subdivisions of the State, and the economic development districts located wholly or partially in the State.

(2) COMPREHENSIVE ECONOMIC DEVELOPMENT STRATEGY.—

As a condition of receipt of assistance for a State plan under this subsection, the State shall have or develop a comprehensive economic development strategy.

(3) COORDINATION.—

Before providing assistance for a State plan under this section, the Secretary shall consider the extent to which the State will consider local and economic development district plans.

(4) COMPREHENSIVE PLANNING PROCESS.—

Any overall State economic development planning assisted under this section shall be a part of a comprehensive planning process that shall consider the provision of public works to—

(A) promote economic development and opportunity;

(B) foster effective transportation access;

(C) enhance and protect the environment;

(D) assist in carrying out the workforce investment strategy of a State;

(E) promote the use of technology in economic development, including access to high-speed telecommunications (including broadband);

(F) address and mitigate economic impacts of extreme weather; and

(G) balance resources through the sound management of physical development.

(5) REPORT TO SECRETARY.—

Each State that receives assistance for the development of a plan under this subsection shall submit to the Secretary an annual report on the planning process assisted under this subsection.

(Pub. L. 89–136, title II, §203, as added Pub. L. 105–393, title I, §102(a), Nov. 13, 1998, 112 Stat. 3602; amended Pub. L. 108–373, title II, §201, Oct. 27, 2004, 118 Stat. 1759; Pub. L. 118–272, div. B, title II,

§2214, Jan. 4, 2025, 138 Stat. 3180.)

§3144. COST SHARING

(a) FEDERAL SHARE.—

Except as provided in subsection (c), the Federal share of the cost of any project carried out under this subchapter shall not exceed—

(1) 60 percent; plus

(2) an additional percent that—

(A) shall not exceed 30 percent; and

(B) is based on the relative needs of the area in which the project will be located, as determined in accordance with regulations promulgated by the Secretary.

(b) NON-FEDERAL SHARE.—

(1) IN GENERAL.—

In determining the amount of the non-Federal share of the cost of a project, the Secretary may provide credit toward the non-Federal share for all contributions both in cash and in-kind, fairly evaluated, including contributions of space, equipment, assumptions of debt, and services.

(2) REGIONAL COMMISSION FUNDS.—

Notwithstanding any other provision of law, any funds contributed by a Regional Commission for a project under this subchapter may be considered to be part of the non-Federal share of the costs of the project.

(c) Increase in Federal share.—

(1) INDIAN TRIBES.—

In the case of a grant to an Indian tribe for a project under this subchapter, the Secretary may increase the Federal share above the percentage specified in subsection (a) up to 100 percent of the cost of the project.

(2) CERTAIN STATES, POLITICAL SUBDIVISIONS, AND NONPROFIT ORGANIZATIONS.—

In the case of a grant to a State, or a political subdivision of a State, that the Secretary determines has exhausted the effective taxing and borrowing capacity of the State or political subdivision or can otherwise document that no local matching funds are reasonably obtainable, or in the case of a grant to a nonprofit organization that the Secretary determines has exhausted the effective borrowing capacity of the nonprofit organization, the Secretary may increase the Federal share above the percentage specified in subsection (a) up to 100 percent of the cost of the project.

(3) TRAINING, RESEARCH, AND TECHNICAL ASSISTANCE.—

In the case of a grant provided under section 3143 or 3147 of this title, the Secretary may increase the Federal share above the percentage specified in subsection (a) up to 100 percent of the cost of the project.

(4) SMALL COMMUNITIES.—

In the case of a grant to a political subdivision of a State (as described in section 3122(6)(A)(iv) of this title) that has a population of fewer than 10,000 residents and meets 1 or more of the eligibility criteria described in section 3161(a) of this title, the Secretary may increase the Federal share under paragraph (1) up to 100 percent of the total cost of the project.

(Pub. L. 89–136, title II, §204, as added Pub. L. 105–393, title I, §102(a), Nov. 13, 1998, 112 Stat. 3603;

amended Pub. L. 108–373, title II, §202, Oct. 27, 2004, 118 Stat. 1759; Pub. L. 118–272, div. B, title II, §2215, Jan. 4, 2025, 138 Stat. 3181.)

§3145. SUPPLEMENTARY GRANTS

(a) DEFINITION OF DESIGNATED FEDERAL GRANT PROGRAM.—

In this section, the term "designated Federal grant program" means any Federal grant program that—

(1) provides assistance in the construction or equipping of public works, public service, or development facilities;

(2) the Secretary designates as eligible for an allocation of funds under this section; and

(3) assists projects that are—

(A) eligible for assistance under this subchapter; and

(B) consistent with a comprehensive economic development strategy.

(b) SUPPLEMENTARY GRANTS.—

Subject to subsection (c), in order to assist eligible recipients in taking advantage of designated Federal grant programs, on the application of an eligible recipient, the Secretary may make a supplementary grant for a project for which the recipient is eligible but for which the recipient cannot provide the required non-Federal share because of the economic situation of the recipient.

(c) REQUIREMENTS APPLICABLE TO SUPPLEMENTARY GRANTS.—

(1) Amount of supplementary grants.—

The share of the project cost supported by a supplementary grant under this section may not exceed the applicable Federal share under section 3144 of this title.

(2) FORM OF SUPPLEMENTARY GRANTS.—

The Secretary shall make supplementary grants by—

(A) the payment of funds made available under this chapter to the heads of the Federal agencies responsible for carrying out the applicable Federal programs; or

(B) the award of funds under this chapter, which will be combined with funds transferred from other Federal agencies in projects administered by the Secretary.

(3) FEDERAL SHARE LIMITATIONS SPECIFIED IN OTHER LAWS.—

Notwithstanding any requirement as to the amount or source of non-Federal funds that may be applicable to a Federal program, funds provided under this section may be used to increase the Federal share for specific projects under the program that are carried out in areas described in section 3161(a) of this title above the Federal share of the cost of the project authorized by the law governing the program.

(Pub. L. 89–136, title II, §205, as added Pub. L. 105–393, title I, §102(a), Nov. 13, 1998, 112 Stat. 3603; amended Pub. L. 108–373, title II, §203, Oct. 27, 2004, 118 Stat. 1760.)

§3146. REGULATIONS ON RELATIVE NEEDS AND ALLOCATIONS

In promulgating rules, regulations, and procedures for assistance under this subchapter, the Secretary shall ensure that—

(1) the relative needs of eligible areas are given adequate consideration by the Secretary, as determined based on, among other relevant factors—

(A) the severity of the rates of unemployment in the eligible areas and the duration of the unemployment;

(B) the per capita income levels, the labor force participation rate, and the extent of underemployment in eligible areas; and

(C) the outmigration of population from eligible areas and the extent to which the outmigration is causing economic injury in the eligible areas;

(2) allocations of assistance under this subchapter are prioritized to ensure that the level of economic distress of an area, rather than a preference for a geographic area or a specific type of economic distress, is the primary factor in allocating the assistance;

(3)(A) rural and urban economically distressed areas are not harmed by the establishment or implementation by the Secretary of a private sector leveraging goal for a project under this subchapter;

(B) any private sector leveraging goal established by the Secretary does not prohibit or discourage grant applicants under this subchapter from public works in, or economic development of, rural or urban economically distressed areas; and

(C) the relevant Committees of Congress are notified prior to making any changes to any private sector leveraging goal; and

(4) grants made under this subchapter promote job creation and retention and will have a high probability of meeting or exceeding applicable performance requirements established in connection with the grants.

(Pub. L. 89–136, title II, §206, as added Pub. L. 105–393, title I, §102(a), Nov. 13, 1998, 112 Stat. 3604; amended Pub. L. 108–373, title II, §204, Oct. 27, 2004, 118 Stat. 1761; Pub. L. 118–272, div. B, title II, §2216, Jan. 4, 2025, 138 Stat. 3181.)

§3147. Grants for training, research, and technical assistance

(a) In general.—

(1) Grants.—

On the application of an eligible recipient, the Secretary may make grants for training, research, and technical assistance, including grants for program evaluation and economic impact analyses, that would be useful in alleviating or preventing conditions of excessive unemployment or underemployment.

(2) Types of assistance.—

Grants under paragraph (1) may be used for—

(A) project planning, project predevelopment, and feasibility studies;

(B) demonstrations of innovative activities or strategic economic development investments;

(C) management and operational assistance;

(D) establishment of university centers;

(E) establishment of business outreach centers;

(F) studies evaluating the needs of, and development potential for, economic growth of areas that the Secretary determines have substantial need for the assistance;

(G) studies that evaluate the effectiveness of coordinating projects funded under this chapter with projects funded under other Acts;

(H) assessment, marketing, and establishment of business clusters; and

(I) other activities determined by the Secretary to be appropriate.

(3) COOPERATION REQUIREMENT.—

In the case of a project assisted under this section that is national or regional in scope, the Secretary may waive the provision in section 3122(6)(A)(vi) of this title requiring a nonprofit organization or association to act in cooperation with officials of a political subdivision of a State.

(b) METHODS OF PROVISION OF ASSISTANCE.—

In providing research and technical assistance under this section, the Secretary, in addition to making grants under subsection (a), may—

(1) provide research and technical assistance through officers or employees of the Department;

(2) pay funds made available to carry out this section to Federal agencies; or

(3) employ private individuals, partnerships, businesses, corporations, or appropriate institutions under contracts entered into for that purpose.

(c) UNIVERSITY CENTERS.—

(1) ESTABLISHMENT.—

In accordance with subsection (a)(2)(D), the Secretary may make grants to institutions of higher education to serve as university centers.

(2) GEOGRAPHIC COVERAGE.—

The Secretary shall ensure that the network of university centers established under this subsection provides services in each State.

(3) DUTIES.—

To the maximum extent practicable, a university center established under this subsection shall—

(A) collaborate with other university centers;

(B) collaborate with economic development districts and other relevant Federal economic development technical assistance and service providers to provide expertise and technical assistance to develop, implement, and support comprehensive economic development strategies and other economic development planning at the local, regional, and State levels, with a focus on innovation, entrepreneurship, workforce development, and regional economic development;

(C) provide technical assistance, business development, and technology transfer services to businesses in the area served by the university center;

(D) establish partnerships with 1 or more commercialization intermediaries that are public or nonprofit technology transfer organizations eligible to receive a grant under section 1862s–9 of this title;

(E) promote local and regional capacity building; and

(F) provide to communities and regions assistance relating to data collection and analysis and other research relating to economic conditions and vulnerabilities that can inform economic development and adjustment strategies.

(4) CONSIDERATION.—

In making grants under this subsection, the Secretary shall consider—

(A) the significant role of regional public universities in supporting economic development in distressed communities through the planning and the implementation of economic development projects and initiatives; and

(B) the location of the university center in or near a distressed community.

(Pub. L. 89–136, title II, §207, as added Pub. L. 105–393, title I, §102(a), Nov. 13, 1998, 112 Stat. 3604; amended Pub. L. 108–373, title II, §205, Oct. 27, 2004, 118 Stat. 1761; Pub. L. 118–272, div. B, title II, §§2211(b), 2217, Jan. 4, 2025, 138 Stat. 3178, 3181.)

§3148. INVESTMENT PRIORITIES

(a) IN GENERAL.—

Subject to subsection (b), for a project to be eligible for assistance under this subchapter, the project shall be consistent with 1 or more of the following investment priorities:

(1) CRITICAL INFRASTRUCTURE.—

Economic development planning or implementation projects that support development of public facilities, including basic public infrastructure, transportation infrastructure, or telecommunications infrastructure.

(2) WORKFORCE.—

Economic development planning or implementation projects that—

(A) support job skills training to meet the hiring needs of the area in which the project is to be carried out and that result in well-paying jobs; or

(B) otherwise promote labor force participation.

(3) INNOVATION AND ENTREPRENEURSHIP.—

Economic development planning or implementation projects that—

(A) support the development of innovation and entrepreneurship-related infrastructure;

(B) promote business development and lending; or

(C) foster the commercialization of new technologies that are creating technology-driven businesses and high-skilled, well-paying jobs of the future.

(4) ECONOMIC RECOVERY RESILIENCE.—

Economic development planning or implementation projects that enhance the ability of an area to withstand and recover from adverse short-term or long-term changes in economic conditions, including effects from industry contractions or economic impacts from natural disasters.

(5) MANUFACTURING.—

Economic development planning or implementation projects that encourage job creation, business expansion, technology and capital upgrades, and productivity growth in manufacturing, including efforts that contribute to the competitiveness and growth of domestic suppliers or the domestic production of innovative, high-value products and production technologies.

(b) CONDITIONS.—

If the Secretary plans to use an investment priority that is not described in subsection (a), the Secretary shall submit to the Committee on Environment and Public Works of the Senate and the Committee on Transportation and Infrastructure of the House of Representatives a written notification that explains the basis for using that investment priority.

(c) SAVINGS CLAUSE.—

Nothing in this section waives any other requirement of this chapter.

(Pub. L. 89–136, title II, §208, as added Pub. L. 118–272, div. B, title II, §2218, Jan. 4, 2025, 138 Stat. 3182.)

§3149. GRANTS FOR ECONOMIC ADJUSTMENT

(a) IN GENERAL.—

On the application of an eligible recipient, the Secretary may make grants for development of public facilities, public services, business development (including funding of a revolving loan fund), planning, technical assistance, training, and any other assistance to alleviate long-term economic deterioration and sudden and severe economic dislocation and further the economic adjustment objectives of this subchapter.

(b) CRITERIA FOR ASSISTANCE.—

The Secretary may provide assistance under this section only if the Secretary determines that—

(1) the project will help the area to meet a special need arising from—

(A) actual or threatened severe unemployment; or

(B) economic adjustment problems resulting from severe changes in economic conditions; and

(2) the area for which a project is to be carried out has a comprehensive economic development strategy and the project is consistent with the strategy, except that this paragraph shall not apply to planning projects.

(c) PARTICULAR COMMUNITY ASSISTANCE.—

Assistance under this section may include assistance provided for activities identified by communities, the economies of which are injured by—

(1) military base closures or realignments, defense contractor reductions in force, or Department of Energy defense-related funding reductions, for help in diversifying their economies through projects to be carried out on Federal Government installations or elsewhere in the communities;

(2) disasters or emergencies, in areas with respect to which a major disaster or emergency has been declared under the Robert T. Stafford Disaster Relief and Emergency Assistance Act (42 U.S.C. 5121 et seq.), for post-disaster economic recovery;

(3) international trade, for help in economic restructuring of the communities;

(4) fishery failures, in areas with respect to which a determination that there is a commercial fishery failure has been made under section 1861a(a) of title 16;

(5) the loss of manufacturing, travel and tourism, natural resource-based, blue economy, or agricultural jobs, for reinvesting in and diversifying the economies of the communities;

(6) economic dislocation in the steel industry due to the closure of a steel plant, primary steel economy contraction events (including temporary layoffs and shifts to part-time work), or job losses in the steel industry or associated with the departure or contraction of the steel industry, for help in economic restructuring of the communities; or

(7) limited water for industrial consumption in areas impacted by decreased water supplies due to drought or extreme heat.

(d) ASSISTANCE TO COAL COMMUNITIES.—

(1) DEFINITIONS.—

In this subsection:

(A) COAL ECONOMY.—

The term "coal economy" means the complete supply chain of coal-reliant industries, including—

    (i) coal mining;

    (ii) coal-fired power plants;

    (iii) transportation or logistics; and

    (iv) manufacturing.

(B) CONTRACTION EVENT.—

The term "contraction event" means the closure of a facility or a reduction in activity relating to a coal-reliant industry, including an industry described in any of clauses (i) through (iv) of subparagraph (A).

(2) AUTHORIZATION.—

On the application of an eligible recipient, the Secretary may make grants for projects in areas adversely impacted by a contraction event in the coal economy.

(3) ELIGIBILITY.—

(A) IN GENERAL.—

In carrying out this subsection, the Secretary shall determine the eligibility of an area based on whether the eligible recipient can reasonably demonstrate that the area—

    (i) has been adversely impacted by a contraction event in the coal economy within the previous 25 years; or

    (ii) will be adversely impacted by a contraction event in the coal economy.

(B) PROHIBITION.—

No regulation or other policy of the Secretary may limit the eligibility of an eligible recipient for a grant under this subsection based on the date of a contraction event except as provided in subparagraph (A)(i).

(C) DEMONSTRATING ADVERSE IMPACT.—

For the purposes of this paragraph, an eligible recipient may demonstrate an adverse impact by demonstrating—

    (i) a loss in employment;

    (ii) a reduction in tax revenue; or

    (iii) any other factor, as determined to be appropriate by the Secretary.

(e) ASSISTANCE TO NUCLEAR HOST COMMUNITIES.—

(1) DEFINITIONS.—

In this subsection:

(A) COMMISSION.—

The term "Commission" means the Nuclear Regulatory Commission.

(B) COMMUNITY ADVISORY BOARD.—

The term "community advisory board" means a community committee or other advisory organization that—

    (i) primarily focuses on the economic impacts of decommissioning activities; and

    (ii) aims to foster communication and information exchange between a licensee planning for and involved in decommissioning activities and members of the community that decommissioning activities may affect.

(C) DECOMMISSION.—

The term "decommission" has the meaning given the term in section 50.2 of title 10, Code of Federal Regulations (or successor regulations).

(D) LICENSEE.—

The term "licensee" has the meaning given the term in section 50.2 of title 10, Code of Federal Regulations (or successor regulations).

(E) NUCLEAR HOST COMMUNITY.—

The term "nuclear host community" means an eligible recipient that has been economically impacted, or reasonably demonstrates to the satisfaction of the Secretary that it will be economically impacted, by a nuclear power plant licensed by the Commission that—

(i) is not co-located with an operating nuclear power plant;

(ii) is at a site with spent nuclear fuel; and

(iii) as of January 4, 2025—

(I) has ceased operations; or

(II) has provided a written notification to the Commission that it will cease operations.

(2) AUTHORIZATION.—

On the application of an eligible recipient, the Secretary may make grants—

(A) to assist with economic development in nuclear host communities; and

(B) to fund community advisory boards in nuclear host communities.

(3) REQUIREMENT.—

In carrying out this subsection, to the maximum extent practicable, the Secretary shall implement the recommendations described in the report submitted to Congress under section 108 of the Nuclear Energy Innovation and Modernization Act (Public Law 115–439; 132 Stat. 5577) entitled "Best Practices for Establishment and Operation of Local Community Advisory Boards Associated with Decommissioning Activities at Nuclear Power Plants".

(4) DISTRIBUTION OF FUNDS.—

The Secretary shall establish a methodology to ensure, to the maximum extent practicable, geographic diversity among grant recipients under this subsection.

(f) SPECIAL PROVISIONS RELATING TO REVOLVING LOAN FUND GRANTS.—

(1) IN GENERAL.—

The Secretary shall promulgate regulations to maintain the proper operation and financial integrity of revolving loan funds established by recipients with assistance under this section.

(2) EFFICIENT ADMINISTRATION.—

The Secretary may—

(A) at the request of a grantee, amend and consolidate grant agreements governing revolving loan funds to provide flexibility with respect to lending areas and borrower criteria;

(B) assign or transfer assets of a revolving loan fund to third party for the purpose of liquidation, and the third party may retain assets of the fund to defray costs related to liquidation; and

(C) take such actions as are appropriate to enable revolving loan fund operators to sell or securitize loans (except that the actions may not include issuance of a

Federal guaranty by the Secretary).

(3) TREATMENT OF ACTIONS.—

An action taken by the Secretary under this subsection with respect to a revolving loan fund shall not constitute a new obligation if all grant funds associated with the original grant award have been disbursed to the recipient.

(4) PRESERVATION OF SECURITIES LAWS.—

(A) Not treated as exempted securities.—

No securities issued pursuant to paragraph (2)(C) shall be treated as exempted securities for purposes of the Securities Act of 1933 (15 U.S.C. 77a et seq.) or the Securities Exchange Act of 1934 (15 U.S.C. 78a et seq.), unless exempted by rule or regulation of the Securities and Exchange Commission.

(B) PRESERVATION.—

Except as provided in subparagraph (A), no provision of this subsection or any regulation promulgated by the Secretary under this subsection supersedes or otherwise affects the application of the securities laws (as the term is defined in section 3(a) of the Securities Exchange Act of 1934 (15 U.S.C. 78c(a))) or the rules, regulations, or orders of the Securities and Exchange Commission or a self-regulatory organization under that Commission.

(g) DISASTER MITIGATION.—

In providing assistance pursuant to subsection (c)(2), if appropriate and as applicable, the Secretary may encourage hazard mitigation in assistance provided pursuant to such subsection.

(Pub. L. 89–136, title II, §209, as added Pub. L. 105–393, title I, §102(a), Nov. 13, 1998, 112 Stat. 3605; amended Pub. L. 108–373, title II, §207, Oct. 27, 2004, 118 Stat. 1762; Pub. L. 115–254, div. D, §1217(a), Oct. 5, 2018, 132 Stat. 3451; Pub. L. 118–272, div. B, title II, §2219, Jan. 4, 2025, 138 Stat. 3183.)

§3150. CHANGED PROJECT CIRCUMSTANCES

In any case in which a grant (including a supplementary grant described in section 3145 of this title) has been made by the Secretary under this subchapter (or made under this chapter, as in effect on the day before the effective date of the Economic Development Administration Reform Act of 1998) for a project, and, after the grant has been made but before completion of the project, the purpose or scope of the project that was the basis of the grant is modified, the Secretary may approve, subject (except for a grant for which funds were obligated in fiscal year 1995) to the availability of appropriations, the use of grant funds for the modified project if the Secretary determines that—

(1) the modified project meets the requirements of this subchapter and is consistent with the comprehensive economic development strategy submitted as part of the application for the grant; and

(2) the modifications are necessary to enhance economic development in the area for which the project is being carried out.

(Pub. L. 89–136, title II, §210, as added Pub. L. 105–393, title I, §102(a), Nov. 13, 1998, 112 Stat. 3606.)

§3151. USE OF FUNDS IN PROJECTS CONSTRUCTED UNDER PROJECTED COST

(a) IN GENERAL.—

In the case of a grant to a recipient for a construction project under section 3141 or 3149 of this title, if the Secretary determines, before closeout of the project, that the cost of the project, based on the designs and specifications that were the basis of the grant, has decreased because of decreases in costs, the Secretary may approve, without further appropriation, the use of the excess funds (or a portion of the excess funds) by the recipient—

(1) to increase the Federal share of the cost of a project under this title to the maximum percentage allowable under section 3144 of this title; or

(2) to improve the project.

(b) OTHER USES OF EXCESS FUNDS.—

Any amount of excess funds remaining after application of subsection (a) may be used by the Secretary for providing assistance under this chapter.

(c) TRANSFERRED FUNDS.—

In the case of excess funds described in subsection (a) in projects using funds transferred from other Federal agencies pursuant to section 3214 of this title, the Secretary shall—

(1) use the funds in accordance with subsection (a), with the approval of the originating agency; or

(2) return the funds to the originating agency.

(Pub. L. 89–136, title II, §211, as added Pub. L. 105–393, title I, §102(a), Nov. 13, 1998, 112 Stat. 3606; amended Pub. L. 108–373, title II, §208, Oct. 27, 2004, 118 Stat. 1763; Pub. L. 111–8, div. G, title I, §1301(b), Mar. 11, 2009, 123 Stat. 829; Pub. L. 111–68, div. A, title I, §1501(a), Oct. 1, 2009, 123 Stat. 2041.)

§3152. REPORTS BY RECIPIENTS

(a) IN GENERAL.—

Each recipient of assistance under this subchapter shall submit reports to the Secretary at such intervals and in such manner as the Secretary shall require by regulation, except that no report shall be required to be submitted more than 10 years after the date of closeout of the assistance award.

(b) CONTENTS.—

Each report shall contain an evaluation of the effectiveness of the economic assistance provided under this subchapter in meeting the need that the assistance was designed to address and in meeting the objectives of this chapter.

(Pub. L. 89–136, title II, §212, as added Pub. L. 105–393, title I, §102(a), Nov. 13, 1998, 112 Stat. 3606.)

§3153. PROHIBITION ON USE OF FUNDS FOR ATTORNEY'S AND CONSULTANT'S FEES

Assistance made available under this subchapter shall not be used directly or indirectly for an attorney's or consultant's fee incurred in connection with obtaining grants and contracts under this subchapter.

(Pub. L. 89–136, title II, §213, as added Pub. L. 105–393, title I, §102(a), Nov. 13, 1998, 112 Stat. 3607.)

§3154. SPECIAL IMPACT AREAS

(a) IN GENERAL.—

On the application of an eligible recipient that is determined by the Secretary to be unable to comply with the requirements of section 3162 of this title, the Secretary may waive, in whole or in part, the requirements of section 3162 of this title and designate the area represented by the recipient as a special impact area.

(b) CONDITIONS.—

The Secretary may make a designation under subsection (a) only after determining that—

(1) the project will fulfill a pressing need of the area; and

(2) the project will—

(A) be useful in alleviating or preventing conditions of excessive unemployment or underemployment; or

(B) assist in providing useful employment opportunities for the unemployed or underemployed residents in the area.

(c) NOTIFICATION.—

At the time of the designation under subsection (a), the Secretary shall submit to the Committee on Environment and Public Works of the Senate and the Committee on Transportation and Infrastructure of the House of Representatives a written notice of the designation, including a justification for the designation.

(Pub. L. 89–136, title II, §214, as added Pub. L. 108–373, title II, §209(a), Oct. 27, 2004, 118 Stat. 1763.)

§3154A. PERFORMANCE AWARDS

(a) IN GENERAL.—

The Secretary may make a performance award in connection with a grant made, on or after October 27, 2004, to an eligible recipient for a project under section 3141 or 3149 of this title.

(b) PERFORMANCE MEASURES.—

(1) REGULATIONS.—

The Secretary shall promulgate regulations to establish performance measures for making performance awards under subsection (a).

(2) CONSIDERATIONS.—

In promulgating regulations under paragraph (1), the Secretary shall consider the inclusion of performance measures that assess—

(A) whether the recipient meets or exceeds scheduling goals;

(B) whether the recipient meets or exceeds job creation goals;

(C) amounts of private sector capital investments leveraged; and

(D) such other factors as the Secretary determines to be appropriate.

(c) AMOUNT OF AWARDS.—

(1) IN GENERAL.—

The Secretary shall base the amount of a performance award made under subsection (a) in connection with a grant on the extent to which a recipient meets or exceeds performance measures established in connection with the grant.

(2) MAXIMUM AMOUNT.—

The amount of a performance award may not exceed 10 percent of the amount of the grant.

(d) Use of awards.—

A recipient of a performance award under subsection (a) may use the award for any eligible purpose under this chapter, in accordance with section 3212 of this title and such regulations as the Secretary may promulgate.

(e) Federal share.—

Notwithstanding section 3144 of this title, the funds of a performance award may be used to pay up to 100 percent of the cost of an eligible project or activity.

(f) Treatment in meeting non-Federal share requirements.—

For the purposes of meeting the non-Federal share requirements under this, or any other, Act the funds of a performance award shall be treated as funds from a non-Federal source.

(g) Terms and conditions.—

In making performance awards under subsection (a), the Secretary shall establish such terms and conditions as the Secretary considers to be appropriate.

(h) Funding.—

The Secretary shall use any amounts made available for economic development assistance programs to carry out this section.

(i) Reporting requirement.—

The Secretary shall include information regarding performance awards made under this section in the annual report required under section 3213 of this title.

(j) Review by Comptroller General.—

(1) Review.—

The Comptroller General shall regularly review the implementation of this section.

(2) Report.—

Not later than 1 year after October 27, 2004, the Comptroller General shall submit to the Committee on Environment and Public Works of the Senate and the Committee on Transportation and Infrastructure of the House of Representatives a report on the findings of the Comptroller on implementation of this subsection.

(Pub. L. 89–136, title II, §215, as added Pub. L. 108–373, title II, §210(a), Oct. 27, 2004, 118 Stat. 1764.)

§3154b. Planning performance awards

(a) In general.—

The Secretary may make a planning performance award in connection with a grant made, on or after October 27, 2004, to an eligible recipient for a project under this subchapter located in an economic development district.

(b) Eligibility.—

The Secretary may make a planning performance award to an eligible recipient under subsection (a) in connection with a grant for a project if the Secretary determines before closeout of the project that—

(1) the recipient actively participated in the economic development activities of the economic development district in which the project is located;

(2) the project is consistent with the comprehensive economic development strategy of the district;

(3) the recipient worked with Federal, State, and local economic development

entities throughout the development of the project; and

(4) the project was completed in accordance with the comprehensive economic development strategy of the district.

(c) MAXIMUM AMOUNT.—

The amount of a planning performance award made under subsection (a) in connection with a grant may not exceed 5 percent of the amount of the grant.

(d) USE OF AWARDS.—

A recipient of a planning performance award under subsection (a) shall use the award to increase the Federal share of the cost of a project under this subchapter.

(e) FEDERAL SHARE.—

Notwithstanding section 3144 of this title, the funds of a planning performance award may be used to pay up to 100 percent of the cost of a project under this subchapter.

(f) FUNDING.—

The Secretary shall use any amounts made available for economic development assistance programs to carry out this section.

(Pub. L. 89–136, title II, §216, as added Pub. L. 108–373, title II, §211(a), Oct. 27, 2004, 118 Stat. 1765.)

§3154C. DIRECT EXPENDITURE OR REDISTRIBUTION BY RECIPIENT

(a) IN GENERAL.—

Subject to subsection (b), a recipient of a grant under section 3141, 3143, or 3147 of this title may directly expend the grant funds or may redistribute the funds in the form of a subgrant to other eligible recipients to fund required components of the scope of work approved for the project.

(b) LIMITATION.—

A recipient may not redistribute grant funds received under section 3141 or 3143 of this title to a for-profit entity.

(c) ECONOMIC ADJUSTMENT.—

Subject to subsection (d), a recipient of a grant under section 3149 of this title may directly expend the grant funds or may redistribute the funds to public and private entities in the form of a grant, loan, loan guarantee, payment to reduce interest on a loan guarantee, or other appropriate assistance.

(d) LIMITATION.—

Under subsection (c), a recipient may not provide any grant to a private for-profit entity.

(Pub. L. 89–136, title II, §217, as added Pub. L. 108–373, title II, §212(a), Oct. 27, 2004, 118 Stat. 1766.)

§3154D. RENEWABLE ENERGY PROGRAM

(a) DEFINITION OF RENEWABLE ENERGY SITE.—

In this section, the term "renewable energy site" means a brownfield site that is redeveloped through the incorporation of 1 or more renewable energy technologies, including solar, wind, geothermal, ocean, and emerging, but proven, renewable energy technologies.

(b) ESTABLISHMENT.—

On the application of an eligible recipient, the Secretary may make a grant for a project for the development of a renewable energy site if the Secretary determines that the project will—

(1) use 1 or more renewable energy technologies described in subsection (a), to develop abandoned or contaminated sites for commercial use; and

(2) improve the commercial and economic opportunities in the area in which the project is located.

(c) SAVINGS CLAUSE.—

To the extent that any portion of a grant awarded under subsection (b) involves remediation, the remediation shall be subject to section 3222 of this title.

(Pub. L. 89–136, title II, §218, as added Pub. L. 108–373, title II, §213(a), Oct. 27, 2004, 118 Stat. 1766; amended Pub. L. 118–272, div. B, title II, §2220, Jan. 4, 2025, 138 Stat. 3185.)

§3154E. WORKFORCE TRAINING GRANTS

(a) IN GENERAL.—

On the application of an eligible recipient, the Secretary may make grants to support the development and expansion of innovative workforce training programs through sectoral partnerships leading to quality jobs and the acquisition of equipment or construction of facilities to support workforce development activities.

(b) ELIGIBLE USES.—

Funds from a grant under this section may be used for—

(1) acquisition or development of land and improvements to house workforce training activities;

(2) acquisition, design and engineering, construction, rehabilitation, alteration, expansion, or improvement of such a facility, including related equipment and machinery;

(3) acquisition of machinery or equipment to support workforce training activities;

(4) planning, technical assistance, and training;

(5) sector partnerships development, program design, and program implementation; and

(6) in the case of an eligible recipient that is a State, subject to subsection (c), a State program to support individual trainees for employment in critical industries with high demand and vacancies necessary for further economic development of the applicable State that—

(A) requires significant post-secondary training; but

(B) does not require a post-secondary degree.

(c) STATE GRANT PILOT PROGRAM.—

(1) IN GENERAL.—

The Secretary may award grants to States for the purpose described in subsection (b)(6).

To be eligible to receive a grant under this subsection, the Chief Executive of a State shall submit to the Secretary an application at such time, in such manner, and containing such information as the Secretary may require, which shall include, at a minimum, the following:

(A) A method for identifying critical industry sectors driving in-State economic growth that face staffing challenges for in-demand jobs and careers.

(B) A governance structure for the implementation of the program established by the State, including defined roles for the consortia of agencies of such State, at a minimum, to include the State departments of economic development, labor, and education, or the State departments or agencies with jurisdiction over those matters.

(C) A strategy for recruiting participants from at least 1 community that meets 1 or more of the criteria described in section 3161(a) of this title.

(D) A plan for how the State will develop a tracking system for eligible programs, participant enrollment, participant outcomes, and an application portal for individual participants.

(3) SELECTION.—

The Secretary shall award not more than 1 grant under this subsection to any State.

(4) ELIGIBLE USES.—

A grant under this subsection may be used for—

(A) necessary costs to carry out the matters described in this subsection, including tuition and stipends for individuals that receive funds under the program established by the applicable State, subject to the requirements described in paragraph (6); and

(B) program implementation, planning, technical assistance, or training.

(5) FEDERAL SHARE.—

Notwithstanding section 3144 of this title, the Federal share of the cost of any award carried out with a grant made under this subsection shall not exceed 70 percent.

(6) PARTICIPANT AMOUNTS.—

A State shall ensure that grant funds provided under this subsection to each individual that receives funds under the program established by the applicable State is the lesser of the following amounts:

(A) In a case in which the individual is also eligible for a Federal Pell Grant under section 1070a of title 20 for enrollment at the applicable training program for any award year of the training program, $11,000 minus the amount of the awarded Federal Pell Grant.

(B) For an individual not described in paragraph (1), the lesser of—

(i) $11,000; and

(ii) the total cost of the training program in which the individual is enrolled, including tuition, fees, career navigation services, textbook costs, expenses related to assessments and exams for certification or licensure, equipment costs, and wage stipends (in the case of a training program that is an earn-and-learn program).

(7) TERMINATION.—

The authority provided under this subsection shall expire on September 30, 2029.

(d) COORDINATION.—

The Secretary shall coordinate the development of new workforce development models with the Secretary of Labor and the Secretary of Education.

(Pub. L. 89–136, title II, §219, as added Pub. L. 118–272, div. B, title II, §2221, Jan. 4, 2025, 138 Stat. 3186.)

§3154F. CONGRESSIONAL NOTIFICATION REQUIREMENTS

(a) IN GENERAL.—

In the case of a project described in subsection (b), the Secretary shall provide to the Committee on Environment and Public Works of the Senate and the Committee on Transportation and Infrastructure of the House of Representatives notice, in accordance with subsection (c), of the award of a grant for the project not less than 3 business days before notifying an eligible recipient of their selection for that award.

(b) PROJECTS DESCRIBED.—

A project referred to in subsection (a) is a project that the Secretary has selected to receive a grant administered by the Economic Development Administration in an amount not less than $100,000.

(c) REQUIREMENTS.—

A notification under subsection (a) shall include—

(1) the name of the project;

(2) the name of the applicant;

(3) the region in which the project is to be carried out;

(4) the State in which the project is to be carried out;

(5) the 1 or more counties or political subdivisions in which the project is to be carried out;

(6) the number of jobs expected to be created or retained as a result of the project;

(7) the estimated date of completion of the project;

(8) the amount of the grant awarded;

(9) a description of the project; and

(10) any additional information, as determined to be appropriate by the Secretary.

(d) PUBLIC AVAILABILITY.—

The Secretary shall make a notification under subsection (a) publicly available not later than 60 days after the date on which the Secretary provides the notice.

(Pub. L. 89–136, title II, §220, as added Pub. L. 118–272, div. B, title II, §2222, Jan. 4, 2025, 138 Stat. 3187.)

§3154G. HIGH-SPEED BROADBAND DEPLOYMENT INITIATIVE

(a) DEFINITIONS.—

In this section:

(1) BROADBAND PROJECT.—

The term "broadband project" means, for the purposes of providing, extending, expanding, or improving high-speed broadband service to further the goals of this chapter—

(A) planning, technical assistance, or training;

(B) the acquisition or development of land; or

(C) the acquisition, design and engineering, construction, rehabilitation, alteration, expansion, or improvement of facilities, including related machinery, equipment, contractual rights, and intangible property.

(2) ELIGIBLE RECIPIENT.—

(A) In general.—

The term "eligible recipient" means an eligible recipient.

(B) INCLUSIONS.—

The term "eligible recipient" includes—

(i) a public-private partnership; and

(ii) a consortium formed for the purpose of providing, extending, expanding, or improving high-speed broadband service between 1 or more eligible recipients and 1 or more for-profit organizations.

(3) HIGH-SPEED BROADBAND.—

The term "high-speed broadband" means the provision of 2-way data transmission with sufficient downstream and upstream speeds to end users to permit effective participation in the economy and to support economic growth, as determined by the Secretary.

(b) BROADBAND PROJECTS.—

(1) IN GENERAL.—

On the application of an eligible recipient, the Secretary may make grants under this subchapter for broadband projects, which shall be subject to the provisions of this section.

(2) CONSIDERATIONS.—

In reviewing applications submitted under paragraph (1), the Secretary shall take into consideration geographic diversity of grants provided, including consideration of underserved markets, in addition to data requested in paragraph (3).

(3) DATA REQUESTED.—

In reviewing an application submitted under paragraph (1), the Secretary shall request from the Federal Communications Commission, the Administrator of the National Telecommunications and Information Administration, the Secretary of Agriculture, and the Appalachian Regional Commission data on—

(A) the level and extent of broadband service that exists in the area proposed to be served; and

(B) the level and extent of broadband service that will be deployed in the area proposed to be served pursuant to another Federal program.

(4) INTEREST IN REAL OR PERSONAL PROPERTY.—

For any broadband project carried out by an eligible recipient that is a public-private partnership or consortium, the Secretary shall require that title to any real or personal property acquired or improved with grant funds, or if the recipient will not acquire title, another possessory interest acceptable to the Secretary, be vested in a public partner or eligible nonprofit organization or association for the useful life of the project, after which title may be transferred to any member of the public-private partnership or consortium in accordance with regulations promulgated by the Secretary.

(5) PROCUREMENT.—

Notwithstanding any other provision of law, no person or entity shall be disqualified from competing to provide goods or services related to a broadband project on the basis that the person or entity participated in the development of the broadband project or in the drafting of specifications, requirements, statements of work, or similar documents related to the goods or services to be provided.

(6) BROADBAND PROJECT PROPERTY.—

(A) IN GENERAL.—

The SECRETARY MAY PERMIT A RECIPIENT OF A GRANT FOR A BROADBAND PROJECT

TO GRANT AN OPTION TO ACQUIRE REAL OR PERSONAL PROPERTY (INCLUDING CONTRACTUAL RIGHTS AND INTANGIBLE PROPERTY) RELATED TO THAT PROJECT TO A THIRD PARTY ON SUCH TERMS AS THE SECRETARY DETERMINES TO BE APPROPRIATE, SUBJECT TO THE CONDITION THAT THE OPTION MAY ONLY BE EXERCISED AFTER THE SECRETARY RELEASES THE FEDERAL INTEREST IN THE PROPERTY.

(B) TREATMENT.—

The grant or exercise of an option described in subparagraph (A) shall not constitute a redistribution of grant funds under section 3154c of this title.

(c) NON-FEDERAL SHARE.—

In determining the amount of the non-Federal share of the cost of a broadband project, the Secretary may provide credit toward the non-Federal share for the present value of allowable contributions over the useful life of the broadband project, subject to the condition that the Secretary may require such assurances of the value of the rights and of the commitment of the rights as the Secretary determines to be appropriate.

(Pub. L. 89–136, title II, §221, as added Pub. L. 118–272, div. B, title II, §2223, Jan. 4, 2025, 138 Stat. 3188.)

§3154H. CRITICAL SUPPLY CHAIN SITE DEVELOPMENT GRANT PROGRAM

(a) IN GENERAL.—

On the application of an eligible recipient, the Secretary may make grants under the "Critical Supply Chain Site Development grant program" (referred to in this section as the "grant program") to carry out site development or expansion projects for the purpose of making the site ready for manufacturing projects.

(b) CONSIDERATIONS.—

In providing a grant to an eligible recipient under the grant program, the Secretary may consider whether—

(1) the proposed improvements to the site will improve economic conditions for rural areas, Tribal communities, or areas that meet 1 or more of the criteria described in section 3161(a) of this title;

(2) the project is consistent with regional economic development plans, which may include a comprehensive economic development strategy;

(3) the eligible recipient has initiatives to prioritize job training and workforce development; and

(4) the project supports industries determined by the Secretary to be of strategic importance to the national or economic security of the United States.

(c) PRIORITY.—

In awarding grants to eligible recipients under the grant program, the Secretary shall give priority to eligible recipients that propose to carry out a project that—

(1) has State, local, private, or nonprofit funds being contributed to assist with site development efforts; and

(2) if the site development or expansion project is carried out, will result in a demonstrated interest in the site by commercial entities or other entities.

(d) Use of funds.—

A grant provided under the grant program may be used for the following activities relating to the development or expansion of a site:

(1) Investments in site utility readiness, including—

(A) construction of on-site utility infrastructure;

(B) construction of last-mile infrastructure, including road infrastructure, water infrastructure, power infrastructure, broadband infrastructure, and other physical last-mile infrastructure;

(C) site grading; and

(D) other activities to extend public utilities or services to a site, as determined appropriate by the Secretary.

(2) Investments in site readiness, including—

(A) land assembly;

(B) environmental reviews;

(C) zoning;

(D) design;

(E) engineering; and

(F) permitting.

(3) Investments in workforce development and sustainability programs, including job training and retraining programs.

(4) Investments to ensure that disadvantaged communities have access to on-site jobs.

(e) PROHIBITION.—

(1) IN GENERAL.—

Subject to paragraph (2), in awarding grants under the grant program, the Secretary shall not require an eligible recipient to demonstrate that a private company or investment has selected the site for development or expansion.

(2) SAFEGUARDS.—

In awarding grants under the grant program, the Secretary shall include necessary safeguards to ensure that—

(A) the site development is fully completed within a reasonable timeframe; and

(B) the eligible recipient has sufficiently demonstrated private sector interest.

(Pub. L. 89–136, title II, §222, as added Pub. L. 118–272, div. B, title II, §2224, Jan. 4, 2025, 138 Stat. 3189.)

SUBCHAPTER III—ELIGIBILITY; COMPREHENSIVE ECONOMIC DEVELOPMENT STRATEGIES

§3161. ELIGIBILITY OF AREAS

(a) IN GENERAL.—

For a project to be eligible for assistance under section 3141 or 3149 of this title, the project shall be located in an area that, on the date of submission of the application, meets 1 or more of the following criteria:

(1) LOW PER CAPITA INCOME.—

The area has a per capita income of 80 percent or less of the national average.

(2) UNEMPLOYMENT RATE ABOVE NATIONAL AVERAGE.—

The area has an unemployment rate that is, for the most recent 24-month period for which data are available, at least 1 percent greater than the national average unemployment rate.

(3) UNEMPLOYMENT, UNDEREMPLOYMENT, OR ECONOMIC ADJUSTMENT PROBLEMS.—
The area is an area that the Secretary determines has experienced or is about to experience a special need arising from actual or threatened severe unemployment, underemployment, or economic adjustment problems resulting from severe short-term or long-term changes in economic conditions.

(4) LOW MEDIAN HOUSEHOLD INCOME.—
The area has a median household income of 80 percent or less of the national average.

(5) WORKFORCE PARTICIPATION.—
The area has—

(A) a labor force participation rate of 90 percent or less of the national average; or

(B) a prime-age employment gap of 5 percent or more.

(6) EXPECTED ECONOMIC DISLOCATION AND DISTRESS FROM ENERGY INDUSTRY TRANSITIONS.—
The area is an area that is expected to experience actual or threatened severe unemployment or economic adjustment problems resulting from severe short-term or long-term changes in economic conditions from energy industries that are experiencing accelerated contraction.

(b) POLITICAL BOUNDARIES OF AREAS.—
An area that meets 1 or more of the criteria of subsection (a), including a small area of poverty or high unemployment within a larger community in less economic distress, shall be eligible for assistance under section 3141 or 3149 of this title without regard to political or other subdivisions or boundaries.

(c) DOCUMENTATION.—

(1) IN GENERAL.—
A determination of eligibility under subsection (a) shall be supported by the most recent Federal data available (including data available from the Bureau of Economic Analysis, the Bureau of Labor Statistics, the Census Bureau, the Bureau of Indian Affairs, or any other Federal source determined by the Secretary to be appropriate), or, if no recent Federal data is available, by the most recent data available through the government of the State in which the area is located.

(2) ACCEPTANCE BY SECRETARY.—
The documentation shall be accepted by the Secretary unless the Secretary determines that the documentation is inaccurate.

(d) Prior designations.—
Any designation of a redevelopment area made before the effective date of the Economic Development Administration Reform Act of 1998 shall not be effective after that effective date.

(e) TRANSPARENCY.—
To the extent the Secretary includes neighboring counties and communities in an economic development district in accordance with subsection (a)(3), the Secretary shall submit to Congress, and make publicly available online, a notification describing the justification for such inclusion and detailing the economic indicators of such

neighboring counties and communities.

(Pub. L. 89–136, title III, §301, as added Pub. L. 105–393, title I, §102(a), Nov. 13, 1998, 112 Stat. 3607; amended Pub. L. 108–373, title III, §301, Oct. 27, 2004, 118 Stat. 1767; Pub. L. 118–272, div. B, title II, §2225, Jan. 4, 2025, 138 Stat. 3191.)

§3162. COMPREHENSIVE ECONOMIC DEVELOPMENT STRATEGIES

(a) IN GENERAL.—

The Secretary may provide assistance under section 3141 or 3149 of this title (except for planning assistance under section 3149 of this title) to an eligible recipient for a project only if the eligible recipient submits to the Secretary, as part of an application for the assistance—

(1) an identification of the economic development problems to be addressed using the assistance;

(2) an identification of the past, present, and projected future economic development investments in the area receiving the assistance and public and private participants and sources of funding for the investments; and

(3)(A) a comprehensive economic development strategy for addressing the economic problems identified under paragraph (1) in a manner that promotes economic development and opportunity, fosters effective transportation access, maximizes effective development and use of the workforce consistent with any applicable State or local workforce investment strategy, promotes the use of technology in economic development (including access to high-speed telecommunications), enhances and protects the environment, including to mitigate and adapt to the economic impacts of extreme weather, and balances resources through sound management of development; and

(B) a description of how the strategy will solve the problems.

(b) APPROVAL OF COMPREHENSIVE ECONOMIC DEVELOPMENT STRATEGY.—

The Secretary shall approve a comprehensive economic development strategy that meets the requirements of subsection (a) to the satisfaction of the Secretary.

(c) APPROVAL OF OTHER PLAN.—

(1) IN GENERAL.—

The Secretary may accept as a comprehensive economic development strategy a satisfactory plan developed under another federally supported program.

(2) EXISTING STRATEGY.—

To the maximum extent practicable, a plan submitted under this paragraph shall be consistent and coordinated with any existing comprehensive economic development strategy for the area.

(d) EXCEPTION.—

This section shall not apply to grants awarded under section 3147 of this title or grants awarded under section 3149(c)(2) of this title for areas to which more than one comprehensive economic development strategy may apply.

(Pub. L. 89–136, title III, §302, as added Pub. L. 105–393, title I, §102(a), Nov. 13, 1998, 112 Stat. 3608; amended Pub. L. 108–373, title III, §302, Oct. 27, 2004, 118 Stat. 1767; Pub. L. 118–272, div. B, title II, §2226, Jan. 4, 2025, 138 Stat. 3191.)

SUBCHAPTER IV—ECONOMIC DEVELOPMENT DISTRICTS

§3171. Designation of economic development districts

(a) In general.—

In order that economic development projects of broad geographic significance may be planned and carried out, the Secretary may designate appropriate economic development districts in the United States, with the concurrence of the States in which the districts will be wholly or partially located, if—

(1) the proposed district is of sufficient size or population, and contains sufficient resources, to foster economic development on a scale involving more than a single area described in section 3161(a) of this title;

(2) the proposed district contains at least 1 area described in section 3161(a) of this title; and

(3) the proposed district has a comprehensive economic development strategy that—

(A) contains a specific program for intra-district cooperation, self-help, and public investment; and

(B) is approved by each affected State and by the Secretary.

(b) Authorities.—

The Secretary may, under regulations promulgated by the Secretary—

(1) invite the States to determine boundaries for proposed economic development districts;

(2) cooperate with the States—

(A) in sponsoring and assisting district economic planning and economic development groups; and

(B) in assisting the district groups in formulating comprehensive economic development strategies for districts; and

(3) encourage participation by appropriate local government entities in the economic development districts.

(Pub. L. 89–136, title IV, §401, as added Pub. L. 105–393, title I, §102(a), Nov. 13, 1998, 112 Stat. 3608.)

§3172. Termination or modification of economic development districts

The Secretary shall, by regulation, promulgate standards for the termination or modification of the designation of economic development districts.

(Pub. L. 89–136, title IV, §402, as added Pub. L. 105–393, title I, §102(a), Nov. 13, 1998, 112 Stat. 3609.)

§3173. Repealed. Pub. L. 108–373, title IV, §401(a), Oct. 27, 2004, 118 Stat. 1767

Section, Pub. L. 89–136, title IV, §403, as added Pub. L. 105–393, title I, §102(a), Nov. 13, 1998, 112 Stat. 3609, related to incentives for projects in economic development districts.

§3174. Provision of comprehensive economic development strategies to Regional Commissions

If any part of an economic development district is in a region covered by 1 or more of the Regional Commissions, the economic development district shall ensure that a copy of the comprehensive economic development strategy of the district is provided to the affected Regional Commission.

(Pub. L. 89–136, title IV, §404, as added Pub. L. 105–393, title I, §102(a), Nov. 13, 1998, 112 Stat. 3609; amended Pub. L. 108–373, title IV, §402(a), Oct. 27, 2004, 118 Stat. 1768.)

§3175. Assistance to parts of economic development districts not in eligible areas

Notwithstanding section 3161 of this title, the Secretary may provide such assistance as is available under this chapter for a project in a part of an economic development district that is not in an area described in section 3161(a) of this title, if the project will be of a substantial direct benefit to an area described in section 3161(a) of this title that is located in the district.

(Pub. L. 89–136, title IV, §405, as added Pub. L. 105–393, title I, §102(a), Nov. 13, 1998, 112 Stat. 3609.)

SUBCHAPTER V—ADMINISTRATION

§3191. Assistant Secretary for Economic Development

(a) In general.—

The Secretary shall carry out this chapter through an Assistant Secretary of Commerce for Economic Development, to be appointed by the President, by and with the advice and consent of the Senate.

(b) Compensation.—

The Assistant Secretary of Commerce for Economic Development shall be compensated at the rate payable for level IV of the Executive Schedule under section 5315 of title 5.

(c) Duties.—

The Assistant Secretary of Commerce for Economic Development shall carry out such duties as the Secretary shall require and shall serve as the administrator of the Economic Development Administration of the Department.

(Pub. L. 89–136, title V, §501, as added Pub. L. 105–393, title I, §102(a), Nov. 13, 1998, 112 Stat. 3610.)

§3192. Economic development information clearinghouse

In carrying out this chapter, the Secretary shall—

(1) maintain a central information clearinghouse on the Internet with—

(A) information on economic development, economic adjustment, disaster recovery, defense conversion, and trade adjustment programs and activities of the Federal Government;

(B) links to State economic development organizations; and

(C) links to other appropriate economic development resources;

(2) assist potential and actual applicants for economic development, economic adjustment, disaster recovery, defense conversion, and trade adjustment assistance under Federal and State laws in locating and applying for the assistance;

(3) assist areas described in section 3161(a) of this title and other areas by providing to interested persons, communities, industries, and businesses in the areas any technical information, market research, or other forms of assistance, information,

or advice that would be useful in alleviating or preventing conditions of excessive unemployment or underemployment in the areas; and

(4) obtain appropriate information from other Federal agencies needed to carry out the duties under this chapter.

(Pub. L. 89–136, title V, §502, as added Pub. L. 105–393, title I, §102(a), Nov. 13, 1998, 112 Stat. 3610; amended Pub. L. 108–373, title V, §501, Oct. 27, 2004, 118 Stat. 1768.)

§3193. CONSULTATION WITH OTHER PERSONS AND AGENCIES

(a) CONSULTATION ON PROBLEMS RELATING TO EMPLOYMENT.—

The Secretary may consult with any persons, including representatives of labor, management, agriculture, and government, who can assist in addressing the problems of area and regional unemployment or underemployment.

(b) CONSULTATION ON ADMINISTRATION OF CHAPTER.—

The Secretary may provide for such consultation with interested Federal agencies as the Secretary determines to be appropriate in the performance of the duties of the Secretary under this chapter.

(Pub. L. 89–136, title V, §503, as added Pub. L. 105–393, title I, §102(a), Nov. 13, 1998, 112 Stat. 3610.)

§3194. ADMINISTRATION, OPERATION, AND MAINTENANCE

The Secretary shall approve Federal assistance under this chapter only if the Secretary is satisfied that the project for which Federal assistance is granted will be properly and efficiently administered, operated, and maintained.

(Pub. L. 89–136, title V, §504, as added Pub. L. 105–393, title I, §102(a), Nov. 13, 1998, 112 Stat. 3610.)

§3195. REPEALED. PUB. L. 108–373, TITLE V, §502(A), OCT. 27, 2004, 118 STAT. 1768

Section, Pub. L. 89–136, title V, §505, as added Pub. L. 105–393, title I, §102(a), Nov. 13, 1998, 112 Stat. 3610, related to businesses desiring Federal contracts.

§3196. PERFORMANCE EVALUATIONS OF GRANT RECIPIENTS

(a) IN GENERAL.—

The Secretary shall conduct an evaluation of each university center and each economic development district that receives grant assistance under this chapter (each referred to in this section as a "grantee") to assess the grantee's performance and contribution toward retention and creation of employment.

(b) PURPOSE OF EVALUATIONS OF UNIVERSITY CENTERS.—

The purpose of the evaluations of university centers under subsection (a) shall be to determine which university centers are performing well and are worthy of continued grant assistance under this chapter, and which should not receive continued assistance, so that university centers that have not previously received assistance may receive assistance.

(c) TIMING OF EVALUATIONS.—

Evaluations under subsection (a) shall be conducted on a continuing basis so that each grantee is evaluated within 3 years after the first award of assistance to the grantee, and at least once every 3 years thereafter, so long as the grantee receives the assistance.

(d) EVALUATION CRITERIA.—

(1) ESTABLISHMENT.—

The Secretary shall establish criteria for use in conducting evaluations under subsection (a).

(2) EVALUATION CRITERIA FOR UNIVERSITY CENTERS.—

The criteria for evaluation of a university center shall, at a minimum, provide for an assessment of the center's contribution to providing technical assistance, conducting applied research, program performance, and disseminating results of the activities of the center.

(3) EVALUATION CRITERIA FOR ECONOMIC DEVELOPMENT DISTRICTS.—

The criteria for evaluation of an economic development district shall, at a minimum, provide for an assessment of management standards, financial accountability, and program performance.

(e) PEER REVIEW.—

In conducting an evaluation of a university center or economic development district under subsection (a), the Secretary shall provide for the participation of at least 1 other university center or economic development district, as appropriate, on a cost-reimbursement basis.

(Pub. L. 89–136, title V, §506, as added Pub. L. 105–393, title I, §102(a), Nov. 13, 1998, 112 Stat. 3611; amended Pub. L. 108–373, title V, §503, Oct. 27, 2004, 118 Stat. 1769.)

§3197. NOTIFICATION OF REORGANIZATION

Not later than 30 days before the date of any reorganization of the offices, programs, or activities of the Economic Development Administration, the Secretary shall provide notification of the reorganization to the Committee on Environment and Public Works and the Committee on Appropriations of the Senate, and the Committee on Transportation and Infrastructure and the Committee on Appropriations of the House of Representatives.

(Pub. L. 89–136, title V, §507, as added Pub. L. 105–393, title I, §102(a), Nov. 13, 1998, 112 Stat. 3611.)

§3198. OFFICE OF TRIBAL ECONOMIC DEVELOPMENT

(a) ESTABLISHMENT.—

There is established within the Economic Development Administration an Office of Tribal Economic Development (referred to in this section as the "Office").

(b) PURPOSES.—

The purposes of the Office shall be—

(1) to coordinate all Tribal economic development activities carried out by the Secretary;

(2) to help Tribal communities access economic development assistance programs, including the assistance provided under this chapter;

(3) to coordinate Tribal economic development strategies and efforts with other Federal agencies; and

(4) to be a participant in any negotiated rulemakings or consultations relating to, or having an impact on, projects, programs, or funding that benefit Tribal communities.

(c) TRIBAL ECONOMIC DEVELOPMENT STRATEGY.—

(1) IN GENERAL.—

Not later than 1 year after January 4, 2025, the Office shall initiate a Tribal consultation process to develop, and not less frequently than every 3 years thereafter, update, a strategic plan for Tribal economic development for the Economic Development Administration.

(2) SUBMISSION TO CONGRESS.—

Not later than 1 year after January 4, 2025, and not less frequently than every 3 years thereafter, the Office shall submit to the Committee on Transportation and Infrastructure of the House of Representatives and the Committee on Environment and Public Works of the Senate the strategic plan for Tribal economic development developed under paragraph (1).

(d) OUTREACH.—

The Secretary shall establish a publicly facing website to help provide a comprehensive, single source of information for Indian tribes, Tribal leaders, Tribal businesses, and citizens in Tribal communities to better understand and access programs that support economic development in Tribal communities, including the economic development programs administered by Federal agencies or departments other than the Department.

(e) DEDICATED STAFF.—

The Secretary shall ensure that the Office has sufficient staff to carry out all outreach activities under this section.

(Pub. L. 89–136, title V, §508, as added Pub. L. 118–272, div. B, title II, §2227, Jan. 4, 2025, 138 Stat. 3192.)

§3199. OFFICE OF DISASTER RECOVERY AND RESILIENCE

(a) ESTABLISHMENT.—

The Secretary shall establish an Office of Disaster Recovery and Resilience—

(1) to direct and implement the post-disaster economic recovery responsibilities of the Economic Development Administration pursuant to subsections (c)(2) and (e) of section 3149 of this title and section 3233 of this title;

(2) to direct and implement economic recovery and enhanced resilience support function activities as directed under the National Disaster Recovery Framework; and

(3) support long-term economic recovery in communities in which a major disaster or emergency has been declared under the Robert T. Stafford Disaster Relief and Emergency Assistance Act (42 U.S.C. 5121 et seq.), or otherwise impacted by an event of national significance, as determined by the Secretary, through—

(A) convening and deploying an economic development assessment team;

(B) hosting or attending convenings related to identification of additional Federal, State, local, and philanthropic entities and resources;

(C) exploring potential flexibilities related to existing awards;

(D) provision of technical assistance through staff or contractual resources; and

(E) other activities determined by the Secretary to be appropriate.

(b) APPOINTMENT AUTHORITIES.—

(1) APPOINTMENT.—

The Secretary is authorized to appoint such temporary personnel as may be necessary to carry out the responsibilities of the Office of Disaster Recovery and

Resilience, without regard to the provisions of subchapter I of chapter 33 of title 5 governing appointments in the competitive service.

(2) CONVERSION OF EMPLOYEES.—

Notwithstanding chapter 33 of title 5, or any other provision of law relating to the examination, certification, and appointment of individuals in the competitive service, a temporary employee appointed under this subsection may be selected by the Secretary for a permanent appointment in the competitive service in the Economic Development Administration under internal competitive promotion procedures if—

(A) the employee has served continuously for at least 2 years under 1 or more appointments under this subsection; and

(B) the employee's performance has been at an acceptable level of performance throughout the period or periods referred to in subparagraph (A).

(3) STATUS UPON CONVERSION.—

An individual converted under this subsection shall become a career-conditional employee, unless the employee has already completed the service requirements for career tenure.

(4) REPORTING.—

For any fiscal year during which the Secretary exercises the authority under this subsection, the Secretary shall submit to the Committee on Environment and Public Works of the Senate and the Committee on Transportation and Infrastructure of the House of Representatives a report that describes the use of that authority including, at a minimum—

(A) the number of employees hired under the authority during the fiscal year;

(B) the positions and grades for which employees were hired;

(C) the number of employees converted to career-conditional;

(D) a description of how the Secretary assessed employee performance to determine the eligibility of the employee for conversion under paragraph (2)(B);

(E) the number of employees who were hired under that authority as temporary employees who have met the continuous service requirements described in subparagraph (A) of paragraph (2) but not the performance requirements described in subparagraph (B) of that paragraph; and

(F) the number of employees who were hired under that authority who have separated from the Economic Development Administration.

(5) RULE OF CONSTRUCTION.—

Nothing in this subsection waives any requirement relating to qualifications of applicants for positions in the Office of Disaster Recovery and Resilience under this subsection.

(6) TERMINATION.—

The authority provided by this subsection shall expire on September 30, 2029.

(c) DISASTER TEAM.—

(1) ESTABLISHMENT.—

As soon as practicable after January 4, 2025, the Secretary shall establish a disaster team (referred to in this section as the "disaster team") for the deployment of individuals to carry out responsibilities of the Office of Disaster Recovery and Resilience after a major disaster or emergency has been declared under the Robert T.

Stafford Disaster Relief and Emergency Assistance Act (42 U.S.C. 5121 et seq.) and the Department has been activated by the Federal Emergency Management Agency.

(2) MEMBERSHIP.—

(A) DESIGNATION OF STAFF.—

As soon as practicable after January 4, 2025, the Secretary shall designate to serve on the disaster team—

(i) employees of the Office of Disaster Recovery and Resilience;

(ii) employees of the Department who are not employees of the Economic Development Administration; and

(iii) in consultation with the heads of other Federal agencies, employees of those agencies, as appropriate.

(B) CAPABILITIES.—

In designating individuals under subparagraph (A), the Secretary shall ensure that the disaster team includes a sufficient quantity of—

(i) individuals who are capable of deploying rapidly and efficiently to respond to major disasters and emergencies; and

(ii) highly trained full-time employees who will lead and manage the disaster team.

(3) TRAINING.—

The Secretary shall ensure that appropriate and ongoing training is provided to members of the disaster team to ensure that the members are adequately trained regarding the programs and policies of the Economic Development Administration relating to post-disaster economic recovery efforts.

(4) EXPENSES.—

In carrying out this section, the Secretary may—

(A) use, with or without reimbursement, any service, equipment, personnel, or facility of any Federal agency with the explicit support of that agency, to the extent such use does not impair or conflict with the authority of the President or the Administrator of the Federal Emergency Management Agency under the Robert T. Stafford Disaster Relief and Emergency Assistance Act (42 U.S.C. 5121 et seq.) to direct Federal agencies in any major disaster or emergency declared under that Act; and

(B) provide members of the disaster team with travel expenses, including per diem in lieu of subsistence, at rates authorized for an employee of an agency under subchapter I of chapter 57 of title 5, while away from the home or regular place of business of the member in the performance of services for, or relating to, the disaster team.

(d) ANNUAL REPORTS.—

Not later than July 1, 2026, and annually thereafter, the Secretary shall submit to the Committee on Environment and Public Works of the Senate and the Committee on Transportation and Infrastructure of the House of Representatives a report that includes—

(1) a summary of the activities of the Office of Disaster Recovery and Resilience and any disaster teams established pursuant to subsection (c);

(2) the number and details of the disasters in which the Office of Disaster Recovery

and Resilience and permanent and temporary personnel, including disaster teams, were involved and deployed;

(3) the locations and length of any deployments;

(4) the number of personnel deployed, broken down by category, including permanent and temporary personnel; and

(5) a breakdown of expenses, with or without reimbursement.

(Pub. L. 89–136, title V, §509, as added Pub. L. 118–272, div. B, title II, §2228, Jan. 4, 2025, 138 Stat. 3192.)

§3200. Technical Assistance Liaisons

(a) In general.—

A Regional Director of a regional office of the Economic Development Administration may designate a staff member to act as a "Technical Assistance Liaison" for any State served by the regional office.

(b) Role.—

A Technical Assistance Liaison shall—

(1) work in coordination with an Economic Development Representative to provide technical assistance, in addition to technical assistance under section 3147 of this title, to eligible recipients that are underresourced communities, as determined by the Technical Assistance Liaison, that submit applications for assistance under subchapter II; and

(2) at the request of an eligible recipient that submitted an application for assistance under subchapter II, provide technical feedback on unsuccessful grant applications.

(c) Technical assistance.—

The Secretary may enter into a contract or cooperative agreement with an eligible recipient for the purpose of providing technical assistance to eligible recipients that are underresourced communities that have submitted or may submit an application for assistance under this chapter.

(Pub. L. 89–136, title V, §510, as added Pub. L. 118–272, div. B, title II, §2229, Jan. 4, 2025, 138 Stat. 3195.)

SUBCHAPTER VI—MISCELLANEOUS

§3211. Powers of Secretary

(a) In general.—

In carrying out the duties of the Secretary under this chapter, the Secretary may—

(1) adopt, alter, and use a seal, which shall be judicially noticed;

(2) subject to the civil service and classification laws, select, employ, appoint, and fix the compensation of such personnel as are necessary to carry out this chapter;

(3) hold such hearings, sit and act at such times and places, and take such testimony, as the Secretary determines to be appropriate;

(4) request directly, from any Federal agency, board, commission, office, or independent establishment, such information, suggestions, estimates, and statistics as the Secretary determines to be necessary to carry out this chapter (and each Federal agency, board, commission, office, or independent establishment may provide such

information, suggestions, estimates, and statistics directly to the Secretary);

(5) under regulations promulgated by the Secretary—

(A) assign or sell at public or private sale, or otherwise dispose of for cash or credit, in the Secretary's discretion and on such terms and conditions and for such consideration as the Secretary determines to be reasonable, any evidence of debt, contract, claim, personal property, or security assigned to or held by the Secretary in connection with assistance provided under this chapter; and

(B) collect or compromise all obligations assigned to or held by the Secretary in connection with that assistance until such time as the obligations are referred to the Attorney General for suit or collection;

(6) deal with, complete, renovate, improve, modernize, insure, rent, or sell for cash or credit, on such terms and conditions and for such consideration as the Secretary determines to be reasonable, any real or personal property conveyed to or otherwise acquired by the Secretary in connection with assistance provided under this chapter;

(7) pursue to final collection, by means of compromise or other administrative action, before referral to the Attorney General, all claims against third parties assigned to the Secretary in connection with assistance provided under this chapter;

(8) acquire, in any lawful manner, any property (real, personal, or mixed, tangible or intangible), to the extent appropriate in connection with assistance provided under this chapter;

(9) in addition to any powers, functions, privileges, and immunities otherwise vested in the Secretary, take any action, including the procurement of the services of attorneys by contract, determined by the Secretary to be necessary or desirable in making, purchasing, servicing, compromising, modifying, liquidating, or otherwise administratively dealing with assets held in connection with financial assistance provided under this chapter;

(10)(A) employ experts and consultants or organizations as authorized by section 3109 of title 5 except that contracts for such employment may be renewed annually;

(B) compensate individuals so employed, including compensation for travel time; and

(C) allow individuals so employed, while away from their homes or regular places of business, travel expenses, including per diem in lieu of subsistence, as authorized by section 5703 of title 5 for persons employed intermittently in the Federal Government service;

(11) establish performance measures for grants and other assistance provided under this chapter, and use the performance measures to evaluate the economic impact of economic development assistance programs under this chapter, which establishment and use of performance measures shall be provided by the Secretary through—

(A) officers or employees of the Department;

(B) the employment of persons under contracts entered into for such purposes; or

(C) grants to persons, using funds made available to carry out this chapter;

(12) conduct environmental reviews and incur necessary expenses to evaluate and monitor the environmental impact of economic development assistance provided and proposed to be provided under this chapter, including expenses associated with

the representation and defense of the actions of the Secretary relating to the environmental impact of the assistance, using any funds made available to carry out section 3147 of this title;

(13) sue and be sued in any court of record of a State having general jurisdiction or in any United States district court, except that no attachment, injunction, garnishment, or other similar process, mesne or final, shall be issued against the Secretary or the property of the Secretary; and

(14) establish such rules, regulations, and procedures as the Secretary considers appropriate for carrying out this chapter.

(b) DEFICIENCY JUDGMENTS.—

The authority under subsection (a)(7) to pursue claims shall include the authority to obtain deficiency judgments or otherwise pursue claims relating to mortgages assigned to the Secretary.

(c) INAPPLICABILITY OF CERTAIN OTHER REQUIREMENTS.—

Section 6101 of title 41 shall not apply to any contract of hazard insurance or to any purchase or contract for services or supplies on account of property obtained by the Secretary as a result of assistance provided under this chapter if the premium for the insurance or the amount of the services or supplies does not exceed $1,000.

(d) PROPERTY INTERESTS.—

(1) IN GENERAL.—

The powers of the Secretary under this section, relating to property acquired by the Secretary in connection with assistance provided under this chapter, shall extend to property interests of the Secretary relating to projects approved under—

(A) this chapter;

(B) title I of the Public Works Employment Act of 1976 (42 U.S.C. 6701 et seq.);

(C) title II of the Trade Act of 1974 (19 U.S.C. 2251 et seq.); and

(D) the Community Emergency Drought Relief Act of 1977 (42 U.S.C. 5184 note; Public Law 95–31).

(2) RELEASE.—

(A) IN GENERAL.—

Except as provided in subparagraph (B), the Secretary may release, in whole or in part, any real property interest, or tangible personal property interest, in connection with a grant after the date that is 20 years after the date on which the grant was awarded.

(B) CERTAIN RELEASES.—

(i) IN GENERAL.—

On written request from a recipient of a grant under section 3149(d) [1] of this title, the Secretary shall release, in accordance with this subparagraph, any Federal interest in connection with the grant, if—

(I) the request is made not less than 7 years after the final disbursement of the original grant;

(II) the recipient has complied with the terms and conditions of the grant to the satisfaction of the Secretary;

(III) any proceeds realized from the grant will be used for 1 or more activities that continue to carry out the economic development purposes of this chapter; and

(IV) the recipient includes in the written request a description of how the recipient will use the proceeds of the grant in accordance with subclause (III).

(ii) DEADLINE.—

(I) IN GENERAL.—

Except as provided in subclause (II), the Secretary shall complete all closeout actions for the grant by not later than 180 days after receipt and acceptance of the written request under clause (i).

(II) EXTENSION.—

The Secretary may extend a deadline under subclause (I) by an additional 180 days if the Secretary determines the extension to be necessary.

(iii) SAVINGS PROVISION.—

Section 3212 of this title shall continue to apply to a project assisted with a grant under section 3149(d) [1] of this title regardless of whether the Secretary releases a Federal interest under clause (i).

(e) POWERS OF CONVEYANCE AND EXECUTION.—

The power to convey and to execute, in the name of the Secretary, deeds of conveyance, deeds of release, assignments and satisfactions of mortgages, and any other written instrument relating to real or personal property or any interest in such property acquired by the Secretary under this chapter may be exercised by the Secretary, or by any officer or agent appointed by the Secretary for that purpose, without the execution of any express delegation of power or power of attorney.

(Pub. L. 89–136, title VI, §601, as added Pub. L. 105–393, title I, §102(a), Nov. 13, 1998, 112 Stat. 3611; amended Pub. L. 116–192, §2, Oct. 30, 2020, 134 Stat. 978.)

[1] *See References in Text note below.*

§3212. MAINTENANCE OF STANDARDS

All laborers and mechanics employed by contractors or subcontractors on projects assisted by the Secretary under this chapter shall be paid wages at rates not less than those prevailing on similar construction in the locality as determined by the Secretary of Labor in accordance with subchapter IV of chapter 31 of title 40. The Secretary shall not extend any financial assistance under this chapter for such a project without first obtaining adequate assurance that these labor standards will be maintained upon the construction work. The Secretary of Labor shall have, with respect to the labor standards specified in this provision, the authority and functions set forth in Reorganization Plan Numbered 14 of 1950 (15 F.R. 3176; 64 Stat. 1267), and section 3145 of title 40.

(Pub. L. 89–136, title VI, §602, formerly title VII, §712, Aug. 26, 1965, 79 Stat. 575; Pub. L. 93–567, title III, §302, Dec. 31, 1974, 88 Stat. 1855; renumbered title VI, §602, and amended Pub. L. 105–393, title I, §102(b)(1), (2), Nov. 13, 1998, 112 Stat. 3616; Pub. L. 108–373, title V, §504, Oct. 27, 2004, 118 Stat. 1769.)

§3213. ANNUAL REPORT TO CONGRESS

(a) IN GENERAL.—

Not later than July 1, 2000, and July 1 of each year thereafter, the Secretary shall submit to Congress a comprehensive and detailed annual report on the activities of the Secretary under this chapter during the most recently completed fiscal year.

(b) INCLUSIONS.—

Each report required under subsection (a) shall—

(1) include a list of all grant recipients by State, including the projected private sector dollar to Federal dollar investment ratio for each grant recipient;

(2) include a discussion of any private sector leveraging goal with respect to grants awarded to—

(A) rural areas and urban economically distressed areas; and

(B) highly distressed areas;

(3) after the completion of a project, include the realized private sector dollar to Federal dollar investment ratio for the project; and

(4)(A) include a list of all of the grants provided by the Economic Development Administration for projects located in, or that primarily benefit, rural areas;

(B) an explanation of the process used to determine how each project referred to in subparagraph (A) would benefit a rural area; and

(C) a certification that each project referred to in subparagraph (A)—

(i) is located in a rural area; or

(ii) will primarily benefit a rural area.

(c) ADDITIONAL REPORTING.—

As part of the annual report to Congress of the Economic Development Administration, the Secretary shall include a report on project completions and close outs for construction awards that includes the following information on individual construction projects:

(1) The award date of the project.

(2) The completion date of the project.

(3) The close out date of the project.

(4) The total amount of the project, including non-Federal cost share and funding from other sources, including a breakdown by source.

(5) The number of jobs anticipated to be created or retained as a result of the investment.

(d) PUBLIC AVAILABILITY.—

Not later than the date of the submission of the report under subsection (c), the Secretary shall make the report under subsection (c) publicly available.

(e) ADDITIONAL REPORTING REQUIREMENT.—

To ensure that projects are meeting expected timelines, not later than 1 year after January 4, 2025, the Secretary shall submit to the Committee on Environment and Public Works of the Senate and the Committee on Transportation and Infrastructure of the House of Representatives a report that, at a minimum—

(1) includes an analysis of Economic Development Administration construction project timeline estimates and actual project durations; and

(2) describes the frequency with which project timelines are delayed and the sources of those delays, including cases in which a project scope or schedule requires an award amendment.

(Pub. L. 89–136, title VI, §603, as added Pub. L. 105–393, title I, §102(a), Nov. 13, 1998, 112 Stat. 3614;

amended Pub. L. 108–373, title VI, §601, Oct. 27, 2004, 118 Stat. 1769; Pub. L. 118–272, div. B, title II, §2230, Jan. 4, 2025, 138 Stat. 3196.)

§3214. Delegation of functions and transfer of funds among Federal agencies

(a) DELEGATION OF FUNCTIONS TO OTHER FEDERAL AGENCIES.—

The Secretary may—

(1) delegate to the heads of other Federal agencies such functions, powers, and duties of the Secretary under this chapter as the Secretary determines to be appropriate; and

(2) authorize the redelegation of the functions, powers, and duties by the heads of the agencies.

(b) Transfer of funds to other Federal agencies.—

Funds authorized to be appropriated to carry out this chapter may be transferred between Federal agencies, if the funds are used for the purposes for which the funds are specifically authorized and appropriated.

(c) Transfer of funds from other Federal agencies.—

(1) IN GENERAL.—

Subject to paragraph (2), for the purposes of this chapter, the Secretary may accept transfers of funds from other Federal agencies if the funds are used for the purposes for which (and in accordance with the terms under which) the funds are specifically authorized and appropriated.

(2) USE OF FUNDS.—

The transferred funds—

(A) shall remain available until expended; and

(B) may, to the extent necessary to carry out this chapter, be transferred to and merged by the Secretary with the appropriations for salaries and expenses.

(Pub. L. 89–136, title VI, §604, as added Pub. L. 105–393, title I, §102(a), Nov. 13, 1998, 112 Stat. 3614.)

§3215. Penalties

(a) FALSE STATEMENTS; SECURITY OVERVALUATION.—

A person that makes any statement that the person knows to be false, or willfully overvalues any security, for the purpose of—

(1) obtaining for the person or for any applicant any financial assistance under this chapter or any extension of the assistance by renewal, deferment, or action, or by any other means, or the acceptance, release, or substitution of security for the assistance;

(2) influencing in any manner the action of the Secretary; or

(3) obtaining money, property, or any thing of value, under this chapter;

shall be fined under title 18, imprisoned not more than 5 years, or both.

(b) EMBEZZLEMENT AND FRAUD-RELATED CRIMES.—

A person that is connected in any capacity with the Secretary in the administration of this chapter and that—

(1) embezzles, abstracts, purloins, or willfully misapplies any funds, securities, or other thing of value, that is pledged or otherwise entrusted to the person;

(2) with intent to defraud the Secretary or any other person or entity, or to deceive any officer, auditor, or examiner—

(A) makes any false entry in any book, report, or statement of or to the Secretary; or

(B) without being duly authorized, draws any order or issue, puts forth, or assigns any note, debenture, bond, or other obligation, or draft, bill of exchange, mortgage, judgment, or decree thereof;

(3) with intent to defraud, participates or shares in or receives directly or indirectly any money, profit, property, or benefit through any transaction, loan, grant, commission, contract, or any other act of the Secretary; or

(4) gives any unauthorized information concerning any future action or plan of the Secretary that might affect the value of securities, or having such knowledge invests or speculates, directly or indirectly, in the securities or property of any company or corporation receiving loans, grants, or other assistance from the Secretary; shall be fined under title 18, imprisoned not more than 5 years, or both.

(Pub. L. 89–136, title VI, §605, as added Pub. L. 105–393, title I, §102(a), Nov. 13, 1998, 112 Stat. 3614.)

§3216. Employment of expediters and administrative employees

Assistance shall not be provided by the Secretary under this chapter to any business unless the owners, partners, or officers of the business—

(1) certify to the Secretary the names of any attorneys, agents, and other persons engaged by or on behalf of the business for the purpose of expediting applications made to the Secretary for assistance of any kind, under this chapter, and the fees paid or to be paid to the person for expediting the applications; and

(2) execute an agreement binding the business, for the 2-year period beginning on the date on which the assistance is provided by the Secretary to the business, to refrain from employing, offering any office or employment to, or retaining for professional services, any person who, on the date on which the assistance or any part of the assistance was provided, or within the 1-year period ending on that date—

(A) served as an officer, attorney, agent, or employee of the Department; and

(B) occupied a position or engaged in activities that the Secretary determines involved discretion with respect to the granting of assistance under this chapter.

(Pub. L. 89–136, title VI, §606, as added Pub. L. 105–393, title I, §102(a), Nov. 13, 1998, 112 Stat. 3615.)

§3217. Maintenance and public inspection of list of approved applications for financial assistance

(a) In general.—

The Secretary shall—

(1) maintain as a permanent part of the records of the Department a list of applications approved for financial assistance under this chapter; and

(2) make the list available for public inspection during the regular business hours of the Department.

(b) Additions to list.—

The following information shall be added to the list maintained under subsection (a) as soon as an application described in subsection (a)(1) is approved:

(1) The name of the applicant and, in the case of a corporate application, the name of each officer and director of the corporation.

(2) The amount and duration of the financial assistance for which application is made.

(3) The purposes for which the proceeds of the financial assistance are to be used.

(Pub. L. 89–136, title VI, §607, as added Pub. L. 105–393, title I, §102(a), Nov. 13, 1998, 112 Stat. 3615.)

§3218. RECORDS AND AUDITS

(a) RECORDKEEPING AND DISCLOSURE REQUIREMENTS.—

Each recipient of assistance under this chapter shall keep such records as the Secretary shall require, including records that fully disclose—

(1) the amount and the disposition by the recipient of the proceeds of the assistance;

(2) the total cost of the project in connection with which the assistance is given or used;

(3) the amount and nature of the portion of the cost of the project provided by other sources; and

(4) such other records as will facilitate an effective audit.

(b) ACCESS TO BOOKS FOR EXAMINATION AND AUDIT.—

The Secretary, the Inspector General of the Department, and the Comptroller General of the United States, or any duly authorized representative, shall have access for the purpose of audit and examination to any books, documents, papers, and records of the recipient that relate to assistance received under this chapter.

(Pub. L. 89–136, title VI, §608, as added Pub. L. 105–393, title I, §102(a), Nov. 13, 1998, 112 Stat. 3616.)

§3219. RELATIONSHIP TO ASSISTANCE UNDER OTHER LAW

Nothing in this chapter authorizes or permits any reduction in the amount of Federal assistance that any State or other entity eligible under this chapter is entitled to receive under any other Act.

(Pub. L. 89–136, title VI, §609, as added Pub. L. 105–393, title I, §102(a), Nov. 13, 1998, 112 Stat. 3616; amended Pub. L. 108–373, title VI, §602, Oct. 27, 2004, 118 Stat. 1769.)

§3220. ACCEPTANCE OF CERTIFICATIONS BY APPLICANTS

Under terms and conditions determined by the Secretary, the Secretary may accept the certifications of an applicant for assistance under this chapter that the applicant meets the requirements of this chapter.

(Pub. L. 89–136, title VI, §610, as added Pub. L. 105–393, title I, §102(a), Nov. 13, 1998, 112 Stat. 3616.)

§3221. BROWNFIELDS REDEVELOPMENT REPORT

(a) DEFINITION OF BROWNFIELD SITE.—

In this section, the term "brownfield site" has the meaning given the term in section

9601(39) of this title.

(b) REPORT.—

(1) IN GENERAL.—

Not later than 1 year after October 27, 2004, the Comptroller General shall prepare a report that evaluates the grants made by the Economic Development Administration for the economic development of brownfield sites.

(2) CONTENTS.—

The report shall—

(A) identify each project conducted during the previous 10-year period in which grant funds have been used for brownfield sites redevelopment activities; and

(B) include for each project a description of—

(i) the type of economic development activities conducted;

(ii) if remediation activities were conducted—

(I) the type of remediation activities; and

(II) the amount of grant money used for those activities in dollars and as a percentage of the total grant award;

(iii) the economic development and environmental standards applied, if applicable;

(iv) the economic development impact of the project;

(v) the role of Federal, State, or local environmental agencies, if any; and

(vi) public participation in the project.

(3) SUBMISSION OF REPORT.—

The Comptroller General shall submit to the Committee on Environment and Public Works of the Senate and the Committee on Transportation and Infrastructure of the House of Representatives a copy of the report.

(Pub. L. 89–136, title VI, §611, as added Pub. L. 108–373, title VI, §603(a), Oct. 27, 2004, 118 Stat. 1769.)

§3222. SAVINGS CLAUSE

To the extent that any portion of grants made under this chapter are used for an economic development project that involves remediation, the remediation shall be conducted in compliance with all applicable Federal, State, and local laws and standards.

(Pub. L. 89–136, title VI, §612, as added Pub. L. 108–373, title VI, §604(a), Oct. 27, 2004, 118 Stat. 1770.)

SUBCHAPTER VII—FUNDING

§3231. GENERAL AUTHORIZATION OF APPROPRIATIONS

(a) GRANTS FOR PUBLIC WORKS AND ECONOMIC DEVELOPMENT.—

There are authorized to be appropriated to carry out section 3141 of this title, to remain available until expended—

(1) $170,000,000 for fiscal year 2025;

(2) $195,000,000 for fiscal year 2026;

(3) $220,000,000 for fiscal year 2027;

(4) $245,000,000 for fiscal year 2028; and

(5) $270,000,000 for fiscal year 2029.

(b) GRANTS FOR PLANNING AND GRANTS FOR ADMINISTRATIVE EXPENSES.—

There are authorized to be appropriated to carry out section 3143 of this title, to remain available until expended—

(1) $90,000,000 for fiscal year 2025;

(2) $100,000,000 for fiscal year 2026;

(3) $110,000,000 for fiscal year 2027;

(4) $120,000,000 for fiscal year 2028; and

(5) $130,000,000 for fiscal year 2029.

(c) GRANTS FOR TRAINING, RESEARCH, AND TECHNICAL ASSISTANCE.—

There are authorized to be appropriated to carry out section 3147 of this title, to remain available until expended—

(1) $25,000,000 for fiscal year 2025;

(2) $30,000,000 for fiscal year 2026;

(3) $35,000,000 for fiscal year 2027;

(4) $40,000,000 for fiscal year 2028; and

(5) $45,000,000 for fiscal year 2029.

(d) GRANTS FOR ECONOMIC ADJUSTMENT.—

There are authorized to be appropriated to carry out section 3149 of this title (other than subsections (d) and (e)), to remain available until expended—

(1) $65,000,000 for fiscal year 2025;

(2) $75,000,000 for fiscal year 2026;

(3) $85,000,000 for fiscal year 2027;

(4) $95,000,000 for fiscal year 2028; and

(5) $105,000,000 for fiscal year 2029.

(e) ASSISTANCE TO COAL COMMUNITIES.—

There is authorized to be appropriated to carry out section 3149(d) of this title $75,000,000 for each of fiscal years 2025 through 2029, to remain available until expended.

(f) ASSISTANCE TO NUCLEAR HOST COMMUNITIES.—

There are authorized to be appropriated to carry out section 3149(e) of this title, to remain available until expended—

(1) to carry out paragraph (2)(A), $35,000,000 for each of fiscal years 2025 through 2029; and

(2) to carry out paragraph (2)(B), $5,000,000 for each of fiscal years 2025 through 2027.

(g) RENEWABLE ENERGY PROGRAM.—

There is authorized to be appropriated to carry out section 3154d of this title $5,000,000 for each of fiscal years 2025 through 2029, to remain available until expended.

(h) WORKFORCE TRAINING GRANTS.—

There is authorized to be appropriated to carry out section 3154e of this title $50,000,000 for each of fiscal years 2025 through 2029, to remain available until expended, of which $10,000,000 for each of fiscal years 2025 through 2029 shall be used to carry out subsection (c) of that section.

(i) CRITICAL SUPPLY CHAIN SITE DEVELOPMENT GRANT PROGRAM.—

There is authorized to be appropriated to carry out section 3154h of this title $20,000,000 for each of fiscal years 2025 through 2029, to remain available until expended.

(j) TECHNICAL ASSISTANCE LIAISONS.—

There is authorized to be appropriated to carry out section 3200 of this title $5,000,000 for each of fiscal years 2025 through 2029, to remain available until expended.

(k) SALARIES AND EXPENSES.—

There are authorized to be appropriated for salaries and expenses of administering this chapter, to remain available until expended—

(1) $33,377,000 for fiscal year 2004; and

(2) such sums as are necessary for each fiscal year thereafter.

(Pub. L. 89–136, title VII, §701, as added Pub. L. 105–393, title I, §102(b)(3), Nov. 13, 1998, 112 Stat. 3617; amended Pub. L. 108–373, title VII, §701, Oct. 27, 2004, 118 Stat. 1771; Pub. L. 118–272, div. B, title II, §2236(a), Jan. 4, 2025, 138 Stat. 3199.)

§3232. AUTHORIZATION OF APPROPRIATIONS FOR DEFENSE CONVERSION ACTIVITIES

(a) IN GENERAL.—

In addition to amounts made available under section 3231 of this title, there are authorized to be appropriated such sums as are necessary to carry out section 3149(c)(1) of this title, to remain available until expended.

(b) PILOT PROJECTS.—

Funds made available under subsection (a) may be used for activities including pilot projects for privatization of, and economic development activities for, closed or realigned military or Department of Energy installations.

(Pub. L. 89–136, title VII, §702, as added Pub. L. 105–393, title I, §102(b)(3), Nov. 13, 1998, 112 Stat. 3617.)

§3233. AUTHORIZATION OF APPROPRIATIONS FOR DISASTER ECONOMIC RECOVERY ACTIVITIES

(a) IN GENERAL.—

In addition to amounts made available under section 3231 of this title, there are authorized to be appropriated such sums as are necessary to carry out section 3149(c)(2) of this title, to remain available until expended.

(b) FEDERAL SHARE.—

The Federal share of the cost of activities funded with amounts made available under subsection (a) shall be up to 100 percent.

(Pub. L. 89–136, title VII, §703, as added Pub. L. 105–393, title I, §102(b)(3), Nov. 13, 1998, 112 Stat. 3617.)

§3234. REPEALED. PUB. L. 118–272, DIV. B, TITLE II, §2236(B), JAN. 4, 2025, 138 STAT. 3201

Section 3234, Pub. L. 89–136, title VII, §704, as added Pub. L. 108–373, title VII,

§3234. Repealed. Pub. L. 118–272, div. B, title II, §2236(b), Jan. 4, 2025, 138 Stat. 3201

CHAPTER 38—PUBLIC WORKS AND ECONOMIC DEVELOPMENT

§702(a), Oct. 27, 2004, 118 Stat. 1771, provided for funding for grants for planning and administrative expenses.

Prior sections 3234 and 3235 were repealed by Pub. L. 105–393, title I, §102(c), Nov. 13, 1998, 112 Stat. 3617.

Section 3234, Pub. L. 89–136, title VIII, §804, as added Pub. L. 93–288, title V, §501, May 22, 1974, 88 Stat. 162, authorized disaster area loan guarantees.

Section 3235, Pub. L. 89–136, title VIII, §805, as added Pub. L. 93–288, title V, §501, May 22, 1974, 88 Stat. 162, authorized provision of technical assistance for facilitation of economic recovery in disaster areas.

A prior section 3236, Pub. L. 89–136, title VIII, §806, as added Pub. L. 93–288, title V, §501, May 22, 1974, 88 Stat. 163, related to authorization of appropriations for subchapter, prior to repeal by Pub. L. 97–35, title XVIII, §1821(a)(10), Aug. 13, 1981, 95 Stat. 766.

Prior sections 3241 to 3246c were repealed by Pub. L. 105–393, title I §102(c), Nov. 13, 1998, 112 Stat. 3617.

Section 3241, Pub. L. 89–136, title IX, §901, as added Pub. L. 93–423, §12, Sept. 27, 1974, 88 Stat. 1164; amended Pub. L. 94–487, title I, §121(a), Oct. 12, 1976, 90 Stat. 2336, stated purpose of former subchapter IX.

Section 3242, Pub. L. 89–136, title IX, §902, as added Pub. L. 93–423, §12, Sept. 27, 1974, 88 Stat. 1164, defined "eligible recipient".

Section 3243, Pub. L. 89–136, title IX, §903, as added Pub. L. 93–423, §12, Sept. 27, 1974, 88 Stat. 1164; amended Pub. L. 94–487, title I, §121(b), (c), Oct. 12, 1976, 90 Stat. 2336, authorized grants to eligible recipients.

Section 3244, Pub. L. 89–136, title IX, §904, as added Pub. L. 93–423, §12, Sept. 27, 1974, 88 Stat. 1165; amended Pub. L. 96–470, title II, §201(c), Oct. 19, 1980, 94 Stat. 2241, required annual reports by recipients and Secretary.

Section 3245, Pub. L. 89–136, title IX, §905, as added Pub. L. 93–423, §12, Sept. 27, 1974, 88 Stat. 1166; amended Pub. L. 94–487, title I, §121(d), Oct. 12, 1976, 90 Stat. 2336; Pub. L. 96–506, §1(10), Dec. 8, 1980, 94 Stat. 2746; Pub. L. 97–35, title XVIII, §1821(a)(11), Aug. 13, 1981, 95 Stat. 766, authorized appropriations.

Section 3246, Pub. L. 89–136, title X, §1001, as added Pub. L. 93–567, title III, §301, Dec. 31, 1974, 88 Stat. 1853, stated the purpose of former subchapter X.

Section 3246a, Pub. L. 89–136, title X, §1002, as added Pub. L. 93–567, title III, §301, Dec. 31, 1974, 88 Stat. 1853; amended Pub. L. 94–487, title I, §122, Oct. 12, 1976, 90 Stat. 2337, defined "eligible area".

Section 3246b, Pub. L. 89–136, title X, §1003, as added Pub. L. 93–567, title III, §301, Dec. 31, 1974, 88 Stat. 1853; amended Pub. L. 94–487, title I, §123, Oct. 12, 1976, 90 Stat. 2337, authorized a job opportunities program.

Section 3246c, Pub. L. 89–136, title X, §1004, as added Pub. L. 93–567, title III, §301, Dec. 31, 1974, 88 Stat. 1854; amended Pub. L. 94–487, title I, §124, Oct. 12, 1976, 90 Stat. 2337, related to program review.

A prior section 3246d, Pub. L. 89–136, title X, §1005, as added Pub. L. 93–567, title III, §301, Dec. 31, 1974, 88 Stat. 1855, related to the limitations on the use of funds appropriated pursuant to section 3246f of this title for programs and projects, prior to repeal by Pub. L. 94–487, title I, §125, Oct. 12, 1976, 90 Stat. 2338.

§3234. Repealed. Pub. L. 118–272, div. B, title II, §2236(b), Jan. 4, 2025, 138 Stat. 3201

CHAPTER 38—PUBLIC WORKS AND
ECONOMIC DEVELOPMENT

Prior sections 3246e to 3246h were repealed by Pub. L. 105–393, title I, §102(c), Nov. 13, 1998, 112 Stat. 3617.

Section 3246e, Pub. L. 89–136, title X, §1005, formerly §1006, as added Pub. L. 93–567, title III, §301, Dec. 31, 1974, 88 Stat. 1855; renumbered §1005 and amended Pub. L. 94–487, title I, §§125, 126, Oct. 12, 1976, 90 Stat. 2338, authorized the prescription of rules, regulations, and procedures.

Section 3246f, Pub. L. 89–136, title X, §1006, formerly §1007, as added Pub. L. 93–567, title III, §301, Dec. 31, 1974, 88 Stat. 1855; renumbered §1006 and amended Pub. L. 94–487, title I, §§125, 127, Oct. 12, 1976, 90 Stat. 2338, authorized appropriations.

Section 3246g, Pub. L. 89–136, title X, §1007, formerly §1008, as added Pub. L. 93–567, title III, §301, Dec. 31, 1976, 88 Stat. 1855; renumbered §1007 and amended Pub. L. 94–487, title I, §§125, 128, Oct. 12, 1976, 90 Stat. 2338; Pub. L. 96–506, §1(11), Dec. 8, 1980, 94 Stat. 2746; Pub. L. 97–35, title XVIII, §1821(a)(12), Aug. 13, 1981, 95 Stat. 766, provided that no further obligation of funds appropriated under former subchapter X could be made by the Secretary of Commerce after Sept. 30, 1981.

Section 3246h, Pub. L. 89–136, title X, §1008, as added Pub. L. 94–487, title I, §129, Oct. 12, 1976, 90 Stat. 2339, provided that a program or project was not ineligible for financial assistance solely because of increased construction costs.

CHAPTER 39—SOLID WASTE DISPOSAL

§§3251 TO 3254F. OMITTED

§3255. REPEALED. PUB. L. 91–512, TITLE I, §104(A), OCT. 26, 1970, 84 STAT. 1228

Section, Pub. L. 89–272, title II, §206, Oct. 20, 1965, 79 Stat. 999, authorized grants to State and interstate agencies for surveys of solid-waste disposal practices and problems, and for development of solid-waste disposal plans.

Economic Development Administration Reuathorization Act of 2004 - Sec. 605

Public Law 108–373

ECONOMIC DEVELOPMENT ADMINISTRATION REAUTHORIZATION ACT OF 2004

Section 605

[Public Law 108-373]

SEC. 605. SENSE OF CONGRESS REGARDING ECONOMIC DEVELOPMENT REPRESENTATIVES.

(a) FINDINGS.— Congress finds that —

(1) planning and coordination among Federal agencies, State and local governments, Indian tribes, and economic development districts is vital to the success of an economic development program;

(2) economic development representatives of the Economic Development Administration provide distressed communities with the technical assistance necessary to foster this planning and coordination; and

(3) in the 5 years preceding the date of enactment of this Act, the number of economic development representatives has declined by almost 25 percent.

(b) SENSE OF CONGRESS.— It is the sense of Congress that the Secretary should maintain a sufficient number of economic development representatives to ensure that the Economic Development Administration is able to provide effective assistance to distressed communities and foster economic growth and development among the States.

★

APPALACHIAN REGIONAL DEVELOPMENT

SUBTITLE IV OF TITLE 40 U.S.C.

SUBTITLE IV—APPALACHIAN REGIONAL DEVELOPMENT

Chapter		Sec.
141.	GENERAL PROVISIONS	14101
143.	APPALACHIAN REGIONAL COMMISSION	14301
145.	SPECIAL APPALACHIAN PROGRAMS	14501
147.	MISCELLANEOUS	14701

CHAPTER 141—GENERAL PROVISIONS

Sec.
14101.   Findings and purposes.
14102.   Definitions.

§14101. FINDINGS AND PURPOSES

(a) 1965 FINDINGS AND PURPOSE.—

(1) FINDINGS.—Congress finds and declares that the Appalachian region of the United States, while abundant in natural resources and rich in potential, lags behind the rest of the Nation in its economic growth and that its people have not shared properly in the Nation's prosperity. The region's uneven past development, with its historical reliance on a few basic industries and a marginal agriculture, has failed to provide the economic base that is a vital prerequisite for vigorous, self-sustaining growth. State and local governments and the people of the region understand their problems and have been working, and will continue to work, purposefully toward their solution. Congress recognizes the comprehensive report of the President's Appalachian Regional Commission documenting these findings and concludes that regionwide development is feasible, desirable, and urgently needed.

(2) PURPOSE.—It is the purpose of this subtitle to assist the region in meeting its special problems, to promote its economic development, and to establish a framework for joint federal and state efforts toward providing the basic facilities essential to its growth and attacking its common problems and meeting its common needs on a coordinated and concerted regional basis. The public investments made in the region under this subtitle shall be concentrated in areas where there is a significant potential for future growth and where the expected return on public dollars invested will be the greatest. States will be responsible for recommending local and state projects within their borders that will receive assistance under this subtitle. As the region obtains the needed physical and transportation facilities and develops its human resources, Congress expects that the region will generate a diversified industry and that the region will then be able to support itself through the workings of a strengthened free enterprise economy.

(b) 1975 FINDINGS AND PURPOSE.—

(1) FINDINGS.—Congress further finds and declares that while substantial progress has been made toward achieving the purposes set out in subsection (a), especially with respect to the provision of essential public facilities, much remains to be accomplished, especially with respect to the provision of essential health, education, and other public services. Congress recognizes that changes and evolving national purposes in the decade since 1965 affect not only the Appalachian region but also its relationship to a nation that on December 31, 1975, is assigning higher priority to conservation and the quality of life, values long cherished within the region. Appalachia as of December 31, 1975, has the opportunity, in accommodating future growth and development, to demonstrate local leadership and coordinated planning so that housing, public services, transportation and other community facilities will be provided in a way congenial to the traditions and beauty of the region and

compatible with conservation values and an enhanced quality of life for the people of the region, and consistent with that goal, the Appalachian region should be able to take advantage of eco-industrial development, which promotes both employment and economic growth and the preservation of natural resources. Congress recognizes also that fundamental changes are occurring in national energy requirements and production, which not only risk short-term dislocations but will undoubtedly result in major long-term effects in the region. It is essential that the opportunities for expanded energy production be used so as to maximize the social and economic benefits and minimize the social and environmental costs to the region and its people.

(2) PURPOSE.—It is also the purpose of this subtitle to provide a framework for coordinating federal, state and local efforts toward—

(A) anticipating the effects of alternative energy policies and practices;

(B) planning for accompanying growth and change so as to maximize the social and economic benefits and minimize the social and environmental costs; and

(C) implementing programs and projects carried out in the region by federal, state, and local governmental agencies so as to better meet the special problems generated in the region by the Nation's energy needs and policies, including problems of transportation, housing, community facilities, and human services.

(c) 1998 FINDINGS AND PURPOSE.—

(1) FINDINGS.—Congress further finds and declares that while substantial progress has been made in fulfilling many of the objectives of this subtitle, rapidly changing national and global economies over the decade ending November 13, 1998, have created new problems and challenges for rural areas throughout the United States and especially for the Appalachian region.

(2) PURPOSE.—In addition to the purposes stated in subsections (a) and (b), it is the purpose of this subtitle—

(A) to assist the Appalachian region in—

(i) providing the infrastructure necessary for economic and human resource development;

(ii) developing the region's industry;

(iii) building entrepreneurial communities;

(iv) generating a diversified regional economy; and

(v) making the region's industrial and commercial resources more competitive in national and world markets;

(B) to provide a framework for coordinating federal, state, and local initiatives to respond to the economic competitiveness challenges in the Appalachian region through—

(i) improving the skills of the region's workforce;

(ii) adapting and applying new technologies for the region's businesses, including eco-industrial development technologies; and

(iii) improving the access of the region's businesses to the technical and financial resources necessary to development of the businesses; and

(C) to address the needs of severely and persistently distressed areas of the Appalachian region and focus special attention on the areas of greatest need so as to provide a fairer opportunity for the people of the region to share the quality of life generally enjoyed by citizens across the United States.

(Pub. L. 107–217, Aug. 21, 2002, 116 Stat. 1252.)

§14102. DEFINITIONS

(a) DEFINITIONS.—In this subtitle—

(1) APPALACHIAN REGION.—The term "Appalachian region" means that area of the eastern United States consisting of the following counties (including any political subdivision located within the area):

(A) In Alabama, the counties of Bibb, Blount, Calhoun, Chambers, Cherokee, Chilton, Clay, Cleburne, Colbert, Coosa, Cullman, De Kalb, Elmore, Etowah, Fayette, Franklin, Hale, Jackson, Jefferson, Lamar, Lauderdale, Lawrence, Limestone, Macon, Madison, Marion, Marshall, Morgan, Pickens, Randolph, St. Clair, Shelby, Talladega, Tallapoosa, Tuscaloosa, Walker, and Winston.

(B) In Georgia, the counties of Banks, Barrow, Bartow, Carroll, Catoosa, Chattooga, Cherokee, Dade, Dawson, Douglas, Elbert, Fannin, Floyd, Forsyth, Franklin, Gilmer, Gordon, Gwinnett, Habersham, Hall, Haralson, Hart, Heard, Jackson, Lumpkin, Madison, Murray, Paulding, Pickens, Polk, Rabun, Stephens, Towns, Union, Walker, White, and Whitfield.

(C) In Kentucky, the counties of Adair, Bath, Bell, Boyd, Breathitt, Carter, Casey, Clark, Clay, Clinton, Cumberland, Edmonson, Elliott, Estill, Fleming, Floyd, Garrard, Green, Greenup, Harlan, Hart, Jackson, Johnson, Knott, Knox, Laurel, Lawrence, Lee, Leslie, Letcher, Lewis, Lincoln, McCreary, Madison, Magoffin, Martin, Menifee, Metcalfe, Monroe, Montgomery, Morgan, Nicholas, Owsley, Perry, Pike, Powell, Pulaski, Robertson, Rockcastle, Rowan, Russell, Wayne, Whitley, and Wolfe.

(D) In Maryland, the counties of Allegany, Garrett, and Washington.

(E) In Mississippi, the counties of Alcorn, Benton, Calhoun, Chickasaw, Choctaw, Clay, Itawamba, Kemper, Lee, Lowndes, Marshall, Monroe, Montgomery, Noxubee, Oktibbeha, Panola, Pontotoc, Prentiss, Tippah, Tishomingo, Union, Webster, Winston, and Yalobusha.

(F) In New York, the counties of Allegany, Broome, Cattaraugus, Chautauqua, Chemung, Chenango, Cortland, Delaware, Otsego, Schoharie, Schuyler, Steuben, Tioga, and Tompkins.

(G) In North Carolina, the counties of Alexander, Alleghany, Ashe, Avery, Buncombe, Burke, Caldwell, Catawba, Cherokee, Clay, Cleveland, Davie, Forsyth, Graham, Haywood, Henderson, Jackson, McDowell, Macon, Madison, Mitchell, Polk, Rutherford, Stokes, Surry, Swain, Transylvania, Watauga, Wilkes, Yadkin, and Yancey.

(H) In Ohio, the counties of Adams, Ashtabula, Athens, Belmont, Brown, Carroll, Clermont, Columbiana, Coshocton, Gallia, Guernsey, Harrison, Highland, Hocking, Holmes, Jackson, Jefferson, Lawrence, Mahoning, Meigs, Monroe, Morgan, Muskingum, Noble, Perry, Pike, Ross, Scioto, Trumbull, Tuscarawas, Vinton, and Washington.

(I) In Pennsylvania, the counties of Allegheny, Armstrong, Beaver, Bedford, Blair, Bradford, Butler, Cambria, Cameron, Carbon, Centre, Clarion, Clearfield,

(d) DELEGATION.—

(1) POWERS AND RESPONSIBILITIES.—Commission powers and responsibilities specified in section 14302(c) and (d) of this title, and the vote of any Commission member, may not be delegated to an individual who is not a Commission member or who is not entitled to vote in Commission meetings.

(2) ALTERNATE FEDERAL COCHAIRMAN.—The alternate to the Federal Cochairman shall perform the functions and duties the Federal Cochairman delegates when not actively serving as the alternate.

(e) EXECUTIVE DIRECTOR.—The Commission has an executive director. The executive director is responsible for carrying out the administrative functions of the Commission, for directing the Commission staff, and for other duties the Commission may assign.

(f) STATUS OF PERSONNEL.—Members, alternates, officers, and employees of the Commission are not federal employees for any purpose, except the Federal Cochairman, the alternate to the Federal Cochairman, the staff of the Federal Cochairman, and federal employees detailed to the Commission under section 14306(a)(3) of this title.

(Pub. L. 107–217, Aug. 21, 2002, 116 Stat. 1256; Pub. L. 112–166, §2(n), Aug. 10, 2012, 126 Stat. 1287.)

[1] *So in original.*

§14302. DECISIONS

(a) REQUIREMENTS FOR APPROVAL.—Except as provided in section 14306(d) of this title, decisions by the Appalachian Regional Commission require the affirmative vote of the Federal Cochairman and of a majority of the state members, exclusive of members representing States delinquent under section 14306(d).

(b) CONSULTATION.—In matters coming before the Commission, the Federal Cochairman, to the extent practicable, shall consult with the federal departments and agencies having an interest in the subject matter.

(c) DECISIONS REQUIRING QUORUM OF STATE MEMBERS.—A decision involving Commission policy, approval of state, regional or subregional development plans or strategy statements, modification or revision of the Appalachian Regional Commission Code, allocation of amounts among the States, or designation of a distressed county or an economically strong county shall not be made without a quorum of state members.

(d) PROJECT AND GRANT PROPOSALS.—The approval of project and grant proposals is a responsibility of the Commission and shall be carried out in accordance with section 14322 of this title.

(Pub. L. 107–217, Aug. 21, 2002, 116 Stat. 1257.)

§14303. FUNCTIONS

(a) IN GENERAL.—In carrying out the purposes of this subtitle, the Appalachian Regional Commission shall—

(1) develop, on a continuing basis, comprehensive and coordinated plans and programs and establish priorities under those plans and programs, giving due consideration to other federal, state, and local planning in the Appalachian region;

(2) conduct and sponsor investigations, research, and studies, including an

Clinton, Columbia, Crawford, Elk, Erie, Fayette, Forest, Fulton, Greene, Huntingdon, Indiana, Jefferson, Juniata, Lackawanna, Lawrence, Luzerne, Lycoming, McKean, Mercer, Mifflin, Monroe, Montour, Northumberland, Perry, Pike, Potter, Schuylkill, Snyder, Somerset, Sullivan, Susquehanna, Tioga, Union, Venango, Warren, Washington, Wayne, Westmoreland, and Wyoming.

(J) In South Carolina, the counties of Anderson, Cherokee, Greenville, Oconee, Pickens, Spartanburg, and Union.

(K) In Tennessee, the counties of Anderson, Bledsoe, Blount, Bradley, Campbell, Cannon, Carter, Claiborne, Clay, Cocke, Coffee, Cumberland, De Kalb, Fentress, Franklin, Grainger, Greene, Grundy, Hamblen, Hamilton, Hancock, Hawkins, Jackson, Jefferson, Johnson, Knox, Lawrence, Lewis, Loudon, McMinn, Macon, Marion, Meigs, Monroe, Morgan, Overton, Pickett, Polk, Putnam, Rhea, Roane, Scott, Sequatchie, Sevier, Smith, Sullivan, Unicoi, Union, Van Buren, Warren, Washington, and White.

(L) In Virginia, the counties of Alleghany, Bath, Bland, Botetourt, Buchanan, Carroll, Craig, Dickenson, Floyd, Giles, Grayson, Henry, Highland, Lee, Montgomery, Patrick, Pulaski, Rockbridge, Russell, Scott, Smyth, Tazewell, Washington, Wise, and Wythe.

(M) All the counties of West Virginia, of which the counties of Brooke, Hancock, Marshall, and Ohio shall be considered to be located in the North Central subregion.

(2) LOCAL DEVELOPMENT DISTRICT.—The term "local development district" means any of the following entities for which the Governor of the State in which the entity is located, or the appropriate state officer, certifies to the Appalachian Regional Commission that the entity has a charter or authority that includes the economic development of counties or parts of counties or other political subdivisions within the region:

(A) a nonprofit incorporated body organized or chartered under the law of the State in which it is located.

(B) a nonprofit agency or instrumentality of a state or local government.

(C) a nonprofit agency or instrumentality created through an interstate compact.

(D) a nonprofit association or combination of bodies, agencies, and instrumentalities described in this paragraph.

(b) CHANGE IN DEFINITION.—The Commission may not propose or consider a recommendation for any change in the definition of the Appalachian region as set forth in this section without a prior resolution by the Committee on Environment and Public Works of the Senate or the Committee on Transportation and Infrastructure of the House of Representatives that directs a study of the change.

(Pub. L. 107–217, Aug. 21, 2002, 116 Stat. 1254; Pub. L. 110–371, §7, Oct. 8, 2008, 122 Stat. 4042; Pub. L. 117–58, div. A, title I, §11506(a), Nov. 15, 2021, 135 Stat. 584.)

CHAPTER 143—APPALACHIAN REGIONAL COMMISSION

SUBCHAPTER I—ORGANIZATION AND ADMINISTRATION

Sec.
14301.   Establishment, membership, and employees.
14302.   Decisions.
14303.   Functions.
14304.   Recommendations.
14305.   Liaison between Federal Government and Commission.
14306.   Administrative powers and expenses.
14307.   Meetings.
14308.   Information.
14309.   Personal financial interests.
14310.   Annual report.

SUBCHAPTER II—FINANCIAL ASSISTANCE

14321.   Grants and other assistance.
14322.   Approval of development plans, strategy statements, and projects.
14323.   Congressional notification.

SUBCHAPTER I—ORGANIZATION AND ADMINISTRATION

§14301. ESTABLISHMENT, MEMBERSHIP, AND EMPLOYEES

(a) ESTABLISHMENT.—There is an Appalachian Regional Commission.

(b) MEMBERSHIP.—

(1) FEDERAL AND STATE MEMBERS.—The Commission is composed of the Federal Cochairman, appointed by the President by and with the advice and consent of the Senate, and the Governor of each participating State in the Appalachian region.

(2) ALTERNATE MEMBERS.—Each state member may have a single alternate, appointed by the Governor from among the members of the Governor's cabinet or the Governor's personal staff. The President,,[1] shall appoint an alternate for the Federal Cochairman. An alternate shall vote in the event of the absence, death, disability, removal, or resignation of the member for whom the individual is an alternate. A state alternate shall not be counted toward the establishment of a quorum of the Commission when a quorum of the state members is required.

(3) COCHAIRMEN.—The Federal Cochairman is one of the two Cochairmen of the Commission. The state members shall elect a Cochairman of the Commission from among themselves for a term of not less than one year.

(c) COMPENSATION.—The Federal Cochairman shall be compensated by the Federal Government at level III of the Executive Schedule as set out in section 5314 of title 5. The Federal Cochairman's alternate shall be compensated by the Government at level V of the Executive Schedule as set out in section 5316 of title 5. Each state member and alternate shall be compensated by the State which they represent at the rate established by law of that State.

inventory and analysis of the resources of the region, and, in cooperation with federal, state, and local agencies, sponsor demonstration projects designed to foster regional productivity and growth;

(3) review and study, in cooperation with the agency involved, federal, state, and local public and private programs and, where appropriate, recommend modifications or additions which will increase their effectiveness in the region;

(4) formulate and recommend, where appropriate, interstate compacts and other forms of interstate cooperation and work with state and local agencies in developing appropriate model legislation;

(5) encourage the formation of, and support, local development districts;

(6) encourage private investment in industrial, commercial, and recreational projects;

(7) serve as a focal point and coordinating unit for Appalachian programs;

(8) provide a forum for consideration of problems of the region and proposed solutions and establish and utilize, as appropriate, citizens and special advisory councils and public conferences;

(9) encourage the use of eco-industrial development technologies and approaches;

(10) seek to coordinate the economic development activities of, and the use of economic development resources by, federal agencies in the region; and

(11) support broadband access in the Appalachian region.

(b) IDENTIFY NEEDS AND GOALS OF SUBREGIONAL AREAS.—In carrying out its functions under this section, the Commission shall identify the characteristics of, and may distinguish between the needs and goals of, appropriate subregional areas, including central, northern, and southern Appalachia.

(Pub. L. 107–217, Aug. 21, 2002, 116 Stat. 1258; Pub. L. 117–58, div. A, title I, §11506(b), Nov. 15, 2021, 135 Stat. 584.)

§14304. RECOMMENDATIONS

The Appalachian Regional Commission may make recommendations to the President and to the Governors and appropriate local officials with respect to—

(1) the expenditure of amounts by federal, state, and local departments and agencies in the Appalachian region in the fields of natural resources, agriculture, education, training, and health and welfare and in other fields related to the purposes of this subtitle; and

(2) additional federal, state, and local legislation or administrative actions as the Commission considers necessary to further the purposes of this subtitle.

(Pub. L. 107–217, Aug. 21, 2002, 116 Stat. 1258.)

§14305. LIAISON BETWEEN FEDERAL GOVERNMENT AND COMMISSION

(a) PRESIDENT.—The President shall provide effective and continuing liaison between the Federal Government and the Appalachian Regional Commission and a coordinated review within the Government of the plans and recommendations submitted by the Commission pursuant to sections 14303 and 14304 of this title.

(b) INTERAGENCY COORDINATING COUNCIL ON APPALACHIA.—In carrying out subsection (a), the President shall establish the Interagency Coordinating Council on

Appalachia, to be composed of the Federal Cochairman and representatives of federal agencies that carry out economic development programs in the Appalachian region. The Federal Cochairman is the Chairperson of the Council.

(Pub. L. 107–217, Aug. 21, 2002, 116 Stat. 1259.)

§14306. ADMINISTRATIVE POWERS AND EXPENSES

(a) POWERS.—To carry out its duties under this subtitle, the Appalachian Regional Commission may—

(1) adopt, amend, and repeal bylaws and regulations governing the conduct of its business and the performance of its functions;

(2) appoint and fix the compensation of an executive director and other personnel as necessary to enable the Commission to carry out its functions, except that the compensation shall not exceed the maximum rate of basic pay for the Senior Executive Service under section 5382 of title 5, including any applicable locality-based comparability payment that may be authorized under section 5304(h)(2)(C) of title 5;

(3) request the head of any federal department or agency to detail to temporary duty with the Commission personnel within the administrative jurisdiction of the head of the department or agency that the Commission may need for carrying out its functions, each detail to be without loss of seniority, pay, or other employee status;

(4) arrange for the services of personnel from any state or local government, subdivision or agency of a state or local government, or intergovernmental agency;

(5)(A) make arrangements, including contracts, with any participating state government for inclusion in a suitable retirement and employee benefit system of Commission personnel who may not be eligible for, or continue in, another governmental retirement or employee benefit system; or

(B) otherwise provide for coverage of its personnel;

(6) accept, use, and dispose of gifts or donations of services or any property;

(7) enter into and perform contracts, leases (including the lease of office space for any term), cooperative agreements, or other transactions, necessary in carrying out its functions, on terms as it may consider appropriate, with any—

(A) department, agency, or instrumentality of the Federal Government;

(B) State or political subdivision, agency, or instrumentality of a State; or

(C) person;

(8) maintain a temporary office in the District of Columbia and establish a permanent office at a central and appropriate location it may select and field offices at other places it may consider appropriate; and

(9) take other actions and incur other expenses as may be necessary or appropriate.

(b) AUTHORIZATIONS.—

(1) DETAIL EMPLOYEES.—The head of a federal department or agency may detail personnel under subsection (a)(3).

(2) ENTER INTO AND PERFORM TRANSACTIONS.—A department, agency, or instrumentality of the Government, to the extent not otherwise prohibited by law, may enter into and perform a contract, lease, cooperative agreement, or other transaction under subsection (a)(7).

(c) RETIREMENT AND OTHER EMPLOYEE BENEFIT PROGRAMS.—The Director of the Office of Personnel Management may contract with the Commission for continued coverage of Commission employees, if the employees are federal employees when they begin Commission employment, in the retirement program and other employee benefit programs of the Government.

(d) EXPENSES.—Administrative expenses of the Commission shall be paid equally by the Government and the States in the Appalachian region, except that the expenses of the Federal Cochairman, the alternate to the Federal Cochairman, and the staff of the Federal Cochairman shall be paid only by the Government. The Commission shall determine the amount to be paid by each State. The Federal Cochairman shall not participate or vote in that determination. Assistance authorized by this subtitle shall not be furnished to any State or to any political subdivision or any resident of any State, and a state member of the Commission shall not participate or vote in any decision by the Commission, while the State is delinquent in payment of its share of administrative expenses.

(Pub. L. 107–217, Aug. 21, 2002, 116 Stat. 1259.)

§14307. MEETINGS

(a) IN GENERAL.—The Appalachian Regional Commission shall conduct at least one meeting each year with the Federal Cochairman and at least a majority of the state members present.

(b) ADDITIONAL MEETINGS BY ELECTRONIC MEANS.—The Commission may conduct additional meetings by electronic means as the Commission considers advisable, including meetings to decide matters requiring an affirmative vote.

(Pub. L. 107–217, Aug. 21, 2002, 116 Stat. 1260.)

§14308. INFORMATION

(a) ACTIONS OF COMMISSION.—To obtain information needed to carry out its duties, the Appalachian Regional Commission shall—

(1) hold hearings, sit and act at times and places, take testimony, receive evidence, and print or otherwise reproduce and distribute so much of its proceedings and reports on the proceedings as the Commission may deem advisable;

(2) arrange for the head of any federal, state, or local department or agency to furnish to the Commission information as may be available to or procurable by the department or agency; and

(3) keep accurate and complete records of its doings and transactions which shall be made available for—

(A) public inspection; and

(B) audit and examination by the Comptroller General or an authorized representative of the Comptroller General.

(b) AUTHORIZATIONS.—

(1) ADMINISTER OATHS.—A Cochairman of the Commission, or any member of the Commission designated by the Commission, may administer oaths when the Commission decides that testimony shall be taken or evidence received under oath.

(2) FURNISH INFORMATION.—The head of any federal, state, or local department or

agency, to the extent not otherwise prohibited by law, may carry out subsection (a)(2).

(c) PUBLIC PARTICIPATION.—Public participation in the development, revision, and implementation of all plans and programs under this subtitle by the Commission, any State, or any local development district shall be provided for, encouraged, and assisted. The Commission shall develop and publish regulations specifying minimum guidelines for public participation, including public hearings.

(Pub. L. 107–217, Aug. 21, 2002, 116 Stat. 1260; Pub. L. 109–284, §6(31), Sept. 27, 2006, 120 Stat. 1213.)

§14309. PERSONAL FINANCIAL INTERESTS

(a) CONFLICT OF INTEREST.—

(1) NO ROLE ALLOWED.—Except as permitted by paragraph (2), an individual who is a state member or alternate, or an officer or employee of the Appalachian Regional Commission, shall not participate personally and substantially as a member, alternate, officer, or employee in any way in any particular matter in which, to the individual's knowledge, any of the following has a financial interest:

(A) the individual.

(B) the individual's spouse, minor child, or partner.

(C) an organization (except a State or political subdivision of a State) in which the individual is serving as an officer, director, trustee, partner, or employee.

(D) any person or organization with whom the individual—

(i) is serving as an officer, director, trustee, partner, or employee; or

(ii) is negotiating or has any arrangement concerning prospective employment.

(2) EXCEPTION.—Paragraph (1) does not apply if the individual first advises the Commission of the nature and circumstances of the particular matter and makes full disclosure of the financial interest and receives in advance a written decision of the Commission that the interest is not so substantial as to be considered likely to affect the integrity of the services which the Commission may expect from the individual.

(3) CRIMINAL PENALTY.—An individual violating this subsection shall be fined under title 18, imprisoned for not more than two years, or both.

(b) ADDITIONAL SOURCES OF SALARY DISALLOWED.—

(1) STATE MEMBER OR ALTERNATE.—A state member or alternate may not receive any salary, or any contribution to, or supplementation of, salary, for services on the Commission from a source other than the State of the member or alternate.

(2) INDIVIDUALS DETAILED TO COMMISSION.—An individual detailed to serve the Commission under section 14306(a)(4) of this title may not receive any salary, or any contribution to, or supplementation of, salary, for services on the Commission from a source other than the state, local, or intergovernmental department or agency from which the individual was detailed or from the Commission.

(3) CRIMINAL PENALTY.—An individual violating this subsection shall be fined under title 18, imprisoned for not more than one year, or both.

(c) FEDERAL COCHAIRMAN, ALTERNATE TO FEDERAL COCHAIRMAN, AND FEDERAL OFFICERS AND EMPLOYEES.—The Federal Cochairman, the alternate to the Federal Cochairman, and any federal officer or employee detailed to duty with the Commission under section 14306(a)(3) of this title are not subject to this section but remain subject to sections 202–209 of title 18.

(d) RESCISSION.—The Commission may declare void and rescind any contract, loan, or grant of or by the Commission in relation to which it finds that there has been a violation of subsection (a)(1) or (b) of this section or any of the provisions of sections 202–209 of title 18.

(Pub. L. 107–217, Aug. 21, 2002, 116 Stat. 1261.)

§14310. ANNUAL REPORT

Not later than six months after the close of each fiscal year, the Appalachian Regional Commission shall prepare and submit to the Governor of each State in the Appalachian region and to the President, for transmittal to Congress, a report on the activities carried out under this subtitle during the fiscal year.

(Pub. L. 107–217, Aug. 21, 2002, 116 Stat. 1262.)

SUBCHAPTER II—FINANCIAL ASSISTANCE

§14321. GRANTS AND OTHER ASSISTANCE

(a) AUTHORIZATION TO MAKE GRANTS.—

(1) IN GENERAL.—The Appalachian Regional Commission may make grants—

(A) for administrative expenses, including the development of areawide plans or action programs and technical assistance activities, of local development districts, but—

(i) the amount of the grant shall not exceed—

(I) 50 percent of administrative expenses;

(II) at the discretion of the Commission, if the grant is to a local development district that has a charter or authority that includes the economic development of a county or a part of a county for which a distressed county designation is in effect under section 14526, 75 percent of administrative expenses; or

(III) at the discretion of the Commission, if the grant is to a local development district that has a charter or authority that includes the economic development of a county or a part of a county for which an at-risk county designation is in effect under section 14526, 70 percent of administrative expenses;

(ii) grants for administrative expenses shall not be made for a state agency certified as a local development district for a period of more than three years beginning on the date the initial grant is made for the development district; and

(iii) the local development district contributions for administrative expenses may be in cash or in kind, fairly evaluated, including space, equipment, and services;

(B) for assistance to States for a period of not more than two years to strengthen the state development planning process for the Appalachian region and the coordination of state planning under this subtitle, the Public Works and Economic Development Act of 1965 (42 U.S.C. 3121 et seq.), and other federal and state programs; and

(C) for investigation, research, studies, evaluations, and assessments of needs, potentials, or attainments of the people of the region, technical assistance, training programs, demonstrations, and the construction of necessary facilities incident to those activities, which will further the purposes of this subtitle.

(2) LIMITATION ON AVAILABLE AMOUNTS.—

(A) IN GENERAL.—Except as provided in subparagraph (B), of the cost of any activity eligible for financial assistance under this section, not more than—

(i) 50 percent may be provided from amounts appropriated to carry out this subtitle;

(ii) in the case of a project to be carried out in a county for which a distressed county designation is in effect under section 14526, 80 percent may be provided from amounts appropriated to carry out this subtitle; or

(iii) in the case of a project to be carried out in a county for which an at-risk county designation is in effect under section 14526, 70 percent may be provided from amounts appropriated to carry out this subtitle.

(B) DISCRETIONARY GRANTS.—

(i) GRANTS TO WHICH PERCENTAGE LIMITATION DOESN'T APPLY.—Discretionary grants made by the Commission to implement significant regional initiatives, to take advantage of special development opportunities, or to respond to emergency economic distress in the region may be made without regard to the percentage limitations specified in subparagraph (A).

(ii) LIMITATION ON AGGREGATE AMOUNT.—For each fiscal year, the aggregate amount of discretionary grants referred to in clause (i) shall not be more than 10 percent of the amount appropriated under section 14703 of this title for the fiscal year, except that a discretionary grant to respond to economic distress directly related to the impacts of the Coronavirus Disease 2019 (COVID–19) shall not be included in such aggregate amount.

(3) SOURCES OF GRANTS.—Grant amounts may be provided entirely from appropriations to carry out this section, in combination with amounts available under other federal or federal grant programs, or from any other source.

(4) FEDERAL SHARE.—Notwithstanding any law limiting the federal share in any other federal or federal grant program, amounts appropriated to carry out this section may be used to increase that federal share, as the Commission decides is appropriate.

(b) ASSISTANCE FOR DEMONSTRATIONS OF ENTERPRISE DEVELOPMENT.—

(1) IN GENERAL.—The Commission may provide assistance under this section for demonstrations of enterprise development, including site acquisition or development where necessary for the feasibility of the project, in connection with the development of the region's energy resources and the development and stimulation of indigenous arts and crafts of the region.

(2) COOPERATION BY FEDERAL AGENCIES.—In carrying out the purposes of this subtitle and in implementing this section, the Secretary of Energy, the Environmental Protection Agency, and other federal agencies shall cooperate with the Commission and shall provide assistance that the Federal Cochairman may request.

(3) AVAILABLE AMOUNTS.—In any fiscal year, not more than—

(A) $3,000,000 shall be obligated for energy resource related demonstrations; and

(B) $2,500,000 shall be obligated for indigenous arts and crafts demonstrations.

(c) RECORDS.—

(1) COMMISSION.—The Commission, as required by the President, shall maintain accurate and complete records of transactions and activities financed with federal amounts and report to the President on the transactions and activities. The records of the Commission with respect to grants are available for audit by the President and the Comptroller General.

(2) RECIPIENTS OF FEDERAL ASSISTANCE.—Recipients of federal assistance under this section, as required by the Commission, shall maintain accurate and complete records of transactions and activities financed with federal amounts and report to the Commission on the transactions and activities. The records are be [1] available for audit by the President, the Comptroller General, and the Commission.

(Pub. L. 107–217, Aug. 21, 2002, 116 Stat. 1262; Pub. L. 110–371, §2(a), Oct. 8, 2008, 122 Stat. 4037; Pub. L. 116–136, div. B, title IV, §14004, Mar. 27, 2020, 134 Stat. 526.)

[1] So in original. Probably should be preceded by "to".

§14322. APPROVAL OF DEVELOPMENT PLANS, STRATEGY STATEMENTS, AND PROJECTS

(a) ANNUAL REVIEW AND APPROVAL REQUIRED.—The Appalachian Regional Commission annually shall review and approve, in accordance with section 14302 of this title, state and regional development plans and strategy statements, and any multistate subregional plans which may be developed.

(b) APPLICATION PROCESS.—An application for a grant or for other assistance for a specific project under this subtitle shall be made through the state member of the Commission representing the applicant. The state member shall evaluate the application for approval. To be approved, the state member must certify, and the Federal Cochairman must determine, that the application—

(1) implements the Commission-approved state development plan;

(2) is included in the Commission-approved strategy statement;

(3) adequately ensures that the project will be properly administered, operated, and maintained; and

(4) otherwise meets the requirements for assistance under this subtitle.

(c) AFFIRMATIVE VOTE REQUIREMENT DEEMED MET.—After the appropriate state development plan and strategy statement are approved, certification by a state member, when joined by an affirmative vote of the Federal Cochairman, is deemed to satisfy the requirements for affirmative votes for decisions under section 14302(a) of this title.

(Pub. L. 107–217, Aug. 21, 2002, 116 Stat. 1264.)

§14323. CONGRESSIONAL NOTIFICATION

(a) IN GENERAL.—In the case of a project described in subsection (b), the Appalachian Regional Commission shall provide to the Committee on Transportation and Infrastructure of the House of Representatives and the Committee on Environment and Public Works of the Senate notice of the award of a grant or other financial assistance not less than 3 full business days before awarding the grant or other financial assistance.

(b) PROJECTS DESCRIBED.—A project referred to in subsection (a) is a project that the Appalachian Regional Commission has selected to receive a grant or other financial assistance under this subtitle in an amount not less than $50,000.

(Added Pub. L. 117–58, div. A, title I, §11506(c)(1), Nov. 15, 2021, 135 Stat. 584.)

CHAPTER 145—SPECIAL APPALACHIAN PROGRAMS

SUBCHAPTER I—PROGRAMS

Sec.
14501.   Appalachian development highway system.
14502.   Demonstration health projects.
14503.   Assistance for proposed low- and middle-income housing projects.
14504.   Telecommunications and technology initiative.
14505.   Entrepreneurship initiative.
14506.   Regional skills partnerships.
14507.   Supplements to federal grant programs.
14508.   Economic and energy development initiative.
14509.   High-speed broadband deployment initiative.
14510.   Drug abuse mitigation initiative.
14511 [1]   Appalachian regional energy hub initiative.

SUBCHAPTER II—ADMINISTRATIVE

14521.   Required level of expenditure.
14522.   Consent of States.
14523.   Program implementation.
14524.   Program development criteria.
14525.   State development planning process.
14526.   Distressed, at-risk, and economically strong counties.

[1] *So in original. Probably should be followed by a period.*

SUBCHAPTER I—PROGRAMS

§14501. APPALACHIAN DEVELOPMENT HIGHWAY SYSTEM

(a) PURPOSE.—To provide a highway system which, in conjunction with the Interstate System and other Federal-aid highways in the Appalachian region, will open up an area with a developmental potential where commerce and communication have been inhibited by lack of adequate access, the Secretary of Transportation may assist in the construction of an Appalachian development highway system and local access roads serving the Appalachian region. Construction on the development highway system shall not be more than three thousand and ninety miles. There shall not be more than 1,400 miles of local access roads that serve specific recreational, residential, educational, commercial, industrial, or similar facilities or facilitate a school consolidation program.

(b) COMMISSION DESIGNATIONS.—

(1) WHAT IS TO BE DESIGNATED.—The Appalachian Regional Commission shall transmit to the Secretary its designations of—

(A) the general corridor location and termini of the development highways;

(B) local access roads to be constructed;

(C) priorities for the construction of segments of the development highways; and

(D) other criteria for the program authorized by this section.

(2) STATE TRANSPORTATION DEPARTMENT RECOMMENDATION REQUIRED.—Before a state member participates in or votes on designations, the member must obtain the recommendations of the state transportation department of the State which the member represents.

(c) ADDITION TO FEDERAL-AID PRIMARY SYSTEM.—When completed, each development highway not already on the Federal-aid primary system shall be added to the system.

(d) USE OF SPECIFIC MATERIALS AND PRODUCTS.—

(1) INDIGENOUS MATERIALS AND PRODUCTS.—In the construction of highways and roads authorized under this section, a State may give special preference to the use of materials and products indigenous to the Appalachian region.

(2) COAL DERIVATIVES.—For research and development in the use of coal and coal products in highway construction and maintenance, the Secretary may require each participating State, to the maximum extent possible, to use coal derivatives in the construction of not more than 10 percent of the roads authorized under this subtitle.

(e) FEDERAL SHARE.—Federal assistance to any construction project under this section shall not be more than 80 percent of the cost of the project.

(f) CONSTRUCTION WITHOUT FEDERAL AMOUNTS.—

(1) PAYMENT OF FEDERAL SHARE.—When a participating State constructs a segment of a development highway without the aid of federal amounts and the construction is in accordance with all procedures and requirements applicable to the construction of segments of Appalachian development highways with those amounts, except for procedures and requirements that limit a State to the construction of projects for which federal amounts have previously been appropriated, the Secretary, on application by the State and with the approval of the Commission, may pay to the State the federal share, which shall not be more than 80 percent of the cost of the construction of the segment, from any amounts appropriated and allocated to the State to carry out this section.

(2) NO COMMITMENT OR OBLIGATION.—This subsection does not commit or obligate the Federal Government to provide amounts for segments of development highways constructed under this subsection.

(g) APPLICATION OF TITLE 23.—

(1) SECTIONS 106(a) AND 118.—Sections 106(a) and 118 of title 23 apply to the development highway system and the local access roads.

(2) CONSTRUCTION AND MAINTENANCE.—States are required to maintain each development highway and local access road as provided for Federal-aid highways in title 23. All other provisions of title 23 that are applicable to the construction and maintenance of Federal-aid primary and secondary highways and which the Secretary decides are not inconsistent with this subtitle shall apply to the system and roads, respectively.

(Pub. L. 107–217, Aug. 21, 2002, 116 Stat. 1265; Pub. L. 108–199, div. F, title I, §123(a), Jan. 23, 2004, 118 Stat. 296.)

§14502. DEMONSTRATION HEALTH PROJECTS

(a) PURPOSE.—To demonstrate the value of adequate health facilities and services to the economic development of the Appalachian region, the Secretary of Health and Human Services may make grants for the planning, construction, equipment, and operation of multi-county demonstration health, nutrition, and child care projects, including hospitals, regional health diagnostic and treatment centers, and other facilities and services necessary for the purposes of this section.

(b) PLANNING GRANTS.—

(1) AUTHORITY TO PROVIDE AMOUNTS AND MAKE GRANTS.—The Secretary may provide amounts to the Appalachian Regional Commission for the support of its Health Advisory Committee and may make grants for expenses of planning necessary for the development and operation of demonstration health projects for the region.

(2) LIMITATION ON AVAILABLE AMOUNTS.—The amount of a grant under this section for planning shall not be more than 75 percent of expenses.

(3) SOURCES OF ASSISTANCE.—The federal contribution may be provided entirely from amounts authorized under this section or in combination with amounts provided under other federal or federal grant programs.

(4) FEDERAL SHARE.—Notwithstanding any provision of law limiting the federal share in those other programs, amounts appropriated to carry out this section may be used to increase the federal share to the maximum percentage cost of a grant authorized by this subsection.

(c) CONSTRUCTION AND EQUIPMENT GRANTS.—

(1) ADDITIONAL USES FOR CONSTRUCTION GRANTS.—Grants under this section for construction may also be used for—

(A) the acquisition of privately owned facilities—

(i) not operated for profit; or

(ii) previously operated for profit if the Commission finds that health services would not otherwise be provided in the area served by the facility if the acquisition is not made; and

(B) initial equipment.

(2) STANDARDS FOR MAKING GRANTS.—Grants under this section for construction shall be made in accordance with section 14523 of this title and shall not be incompatible with the applicable provisions of title VI of the Public Health Service Act (42 U.S.C. 291 et seq.), the Developmental Disabilities Assistance and Bill of Rights Act of 2000 (42 U.S.C. 15001 et seq.), and other laws authorizing grants for the construction of health-related facilities, without regard to any provisions in those laws relating to appropriation authorization ceilings or to allotments among the States.

(3) LIMITATION ON AVAILABLE AMOUNTS.—A grant for the construction or equipment of any component of a demonstration health project shall not be more than 80 percent of the cost.

(4) SOURCES OF ASSISTANCE.—The federal contribution may be provided entirely from amounts authorized under this section or in combination with amounts provided under other federal grant programs for the construction or equipment of health-related facilities.

(5) FEDERAL SHARE.—Notwithstanding any provision of law limiting the federal share in those other programs, amounts authorized under this section may be used to

increase federal grants for component facilities of a demonstration health project to a maximum of 80 percent of the cost of the facilities.

(d) OPERATION GRANTS.—

(1) STANDARDS FOR MAKING GRANTS.—A grant for the operation of a demonstration health project shall not be made—

(A) unless the facility is publicly owned, or owned by a public or private nonprofit organization, and is not operated for profit;

(B) after five years following the commencement of the initial grant for operation of the project, except that child development demonstrations assisted under this section during fiscal year 1979 may be approved under section 14322 of this title for continued support beyond that period, on request of the State, if the Commission finds that no federal, state, or local amounts are available to continue the project; and

(C) unless the Secretary of Health and Human Services is satisfied that the operation of the project will be conducted under efficient management practices designed to obviate operating deficits.

(2) LIMITATION ON AVAILABLE AMOUNTS.—Grants under this section for the operation (including initial operating amounts and operating deficits, which include the cost of attracting, training, and retaining qualified personnel) of a demonstration health project, whether or not constructed with amounts authorized to be appropriated by this section, may be made for up to—

(A) 50 percent of the cost of that operation;

(B) in the case of a project to be carried out in a county for which a distressed county designation is in effect under section 14526, 80 percent of the cost of that operation; or

(C) in the case of a project to be carried out for a county for which an at-risk county designation is in effect under section 14526, 70 percent of the cost of that operation.

(3) SOURCES OF ASSISTANCE.—The federal contribution may be provided entirely from amounts appropriated to carry out this section or in combination with amounts provided under other federal grant programs for the operation of health related facilities and the provision of health and child development services, including parts A and B of title IV and title XX of the Social Security Act (42 U.S.C. 601 et seq., 620 et seq., 1397 et seq.).

(4) FEDERAL SHARE.—Notwithstanding any provision of law limiting the federal share in those other programs, amounts appropriated to carry out this section may be used to increase federal grants for operating components of a demonstration health project to the maximum percentage cost of a grant authorized by this subsection.

(5) STATE DEEMED TO MEET REQUIREMENT OF PROVIDING ASSISTANCE OR SERVICES ON STATEWIDE BASIS.—Notwithstanding any provision of the Social Security Act (42 U.S.C. 301 et seq.) requiring assistance or services on a statewide basis, a State providing assistance or services under a federal grant program described in paragraph (2) in any area of the region approved by the Commission is deemed to be meeting that requirement.

(e) GRANT SOURCES AND USE OF GRANTS IN COMPUTING ALLOTMENTS.—Grants under this section—

(1) shall be made only out of amounts specifically appropriated for the purpose of carrying out this subtitle; and

(2) shall not be taken into account in computing allotments among the States under any other law.

(f) MAXIMUM COMMISSION CONTRIBUTION.—

(1) IN GENERAL.—Subject to paragraphs (2) and (3), the Commission may contribute not more than 50 percent of any project cost eligible for financial assistance under this section from amounts appropriated to carry out this subtitle.

(2) DISTRESSED COUNTIES.—The maximum Commission contribution for a project to be carried out in a county for which a distressed county designation is in effect under section 14526 of this title may be increased to the lesser of—

(A) 80 percent; or

(B) the maximum federal contribution percentage authorized by this section.

(3) AT-RISK COUNTIES.—The maximum Commission contribution for a project to be carried out in a county for which an at-risk county designation is in effect under section 14526 may be increased to the lesser of—

(A) 70 percent; or

(B) the maximum Federal contribution percentage authorized by this section.

(g) EMPHASIS ON OCCUPATIONAL DISEASES FROM COAL MINING.—To provide for the further development of the Appalachian region's human resources, grants under this section shall give special emphasis to programs and research for the early detection, diagnosis, and treatment of occupational diseases arising from coal mining, such as black lung.

(Pub. L. 107–217, Aug. 21, 2002, 116 Stat. 1266; Pub. L. 110–371, §2(b), Oct. 8, 2008, 122 Stat. 4038.)

§14503. ASSISTANCE FOR PROPOSED LOW- AND MIDDLE-INCOME HOUSING PROJECTS

(a) APPALACHIAN HOUSING FUND.—

(1) ESTABLISHMENT.—There is an Appalachian Housing Fund.

(2) SOURCE AND USE OF AMOUNTS IN FUND.—Amounts allocated to the Secretary of Housing and Urban Development for the purposes of this section shall be deposited in the Fund. The Secretary shall use the Fund as a revolving fund to carry out those purposes. Amounts in the Fund not needed for current operation may be invested in bonds or other obligations the Federal Government guarantees as to principal and interest. General expenses of administration of this section may be charged to the Fund.

(b) PURPOSE.—To encourage and facilitate the construction or rehabilitation of housing to meet the needs of low- and moderate-income families and individuals, the Secretary may make grants and loans from the Fund, under terms and conditions the Secretary may prescribe. The grants and loans may be made to nonprofit, limited dividend, or cooperative organizations and public bodies and are for planning and obtaining federally insured mortgage financing or other financial assistance for housing construction or rehabilitation projects for low- and moderate-income families and individuals, in any area of the Appalachian region the Appalachian Regional Commission establishes, under—

(1) section 221 of the National Housing Act (12 U.S.C. 1715l);

(2) section 8 of the United States Housing Act of 1937 (42 U.S.C. 1437f);

(3) section 515 of the Housing Act of 1949 (42 U.S.C. 1485); or

(4) any other law of similar purpose administered by the Secretary or any other department, agency, or instrumentality of the Federal Government or a state government.

(c) PROVIDING AMOUNTS TO STATES FOR GRANTS AND LOANS.—The Secretary or the Commission may provide amounts to the States for making grants and loans to nonprofit, limited dividend, or cooperative organizations and public bodies for the purposes for which the Secretary may provide amounts under this section.

(d) LOANS.—

(1) LIMITATION ON AVAILABLE AMOUNTS.—A loan under subsection (b) for the cost of planning and obtaining financing (including the cost of preliminary surveys and analyses of market needs, preliminary site engineering and architectural fees, site options, application and mortgage commitment fees, legal fees, and construction loan fees and discounts) of a project described in that subsection may be made for up to—

(A) 50 percent of that cost;

(B) in the case of a project to be carried out in a county for which a distressed county designation is in effect under section 14526, 80 percent of that cost; or

(C) in the case of a project to be carried out for a county for which an at-risk county designation is in effect under section 14526, 70 percent of that cost.

(2) INTEREST.—A loan shall be made without interest, except that a loan made to an organization established for profit shall bear interest at the prevailing market rate authorized for an insured or guaranteed loan for that type of project.

(3) PAYMENT.—The Secretary shall require payment of a loan made under this section, under terms and conditions the Secretary may require, no later than on completion of the project. Except for a loan to an organization established for profit, the Secretary may cancel any part of a loan made under this section on determining that a permanent loan to finance the project cannot be obtained in an amount adequate for repayment of a loan made under this section.

(e) GRANTS.—

(1) IN GENERAL.—A grant under this section for expenses incidental to planning and obtaining financing for a project under this section that the Secretary considers to be unrecoverable from the proceeds of a permanent loan made to finance the project shall—

(A) not be made to an organization established for profit; and

(B) except as provided in paragraph (2), not exceed—

(i) 50 percent of those expenses;

(ii) in the case of a project to be carried out in a county for which a distressed county designation is in effect under section 14526, 80 percent of those expenses; or

(iii) in the case of a project to be carried out in a county for which an at-risk county designation is in effect under section 14526, 70 percent of those expenses.

(2) SITE DEVELOPMENT COSTS AND OFFSITE IMPROVEMENTS.—The Secretary may

make grants and commitments for grants, and may advance amounts under terms and conditions the Secretary may require, to nonprofit, limited dividend, or cooperative organizations and public bodies for reasonable site development costs and necessary offsite improvements, such as sewer and water line extensions, when the grant, commitment, or advance is essential to the economic feasibility of a housing construction or rehabilitation project for low- and moderate-income families and individuals which otherwise meets the requirements for assistance under this section. A grant under this paragraph for—

(A) the construction of housing shall not be more than 10 percent of the cost of the project; and

(B) the rehabilitation of housing shall not be more than 10 percent of the reasonable value of the rehabilitation housing, as determined by the Secretary.

(f) INFORMATION, ADVICE, AND TECHNICAL ASSISTANCE.—The Secretary or the Commission may provide, or contract with public or private organizations to provide, information, advice, and technical assistance with respect to the construction, rehabilitation, and operation by nonprofit organizations of housing for low- or moderate- income families in areas of the region the Commission establishes.

(g) APPLICATION OF CERTAIN PROVISIONS.—Programs and projects assisted under this section are subject to the provisions cited in section 14701 of this title to the extent provided in the laws authorizing assistance for low- and moderate-income housing.

(Pub. L. 107–217, Aug. 21, 2002, 116 Stat. 1268; Pub. L. 110–371, §2(c), Oct. 8, 2008, 122 Stat. 4038.)

§14504. TELECOMMUNICATIONS AND TECHNOLOGY INITIATIVE

(a) PROJECTS TO BE ASSISTED.—The Appalachian Regional Commission may provide technical assistance, make grants, enter into contracts, or otherwise provide amounts to persons or entities in the region for projects—

(1) to increase affordable access to advanced telecommunications, entrepreneurship, and management technologies or applications in the region;

(2) to provide education and training in the use of telecommunications and technology;

(3) to develop programs to increase the readiness of industry groups and businesses in the region to engage in electronic commerce; or

(4) to support entrepreneurial opportunities for businesses in the information technology sector.

(b) LIMITATION ON AVAILABLE AMOUNTS.—Of the cost of any activity eligible for a grant under this section, not more than—

(1) 50 percent may be provided from amounts appropriated to carry out this section;

(2) in the case of a project to be carried out in a county for which a distressed county designation is in effect under section 14526, 80 percent may be provided from amounts appropriated to carry out this section; or

(3) in the case of a project to be carried out in a county for which an at-risk county designation is in effect under section 14526, 70 percent may be provided from amounts appropriated to carry out this section.

(c) SOURCES OF ASSISTANCE.—Assistance under this section may be provided entirely from amounts made available to carry out this section, in combination with amounts made available under other federal programs, or from any other source.

(d) FEDERAL SHARE.—Notwithstanding any provision of law limiting the federal share under any other federal program, amounts made available to carry out this section may be used to increase that federal share, as the Commission decides is appropriate.

(Pub. L. 107–217, Aug. 21, 2002, 116 Stat. 1270; Pub. L. 110–371, §2(d), Oct. 8, 2008, 122 Stat. 4039.)

§14505. ENTREPRENEURSHIP INITIATIVE

(a) BUSINESS INCUBATOR SERVICE.—In this section, the term "business incubator service" means a professional or technical service necessary for the initiation and initial sustainment of the operations of a newly established business, including a service such as—

(1) a legal service, including aid in preparing a corporate charter, partnership agreement, or basic contract;

(2) a service in support of the protection of intellectual property through a patent, a trademark, or any other means;

(3) a service in support of the acquisition and use of advanced technology, including the use of Internet services and Web-based services; and

(4) consultation on strategic planning, marketing, or advertising.

(b) PROJECTS TO BE ASSISTED.—The Appalachian Regional Commission may provide technical assistance, make grants, enter into contracts, or otherwise provide amounts to persons or entities in the region for projects—

(1) to support the advancement of, and provide, entrepreneurial training and education for youths, students, and businesspersons;

(2) to improve access to debt and equity capital by such means as facilitating the establishment of development venture capital funds;

(3) to aid communities in identifying, developing, and implementing development strategies for various sectors of the economy;

(4) to develop a working network of business incubators; and

(5) to support entities that provide business incubator services.

(c) LIMITATION ON AVAILABLE AMOUNTS.—Of the cost of any activity eligible for a grant under this section, not more than—

(1) 50 percent may be provided from amounts appropriated to carry out this section;

(2) in the case of a project to be carried out in a county for which a distressed county designation is in effect under section 14526, 80 percent may be provided from amounts appropriated to carry out this section; or

(3) in the case of a project to be carried out in a county for which an at-risk county designation is in effect under section 14526, 70 percent may be provided from amounts appropriated to carry out this section.

(d) SOURCES OF ASSISTANCE.—Assistance under this section may be provided entirely from amounts made available to carry out this section, in combination with amounts made available under other federal programs, or from any other source.

(e) FEDERAL SHARE.—Notwithstanding any provision of law limiting the federal share under any other federal program, amounts made available to carry out this section may be used to increase that federal share, as the Commission decides is appropriate.

(Pub. L. 107–217, Aug. 21, 2002, 116 Stat. 1271; Pub. L. 110–371, §2(e), Oct. 8, 2008, 122 Stat. 4039.)

§14506. REGIONAL SKILLS PARTNERSHIPS

(a) ELIGIBLE ENTITY.—In this section, the term "eligible entity" means a consortium that—

(1) is established to serve one or more industries in a specified geographic area; and

(2) consists of representatives of—

(A) businesses (or a nonprofit organization that represents businesses);

(B) labor organizations;

(C) State and local governments; or

(D) educational institutions.

(b) PROJECTS TO BE ASSISTED.—The Appalachian Regional Commission may provide technical assistance, make grants, enter into contracts, or otherwise provide amounts to eligible entities in the region for projects to improve the job skills of workers for a specified industry, including projects for—

(1) the assessment of training and job skill needs for the industry;

(2) the development of curricula and training methods, including, in appropriate cases, electronic learning or technology-based training;

(3) the identification of training providers;

(4) the development of partnerships between the industry and educational institutions, including community colleges;

(5) the development of apprenticeship programs;

(6) the development of training programs for workers, including dislocated workers; and

(7) the development of training plans for businesses.

(c) ADMINISTRATIVE COSTS.—An eligible entity may use not more than 10 percent of amounts made available to the eligible entity under subsection (b) to pay administrative costs associated with the projects described in subsection (b).

(d) LIMITATION ON AVAILABLE AMOUNTS.—Of the cost of any activity eligible for a grant under this section, not more than—

(1) 50 percent may be provided from amounts appropriated to carry out this section;

(2) in the case of a project to be carried out in a county for which a distressed county designation is in effect under section 14526, 80 percent may be provided from amounts appropriated to carry out this section; or

(3) in the case of a project to be carried out in a county for which an at-risk county designation is in effect under section 14526, 70 percent may be provided from amounts appropriated to carry out this section.

(e) SOURCES OF ASSISTANCE.—Assistance under this section may be provided entirely from amounts made available to carry out this section, in combination with amounts made available under other federal programs, or from any other source.

(f) FEDERAL SHARE.—Notwithstanding any provision of law limiting the federal share under any other federal program, amounts made available to carry out this section may be used to increase that Federal share, as the Commission decides is appropriate.

(Pub. L. 107–217, Aug. 21, 2002, 116 Stat. 1271; Pub. L. 110–371, §2(f), Oct. 8, 2008, 122 Stat. 4039.)

§14507. SUPPLEMENTS TO FEDERAL GRANT PROGRAMS

(a) DEFINITION.—

(1) FEDERAL GRANT PROGRAMS.—In this section, the term "federal grant programs"—

(A) means any federal grant program that provides assistance for the acquisition or development of land, the construction or equipment of facilities, or other community or economic development or economic adjustment activities, including a federal grant program authorized by—

(i) the Consolidated Farm and Rural Development Act (7 U.S.C. 1921 et seq.);

(ii) chapter 2003 of title 54;

(iii) the Watershed Protection and Flood Prevention Act (16 U.S.C. 1001 et seq.);

(iv) the Carl D. Perkins Career and Technical Education Act of 2006 (20 U.S.C. 2301 et seq.);

(v) the Federal Water Pollution Control Act (33 U.S.C. 1251 et seq.) (known as the Clean Water Act);

(vi) title VI of the Public Health Services Act (42 U.S.C. 291 et seq.);

(vii) sections 201 and 209 of the Public Works and Economic Development Act of 1965 (42 U.S.C. 3141, 3149);

(viii) title I of the Housing and Community Development Act of 1974 (42 U.S.C. 5301 et seq.); and

(ix) part IV of title III of the Communications Act of 1934 (47 U.S.C. 390 et seq.); but

(B) does not include—

(i) the program for the construction of the development highway system authorized by section 14501 of this title or any other program relating to highway or road construction authorized by title 23; or

(ii) any other program to the extent that financial assistance other than a grant is authorized.

(2) CERTAIN SEWAGE TREATMENT WORKS DEEMED CONSTRUCTED WITH FEDERAL GRANT ASSISTANCE.—For the purpose of this section, any sewage treatment works constructed pursuant to title II of the Federal Water Pollution Control Act (33 U.S.C. 1281 et seq.) (known as the Clean Water Act) without federal grant assistance under that title is deemed to be constructed with that assistance.

(b) PURPOSE.—To enable the people, States, and local communities of the Appalachian region, including local development districts, to take maximum advantage of federal grant programs for which they are eligible but for which, because of their economic situation, they cannot supply the required matching share, or for which there are insufficient amounts available under the federal law authorizing the programs to meet pressing needs of the region, the Federal Cochairman may use amounts made available to carry out this section—

(1) for any part of the basic federal contribution to projects or activities under the

federal grant programs authorized by federal laws; and

(2) to increase the federal contribution to projects and activities under the programs above the fixed maximum part of the cost of the projects or activities otherwise authorized by the applicable law.

(c) CERTIFICATION REQUIRED.—For a program, project, or activity for which any part of the basic federal contribution to the project or activity under a federal grant program is proposed to be made under subsection (b), the contribution shall not be made until the responsible federal official administering the federal law authorizing the contribution certifies that the program, project, or activity meets the applicable requirements of the federal law and could be approved for federal contribution under that law if amounts were available under the law for the program, project, or activity.

(d) LIMITATIONS IN OTHER LAWS INAPPLICABLE.—Amounts provided pursuant to this subtitle are available without regard to any limitations on areas eligible for assistance or authorizations for appropriation in any other law.

(e) ACCEPTANCE OF CERTAIN MATERIAL.—For a supplemental grant for a project or activity under a federal grant program, the Federal Cochairman shall accept any finding, report, certification, or documentation required to be submitted to the head of the department, agency, or instrumentality of the Federal Government responsible for the administration of the program.

(f) FEDERAL SHARE.—The federal portion of the cost of a project or activity shall not—

(1) be increased to more than the percentages the Commission establishes; nor

(2) be more than 80 percent of the cost.

(g) MAXIMUM COMMISSION CONTRIBUTION.—

(1) IN GENERAL.—Subject to paragraphs (2) and (3), the Commission may contribute not more than 50 percent of a project or activity cost eligible for financial assistance under this section from amounts appropriated to carry out this subtitle.

(2) DISTRESSED COUNTIES.—The maximum Commission contribution for a project or activity to be carried out in a county for which a distressed county designation is in effect under section 14526 of this title may be increased to 80 percent.

(3) AT-RISK COUNTIES.—The maximum Commission contribution for a project to be carried out in a county for which an at-risk county designation is in effect under section 14526 may be increased to 70 percent.

(Pub. L. 107–217, Aug. 21, 2002, 116 Stat. 1272; Pub. L. 109–270, §2(j), Aug. 12, 2006, 120 Stat. 748; Pub. L. 110–371, §2(g), Oct. 8, 2008, 122 Stat. 4040; Pub. L. 113–287, §5(j)(7), Dec. 19, 2014, 128 Stat. 3269.)

§14508. ECONOMIC AND ENERGY DEVELOPMENT INITIATIVE

(a) PROJECTS TO BE ASSISTED.—The Appalachian Regional Commission may provide technical assistance, make grants, enter into contracts, or otherwise provide amounts to persons or entities in the Appalachian region for projects and activities—

(1) to promote energy efficiency in the Appalachian region to enhance the economic competitiveness of the Appalachian region;

(2) to increase the use of renewable energy resources, particularly biomass, in the Appalachian region to produce alternative transportation fuels, electricity, and heat;

and

(3) to support the development of regional, conventional energy resources to produce electricity and heat through advanced technologies that achieve a substantial reduction in emissions, including greenhouse gases, over the current baseline.

(b) LIMITATION ON AVAILABLE AMOUNTS.—Of the cost of any activity eligible for a grant under this section, not more than—

(1) 50 percent may be provided from amounts appropriated to carry out this section;

(2) in the case of a project to be carried out in a county for which a distressed county designation is in effect under section 14526, 80 percent may be provided from amounts appropriated to carry out this section; or

(3) in the case of a project to be carried out in a county for which an at-risk county designation is in effect under section 14526, 70 percent may be provided from amounts appropriated to carry out this section.

(c) SOURCES OF ASSISTANCE.—Subject to subsection (b), grants provided under this section may be provided from amounts made available to carry out this section in combination with amounts made available under other Federal programs or from any other source.

(d) FEDERAL SHARE.—Notwithstanding any provision of law limiting the Federal share under any other Federal program, amounts made available to carry out this section may be used to increase that Federal share, as the Commission decides is appropriate.

(Added Pub. L. 110–371, §3(a), Oct. 8, 2008, 122 Stat. 4040.)

§14509. HIGH-SPEED BROADBAND DEPLOYMENT INITIATIVE

(a) IN GENERAL.—The Appalachian Regional Commission may provide technical assistance, make grants, enter into contracts, or otherwise provide amounts to individuals or entities in the Appalachian region for projects and activities to increase affordable access to broadband networks throughout the Appalachian region.

(b) ELIGIBLE PROJECTS AND ACTIVITIES.—A project or activity eligible to be carried out under this section is a project or activity—

(1) to conduct research, analysis, and training to increase broadband adoption efforts in the Appalachian region; or

(2) for the construction and deployment of broadband service-related infrastructure in the Appalachian region.

(c) LIMITATION ON AVAILABLE AMOUNTS.—Of the cost of any activity eligible for a grant under this section—

(1) not more than 50 percent may be provided from amounts appropriated to carry out this section; and

(2) notwithstanding paragraph (1)—

(A) in the case of a project to be carried out in a county for which a distressed county designation is in effect under section 14526, not more than 80 percent may be provided from amounts appropriated to carry out this section; and

(B) in the case of a project to be carried out in a county for which an at-risk designation is in effect under section 14526, not more than 70 percent may be provided from amounts appropriated to carry out this section.

(d) SOURCES OF ASSISTANCE.—Subject to subsection (c), a grant provided under this section may be provided from amounts made available to carry out this section in combination with amounts made available—

(1) under any other Federal program; or

(2) from any other source.

(e) FEDERAL SHARE.—Notwithstanding any provision of law limiting the Federal share under any other Federal program, amounts made available to carry out this section may be used to increase that Federal share, as the Appalachian Regional Commission determines to be appropriate.

(f) REQUEST FOR DATA.—Before making a grant for a project or activity described in subsection (b)(2), the Appalachian Regional Commission shall request from the Federal Communications Commission, the National Telecommunications and Information Administration, the Economic Development Administration, and the Department of Agriculture data on—

(1) the level and extent of broadband service that exists in the area proposed to be served by the broadband service-related infrastructure; and

(2) the level and extent of broadband service that will be deployed in the area proposed to be served by the broadband service-related infrastructure pursuant to another Federal program.

(g) REQUIREMENT.—For each fiscal year, not less than 65 percent of the amounts made available to carry out this section shall be used for grants for projects and activities described in subsection (b)(2).

(Added Pub. L. 114–94, div. A, title I, §1436(a)(1), Dec. 4, 2015, 129 Stat. 1430; amended Pub. L. 117–58, div. A, title I, §11506(d), Nov. 15, 2021, 135 Stat. 584.)

§14510. DRUG ABUSE MITIGATION INITIATIVE

(a) IN GENERAL.—The Appalachian Regional Commission may provide technical assistance to, make grants to, enter into contracts with, or otherwise provide amounts to individuals or entities in the Appalachian region for projects and activities to address drug abuse, including opioid abuse, in the region, including projects and activities—

(1) to facilitate the sharing of best practices among States, counties, and other experts in the region with respect to reducing such abuse;

(2) to initiate or expand programs designed to eliminate or reduce the harm to the workforce and economic growth of the region that results from such abuse;

(3) to attract and retain relevant health care services, businesses, and workers; and

(4) to develop relevant infrastructure, including broadband infrastructure that supports the use of telemedicine.

(b) LIMITATION ON AVAILABLE AMOUNTS.—Of the cost of any activity eligible for a grant under this section—

(1) not more than 50 percent may be provided from amounts appropriated to carry out this section; and

(2) notwithstanding paragraph (1)—

(A) in the case of a project to be carried out in a county for which a distressed county designation is in effect under section 14526, not more than 80 percent may be provided from amounts appropriated to carry out this section; and

(B) in the case of a project to be carried out in a county for which an at-risk designation is in effect under section 14526, not more than 70 percent may be provided from amounts appropriated to carry out this section.

(c) SOURCES OF ASSISTANCE.—Subject to subsection (b), a grant provided under this section may be provided from amounts made available to carry out this section in combination with amounts made available—

(1) under any other Federal program (subject to the availability of subsequent appropriations); or

(2) from any other source.

(d) FEDERAL SHARE.—Notwithstanding any provision of law limiting the Federal share under any other Federal program, amounts made available to carry out this section may be used to increase that Federal share, as the Appalachian Regional Commission determines to be appropriate.

(Added Pub. L. 115–271, title VIII, §8062(a), Oct. 24, 2018, 132 Stat. 4094.)

§14511. APPALACHIAN REGIONAL ENERGY HUB INITIATIVE

(a) IN GENERAL.—The Appalachian Regional Commission may provide technical assistance to, make grants to, enter into contracts with, or otherwise provide amounts to individuals or entities in the Appalachian region for projects and activities—

(1) to conduct research and analysis regarding the economic impact of an ethane storage hub in the Appalachian region that supports a more-effective energy market performance due to the scale of the project, such as a project with the capacity to store and distribute more than 100,000 barrels per day of hydrocarbon feedstock with a minimum gross heating value of 1,700 Btu per standard cubic foot;

(2) with the potential to significantly contribute to the economic resilience of the area in which the project is located; and

(3) that will help establish a regional energy hub in the Appalachian region for natural gas and natural gas liquids, including hydrogen produced from the steam methane reforming of natural gas feedstocks.

(b) LIMITATION ON AVAILABLE AMOUNTS.—Of the cost of any project or activity eligible for a grant under this section—

(1) except as provided in paragraphs (2) and (3), not more than 50 percent may be provided from amounts made available to carry out this section;

(2) in the case of a project or activity to be carried out in a county for which a distressed county designation is in effect under section 14526, not more than 80 percent may be provided from amounts made available to carry out this section; and

(3) in the case of a project or activity to be carried out in a county for which an at-risk county designation is in effect under section 14526, not more than 70 percent may be provided from amounts made available to carry out this section.

(c) SOURCES OF ASSISTANCE.—Subject to subsection (b), a grant provided under this section may be provided from amounts made available to carry out this section, in combination with amounts made available—

(1) under any other Federal program; or

(2) from any other source.

(d) FEDERAL SHARE.—Notwithstanding any provision of law limiting the Federal share under any other Federal program, amounts made available to carry out this section may be used to increase that Federal share, as the Appalachian Regional Commission determines to be appropriate.

(Added Pub. L. 117–58, div. A, title I, §11506(e)(1), Nov. 15, 2021, 135 Stat. 585.)

SUBCHAPTER II—ADMINISTRATIVE

§14521. REQUIRED LEVEL OF EXPENDITURE

A State or political subdivision of a State is not eligible to receive benefits under this subtitle unless the aggregate expenditure of state amounts, except expenditures for participation in the Dwight D. Eisenhower System of Interstate and Defense Highways and local and federal amounts, for the benefit of the area within the State located in the Appalachian region is maintained at a level which does not fall below the average level of those expenditures for the State's last two full fiscal years prior to March 9, 1965. In computing the level, a State's past expenditure for participation in the Dwight D. Eisenhower System of Interstate and Defense Highways and expenditures of local and federal amounts shall not be included. The Commission shall recommend to the President a lesser requirement when it finds that a substantial population decrease in that part of a State which lies within the region would not justify a state expenditure equal to the average level of the last two years or when it finds that a State's average level of expenditure in an individual program has been disproportionate to the present need for that part of the State.

(Pub. L. 107–217, Aug. 21, 2002, 116 Stat. 1274.)

§14522. CONSENT OF STATES

This subtitle does not require a State to engage in or accept a program under this subtitle without its consent.

(Pub. L. 107–217, Aug. 21, 2002, 116 Stat. 1274.)

§14523. PROGRAM IMPLEMENTATION

(a) REQUIREMENTS.—A program or project authorized under this chapter shall not be implemented until—

(1) the responsible federal official has decided that applications and plans relating to the program or project are not incompatible with the provisions and objectives of federal laws that the official administers that are not inconsistent with this subtitle; and

(2) the Appalachian Regional Commission has approved the program or project and has determined that it—

(A) meets the applicable criteria under section 14524 of this title and the requirements of the development planning process under section 14525 of this title; and

(B) will contribute to the development of the Appalachian region.

(b) DECISION IS CONTROLLING.—A decision under subsection (a)(2) is controlling and shall be accepted by the federal agencies.

(Pub. L. 107–217, Aug. 21, 2002, 116 Stat. 1274.)

§14524. PROGRAM DEVELOPMENT CRITERIA

(a) FACTORS TO BE CONSIDERED.—In considering programs and projects to be given assistance under this subtitle, and in establishing a priority ranking of the requests for assistance presented to the Appalachian Regional Commission, the Commission shall follow procedures that will ensure consideration of—

(1) the relationship of the project or class of projects to overall regional development, including its location in a severely and persistently distressed county or area;

(2) the population and area to be served by the project or class of projects, including the per capita market income and the unemployment rates in the area;

(3) the relative financial resources available to the State or political subdivisions or instrumentalities of the State that seek to undertake the project;

(4) the importance of the project or class of projects in relation to other projects or classes of projects that may be in competition for the same amounts;

(5) the prospects that the project for which assistance is sought will improve, on a continuing rather than a temporary basis, the opportunities for employment, the average level of income, or the economic and social development of the area served by the project; and

(6) the extent to which the project design provides for detailed outcome measurements by which grant expenditures may be evaluated.

(b) LIMITATION ON USE.—Financial assistance made available under this subtitle shall not be used to assist establishments relocating from one area to another.

(c) DETERMINATION REQUIRED BEFORE AMOUNTS MAY BE PROVIDED.—Amounts may be provided for programs and projects in a State under this subtitle only if the Commission determines that the level of federal and state financial assistance under other laws for the same type of programs or projects in that part of the State within the Appalachian region will not be diminished in order to substitute amounts authorized by this subtitle.

(d) MINIMUM AMOUNT OF ASSISTANCE TO DISTRESSED COUNTIES AND AREAS.—For each fiscal year, not less than 50 percent of the amount of grant expenditures the Commission approves shall support activities or projects that benefit severely and persistently distressed counties and areas.

(Pub. L. 107–217, Aug. 21, 2002, 116 Stat. 1275.)

§14525. STATE DEVELOPMENT PLANNING PROCESS

(a) STATE DEVELOPMENT PLAN.—Pursuant to policies the Appalachian Regional Commission establishes, each state member shall submit a development plan for the area of the State within the Appalachian region. The plan shall—

(1) be submitted according to a schedule the Commission prescribes;

(2) reflect the goals, objectives, and priorities identified in the regional development plan and in any subregional development plan that may be approved for the subregion of which the State is a part;

(3) describe the state organization and continuous process for Appalachian

development planning, including—

(A) the procedures established by the State for the participation of local development districts in the process;

(B) how the process is related to overall statewide planning and budgeting processes; and

(C) the method of coordinating planning and projects in the region under this subtitle, the Public Works and Economic Development Act of 1965 (42 U.S.C. 3121 et seq.), and other federal, state, and local programs;

(4) set forth the goals, objectives, and priorities of the State for the region, as established by the Governor, and identify the needs on which the goals, objectives, and priorities are based; and

(5) describe the development strategies for achieving the goals, objectives, and priorities, including funding sources, and recommendations for specific projects to receive assistance under this subtitle.

(b) AREAWIDE ACTION PROGRAMS.—The Commission shall encourage the preparation and execution of areawide action programs that specify interrelated projects and schedules of actions, the necessary agency funding, and other commitments to implement the programs. The programs shall make appropriate use of existing plans affecting the area.

(c) LOCAL DEVELOPMENT DISTRICTS.—Local development districts certified by the State as described in section 14102(a)(2) of this title provide the linkage between state and substate planning and development. The districts shall assist the States in the coordination of areawide programs and projects and may prepare and adopt areawide plans or action programs. In carrying out the development planning process, including the selection of programs and projects for assistance, States shall consult with local development districts, local units of government, and citizen groups and shall consider the goals, objectives, priorities, and recommendations of those bodies.

(d) FEDERAL RESPONSIBILITIES.—To the maximum extent practicable, federal departments, agencies, and instrumentalities undertaking or providing financial assistance for programs or projects in the region shall—

(1) take into account the policies, goals, and objectives the Commission and its member States establish pursuant to this subtitle;

(2) recognize Appalachian state development strategies approved by the Commission as satisfying requirements for overall economic development planning under the programs or projects; and

(3) accept the boundaries and organization of any local development district certified under this subtitle that the Governor may designate as the areawide agency required under any of those programs undertaken or assisted by those federal departments, agencies, and instrumentalities.

(Pub. L. 107–217, Aug. 21, 2002, 116 Stat. 1275.)

§14526. DISTRESSED, AT-RISK, AND ECONOMICALLY STRONG COUNTIES

(a) DESIGNATIONS.—

(1) IN GENERAL.—The Appalachian Regional Commission, in accordance with criteria the Commission may establish, each year shall—

(A) designate as "distressed counties" those counties in the Appalachian region that are the most severely and persistently distressed;

(B) designate as "at-risk counties" those counties in the Appalachian region that are most at risk of becoming economically distressed; and

(C) designate two categories of economically strong counties, consisting of—

(i) "competitive counties", which shall be those counties in the region that are approaching economic parity with the rest of the United States; and

(ii) "attainment counties", which shall be those counties in the region that have attained or exceeded economic parity with the rest of the United States.

(2) ANNUAL REVIEW OF DESIGNATIONS.—The Commission shall—

(A) conduct an annual review of each designation of a county under paragraph (1) to determine if the county still meets the criteria for the designation; and

(B) renew the designation for another one-year period only if the county still meets the criteria.

(b) DISTRESSED COUNTIES.—In program and project development and implementation and in the allocation of appropriations made available to carry out this subtitle, the Commission shall give special consideration to the needs of counties for which a distressed county designation is in effect under this section.

(c) ECONOMICALLY STRONG COUNTIES.—

(1) COMPETITIVE COUNTIES.—Except as provided in paragraphs (3) and (4), assistance under this subtitle for a project that is carried out in a county for which a competitive county designation is in effect under this section shall not be more than 30 percent of the project cost.

(2) ATTAINMENT COUNTIES.—Except as provided in paragraphs (3) and (4), amounts may not be provided under this subtitle for a project that is carried out in a county for which an attainment county designation is in effect under this section.

(3) EXCEPTIONS.—Paragraphs (1) and (2) do not apply to—

(A) a project on the Appalachian development highway system authorized by section 14501 of this title;

(B) a local development district administrative project assisted under section 14321(a)(1)(A) of this title; or

(C) a multicounty project that is carried out in at least two counties designated under this section if—

(i) at least one of the participating counties is designated as a distressed county under this section; and

(ii) the project will be of substantial direct benefit to at least one distressed county.

(4) WAIVER.—

(A) IN GENERAL.—The Commission may waive the requirements of paragraphs (1) and (2) for a project when the recipient of assistance for the project shows the existence of any of the following:

(i) a significant pocket of distress in the part of the county in which the project is carried out.

(ii) a significant potential benefit from the project in at least one area of the region outside the designated county.

(B) Reports to Congress.—The Commission shall submit to the Committee on Environment and Public Works of the Senate and the Committee on Transportation and Infrastructure of the House of Representatives an annual report describing each waiver granted under subparagraph (A) during the period covered by the report.

(Pub. L. 107–217, Aug. 21, 2002, 116 Stat. 1277; Pub. L. 110–371, §4(a), Oct. 8, 2008, 122 Stat. 4041.)

CHAPTER 147—MISCELLANEOUS

Sec.
14701. Applicable labor standards.
14702. Nondiscrimination.
14703. Authorization of appropriations.
14704. Termination.

§14701. APPLICABLE LABOR STANDARDS

All laborers and mechanics employed by contractors or subcontractors in the construction, alteration, or repair, including painting and decorating, of projects, buildings, and works which are financially assisted through federal amounts authorized under this subtitle shall be paid wages at rates not less than those prevailing on similar construction in the locality as the Secretary of Labor determines in accordance with sections 3141–3144, 3146, and 3147 of this title. With respect to those labor standards, the Secretary has the authority and functions set forth in Reorganization Plan Numbered 14 of 1950 (eff. May 24, 1950, 64 Stat. 1267) and section 3145 of this title.

(Pub. L. 107–217, Aug. 21, 2002, 116 Stat. 1278.)

§14702. NONDISCRIMINATION

An individual in the United States shall not, because of sex, be excluded from participation in, be denied the benefits of, or be subjected to discrimination under, a program or activity receiving federal financial assistance under this subtitle.

(Pub. L. 107–217, Aug. 21, 2002, 116 Stat. 1278.)

§14703. AUTHORIZATION OF APPROPRIATIONS

(a) IN GENERAL.—In addition to amounts made available under section 14501, there is authorized to be appropriated to the Appalachian Regional Commission to carry out this subtitle—

(1) $87,000,000 for fiscal year 2008;

(2) $100,000,000 for fiscal year 2009;

(3) $105,000,000 for fiscal year 2010;

(4) $108,000,000 for fiscal year 2011;

(5) $110,000,000 for each of fiscal years 2012 through 2021; and

(6) $200,000,000 for each of fiscal years 2022 through 2026.

(b) ECONOMIC AND ENERGY DEVELOPMENT INITIATIVE.—Of the amounts made available under subsection (a), the following amounts may be used to carry out section 14508—

(1) $12,000,000 for fiscal year 2008;

(2) $12,500,000 for fiscal year 2009;

(3) $13,000,000 for fiscal year 2010;

(4) $13,500,000 for fiscal year 2011; and

(5) $14,000,000 for fiscal year 2012.

(c) HIGH-SPEED BROADBAND DEPLOYMENT INITIATIVE.—Of the amounts made available under subsection (a), $20,000,000 may be used to carry out section 14509 for each of fiscal years 2022 through 2026.

(d) APPALACHIAN REGIONAL ENERGY HUB INITIATIVE.—Of the amounts made available under subsection (a), $5,000,000 shall be used to carry out section 14511 for each of fiscal years 2022 through 2026.

(e) AVAILABILITY.—Amounts made available under subsection (a) remain available until expended.

(f) ALLOCATION OF FUNDS.—Funds approved by the Appalachian Regional Commission for a project in a State in the Appalachian region pursuant to a congressional directive shall be derived from the total amount allocated to the State by the Appalachian Regional Commission from amounts appropriated to carry out this subtitle.

(Pub. L. 107–217, Aug. 21, 2002, 116 Stat. 1278; Pub. L. 110–371, §5, Oct. 8, 2008, 122 Stat. 4041; Pub. L. 114–94, div. A, title I, §1436(b), Dec. 4, 2015, 129 Stat. 1431; Pub. L. 116–159, div. B, title I, §1107(a), Oct. 1, 2020, 134 Stat. 727; Pub. L. 117–58, div. A, title I, §11506(f), Nov. 15, 2021, 135 Stat. 586.)

§14704. TERMINATION

This subtitle, except sections 14102(a)(1) and (b) and 14501, ceases to be in effect on October 1, 2026.

(Pub. L. 107–217, Aug. 21, 2002, 116 Stat. 1278; Pub. L. 109–289, div. B, title II, §20326, as added Pub. L. 110–5, §2, Feb. 15, 2007, 121 Stat. 22; Pub. L. 110–371, §6, Oct. 8, 2008, 122 Stat. 4042; Pub. L. 114–94, div. A, title I, §1436(c), Dec. 4, 2015, 129 Stat. 1431; Pub. L. 116–159, div. B, title I, §1107(b), Oct. 1, 2020, 134 Stat. 727; Pub. L. 117–58, div. A, title I, §11506(g), Nov. 15, 2021, 135 Stat. 586.)

REGIONAL ECONOMIC AND INFRASTRUCTURE DEVELOPMENT

SUBTITLE V OF TITLE 40 U.S.C.

TITLE 40, SUBTITLE V, UNITED STATES CODE

SUBTITLE V—REGIONAL ECONOMIC AND INFRASTRUCTURE DEVELOPMENT

This title was enacted by Pub. L. 107–217, §1, Aug. 21, 2002, 116 Stat. 1062

Chapter		Sec.
151.	**GENERAL PROVISIONS**	**15101**
153.	**REGIONAL COMMISSIONS**	**15301**
155.	**FINANCIAL ASSISTANCE**	**15501**
157.	**ADMINISTRATIVE PROVISIONS**	**15701**
159.	**Additional Regional Commission Programs** [1]	**15901**

[1] *So in original. Probably should be capitalized.*

CHAPTER 151—GENERAL PROVISIONS

Sec.

15101.   Definitions.

§15101. DEFINITIONS

In this subtitle, the following definitions apply:

(1) COMMISSION.—The term "Commission" means a Commission or Authority established under section 15301.

(2) LOCAL DEVELOPMENT DISTRICT.—The term "local development district" means an entity that—

(A)(i) is an economic development district that is—

(I) in existence on the date of the enactment of this chapter; and

(II) located in the region; or

(ii) if an entity described in clause (i) does not exist—

(I) is organized and operated in a manner that ensures broad-based community participation and an effective opportunity for local officials, community leaders, and the public to contribute to the development and implementation of programs in the region;

(II) is governed by a policy board with at least a simple majority of members consisting of—

(aa) elected officials; or

(bb) designees or employees of a general purpose unit of local government that have been appointed to represent the unit of local government; and

(III) is certified by the Governor or appropriate State officer as having a charter or authority that includes the economic development of counties, portions of counties, or other political subdivisions within the region; and

(B) has not, as certified by the Federal Cochairperson—

(i) inappropriately used Federal grant funds from any Federal source; or

(ii) appointed an officer who, during the period in which another entity inappropriately used Federal grant funds from any Federal source, was an officer of the other entity.

(3) FEDERAL GRANT PROGRAM.—The term "Federal grant program" means a Federal grant program to provide assistance in carrying out economic and community development activities.

(4) INDIAN TRIBE.—The term "Indian tribe" has the meaning given the term in section 4 of the Indian Self-Determination and Education Assistance Act (25 U.S.C. 450b).[1]

(5) NONPROFIT ENTITY.—The term "nonprofit entity" means any organization described in section 501(c) of the Internal Revenue Code of 1986 and exempt from taxation under 501(a) of that Code that has been formed for the purpose of economic development.

(6) REGION.—The term "region" means the area covered by a Commission as described in subchapter II of chapter 157.[2]

(Added Pub. L. 110–234, title XIV, §14217(a)(2), May 22, 2008, 122 Stat. 1468, and Pub. L. 110–246, §4(a), title XIV, §14217(a)(2), June 18, 2008, 122 Stat. 1664, 2230; amended Pub. L. 117–328, div. O, title IV, §401(a)(2), Dec. 29, 2022, 136 Stat. 5228.)

[1] *See References in Text note below.*

[2] *So in original. Probably means chapter 4 of this subtitle.*

CHAPTER 153—REGIONAL COMMISSIONS

Sec.
15301. Establishment, membership, and employees.
15302. Decisions.
15303. Functions.
15304. Administrative powers and expenses.
15305. Meetings.
15306. Personal financial interests.
15307. Tribal participation.
15308. Transfer of funds among Federal agencies.
15309. Annual reports.[1]

[1] So in original. Does not conform to section catchline.

§15301. ESTABLISHMENT, MEMBERSHIP, AND EMPLOYEES

(a) ESTABLISHMENT.—There are established the following regional Commissions:

(1) The Southeast Crescent Regional Commission.

(2) The Southwest Border Regional Commission.

(3) The Northern Border Regional Commission.

(4) The Great Lakes Authority.

(5) The Mid-Atlantic Regional Commission.

(6) The Southern New England Regional Commission.

(b) MEMBERSHIP.—

(1) FEDERAL AND STATE MEMBERS.—Each Commission shall be composed of the following members:

(A) A Federal Cochairperson, to be appointed by the President, by and with the advice and consent of the Senate.

(B) The Governor of each participating State in the region of the Commission.

(2) ALTERNATE MEMBERS.—

(A) ALTERNATE FEDERAL COCHAIRPERSON.—The President shall appoint an alternate Federal Cochairperson for each Commission. The alternate Federal Cochairperson, when not actively serving as an alternate for the Federal Cochairperson, shall perform such functions and duties as are delegated by the Federal Cochairperson.

(B) STATE ALTERNATES.—The State member of a participating State may have a single alternate, who shall be appointed by the Governor of the State from among the members of the Governor's cabinet or personal staff.

(C) VOTING.—

(i) IN GENERAL.—An alternate member shall vote in the case of the absence, death, disability, removal, or resignation of the Federal or State member for which the alternate member is an alternate.

(ii) STATE ALTERNATES.—If the alternate State member is unable to vote in accordance with clause (i), the alternate State member may delegate voting authority to a designee, subject to the condition that the executive director shall be notified, in writing, of the designation not less than 1 week before the applicable vote is to take place.

(3) COCHAIRPERSONS.—A Commission shall be headed by—

(A) the Federal Cochairperson, who shall serve as a liaison between the Federal Government and the Commission; and

(B) a State Cochairperson, who shall be a Governor of a participating State in the region and shall be elected by the State members for a term of not less than 1 year.

(4) CONSECUTIVE TERMS.—A State member may not be elected to serve as State Cochairperson for more than 2 consecutive terms.

(c) COMPENSATION.—

(1) FEDERAL COCHAIRPERSONS.—Each Federal Cochairperson shall be compensated by the Federal Government at level III of the Executive Schedule as set out in section 5314 of title 5.

(2) ALTERNATE FEDERAL COCHAIRPERSONS.—Each Federal Cochairperson's alternate shall be compensated by the Federal Government at level V of the Executive Schedule as set out in section 5316 of title 5.

(3) STATE MEMBERS AND ALTERNATES.—Each State member and alternate shall be compensated by the State that they represent at the rate established by the laws of that State.

(d) EXECUTIVE DIRECTOR AND STAFF.—

(1) IN GENERAL.—A Commission shall appoint and fix the compensation of an executive director and such other personnel as are necessary to enable the Commission to carry out its duties. Compensation under this paragraph may not exceed the maximum rate of basic pay established for the Senior Executive Service under section 5382 of title 5, including any applicable locality-based comparability payment that may be authorized under section 5304(h)(2)(C) of that title.

(2) EXECUTIVE DIRECTOR.—The executive director shall be responsible for carrying out the administrative duties of the Commission, directing the Commission staff, and such other duties as the Commission may assign.

(e) NO FEDERAL EMPLOYEE STATUS.—No member, alternate, officer, or employee of a Commission (other than the Federal Cochairperson, the alternate Federal Cochairperson, staff of the Federal Cochairperson, and any Federal employee detailed to the Commission) shall be considered to be a Federal employee for any purpose.

(f) SUCCESSION.—Subject to the time limitations under section 3346 of title 5, the Federal Cochairperson may designate an employee of the Commission to perform the functions and duties of the office of the Federal Cochairperson temporarily in an acting capacity if both the Federal Cochairperson and the alternate Federal Cochairperson die, resign, or otherwise are unable to perform the functions and duties of their offices.

(Added Pub. L. 110–234, title XIV, §14217(a)(2), May 22, 2008, 122 Stat. 1469, and Pub. L. 110–246, §4(a), title XIV, §14217(a)(2), June 18, 2008, 122 Stat. 1664, 2231; amended Pub. L. 115–334, title VI, §6304(f), Dec. 20, 2018, 132 Stat. 4752; Pub. L. 117–328, div. O, title IV, §401(a)(1), Dec. 29, 2022, 136 Stat. 5228; Pub. L. 118–272, div. B, title II, §§2242(a), 2249(a), 2250(a), Jan. 4, 2025, 138 Stat. 3202, 3209.)

§15302. DECISIONS

(a) REQUIREMENTS FOR APPROVAL.—Except as provided in section 15304(c)(3), decisions by the Commission shall require the affirmative vote of the Federal Cochairperson and a majority of the State members or alternate State members, including designees (exclusive of members representing States delinquent under section 15304(c)(3)(C)).

(b) CONSULTATION.—In matters coming before the Commission, the Federal Cochairperson shall, to the extent practicable, consult with the Federal departments and agencies having an interest in the subject matter.

(c) QUORUMS.—

(1) IN GENERAL.—Subject to paragraph (2), a Commission shall determine what constitutes a quorum for meetings of the Commission.

(2) REQUIREMENTS.—Any quorum for meetings of a Commission shall include—

(A) the Federal Cochairperson or the alternate Federal Cochairperson; and

(B) a majority of State members or alternate State members, including designees (exclusive of members representing States delinquent under section 15304(c)(3)(C)).

(d) PROJECTS AND GRANT PROPOSALS.—The approval of project and grant proposals shall be a responsibility of each Commission and shall be carried out in accordance with section 15503.

(Added Pub. L. 110–234, title XIV, §14217(a)(2), May 22, 2008, 122 Stat. 1470, and Pub. L. 110–246, §4(a), title XIV, §14217(a)(2), June 18, 2008, 122 Stat. 1664, 2232; amended Pub. L. 118–272, div. B, title II, §2242(b), Jan. 4, 2025, 138 Stat. 3202.)

§15303. FUNCTIONS

A Commission shall—

(1) assess the needs and assets of its region based on available research, demonstration projects, investigations, assessments, and evaluations of the region prepared by Federal, State, and local agencies, universities, local development districts, and other nonprofit groups;

(2) develop, on a continuing basis, comprehensive and coordinated economic and infrastructure development strategies to establish priorities and approve grants for the economic development of its region, giving due consideration to other Federal, State, and local planning and development activities in the region;

(3) not later than one year after the date of the enactment of this section, and after taking into account State plans developed under section 15502, establish priorities in an economic and infrastructure development plan for its region, including 5-year regional outcome targets;

(4)(A) enhance the capacity of, and provide support for, local development districts in its region; or

(B) if no local development district exists in an area in a participating State in the region, foster the creation of a local development district;

(5) encourage private investment in industrial, commercial, and other economic development projects in its region;

(6) cooperate with and assist State governments with the preparation of economic

and infrastructure development plans and programs for participating States;

(7) formulate and recommend to the Governors and legislatures of States that participate in the Commission forms of interstate cooperation and, where appropriate, international cooperation; and

(8) work with State and local agencies in developing appropriate model legislation to enhance local and regional economic development.

(Added Pub. L. 110–234, title XIV, §14217(a)(2), May 22, 2008, 122 Stat. 1470, and Pub. L. 110–246, §4(a), title XIV, §14217(a)(2), June 18, 2008, 122 Stat. 1664, 2232.)

§15304. ADMINISTRATIVE POWERS AND EXPENSES

(a) POWERS.—In carrying out its duties under this subtitle, a Commission may—

(1) hold such hearings, sit and act at such times and places, take such testimony, receive such evidence, and print or otherwise reproduce and distribute a description of the proceedings and reports on actions by the Commission as the Commission considers appropriate;

(2) authorize, through the Federal or State Cochairperson or any other member of the Commission designated by the Commission, the administration of oaths if the Commission determines that testimony should be taken or evidence received under oath;

(3) request from any Federal, State, or local agency such information as may be available to or procurable by the agency that may be of use to the Commission in carrying out the duties of the Commission;

(4) adopt, amend, and repeal bylaws and rules governing the conduct of business and the performance of duties by the Commission;

(5) request the head of any Federal agency, State agency, or local government to detail to the Commission such personnel as the Commission requires to carry out its duties, each such detail to be without loss of seniority, pay, or other employee status, which may be done without a requirement for the Commission to reimburse the agency or local government;

(6) provide for coverage of Commission employees in a suitable retirement and employee benefit system by making arrangements or entering into contracts with any participating State government or otherwise providing retirement and other employee coverage;

(7) accept, use, and dispose of gifts or donations or services or real, personal, tangible, or intangible property;

(8) collect fees for services provided and retain and expend such fees;

(9) enter into and perform such contracts, cooperative agreements, or other transactions as are necessary to carry out Commission duties, including any contracts or cooperative agreements with a department, agency, or instrumentality of the United States, a State (including a political subdivision, agency, or instrumentality of the State), or a person, firm, association, or corporation; and

(10) establish and maintain a central office at such location in its region as the Commission may select.

(b) FEDERAL AGENCY COOPERATION.—A Federal agency shall—

(1) cooperate with a Commission; and

(2) provide, to the extent practicable, on request of the Federal Cochairperson, appropriate assistance in carrying out this subtitle, in accordance with applicable Federal laws (including regulations).

(c) ADMINISTRATIVE EXPENSES.—

(1) IN GENERAL.—Subject to paragraph (2), the administrative expenses of a Commission shall be paid—

(A) by the Federal Government, in an amount equal to 50 percent of the administrative expenses of the Commission; and

(B) by the States participating in the Commission, in an amount equal to 50 percent of the administrative expenses.

(2) EXPENSES OF THE FEDERAL COCHAIRPERSON.—All expenses of the Federal Cochairperson, including expenses of the alternate and staff of the Federal Cochairperson, shall be paid by the Federal Government.

(3) STATE SHARE.—

(A) IN GENERAL.—Subject to subparagraph (B), the share of administrative expenses of a Commission to be paid by each State of the Commission shall be determined by a majority vote of the State members of the Commission.

(B) NO FEDERAL PARTICIPATION.—The Federal Cochairperson shall not participate or vote in any decision under subparagraph (A).

(C) DELINQUENT STATES.—During any period in which a State is more than 1 year delinquent in payment of the State's share of administrative expenses of the Commission under this subsection—

(i) no assistance under this subtitle shall be provided to the State (including assistance to a political subdivision or a resident of the State) for any project not approved as of the date of the commencement of the delinquency; and

(ii) no member of the Commission from the State shall participate or vote in any action by the Commission.

(4) EFFECT ON ASSISTANCE.—A State's share of administrative expenses of a Commission under this subsection shall not be taken into consideration when determining the amount of assistance provided to the State under this subtitle.

(Added Pub. L. 110–234, title XIV, §14217(a)(2), May 22, 2008, 122 Stat. 1471, and Pub. L. 110–246, §4(a), title XIV, §14217(a)(2), June 18, 2008, 122 Stat. 1664, 2233; amended Pub. L. 115–334, title VI, §6304(a), Dec. 20, 2018, 132 Stat. 4749; Pub. L. 118–272, div. B, title II, §2242(c), Jan. 4, 2025, 138 Stat. 3203.)

§15305. MEETINGS

(a) INITIAL MEETING.—Each Commission shall hold an initial meeting not later than 180 days after the date of the enactment of this section.

(b) ANNUAL MEETING.—Each Commission shall conduct at least 1 meeting each year with—

(1) the Federal Cochairperson; and

(2) at least a majority of the State members or alternate State members (including designees) present in-person or via electronic means.

(c) ADDITIONAL MEETINGS.—Each Commission shall conduct additional meetings at such times as it determines and may conduct such meetings by electronic means.

(Added Pub. L. 110–234, title XIV, §14217(a)(2), May 22, 2008, 122 Stat. 1473, and Pub. L. 110–246, §4(a), title XIV, §14217(a)(2), June 18, 2008, 122 Stat. 1664, 2235; amended Pub. L. 118–272, div. B, title II, §2242(d), Jan. 4, 2025, 138 Stat. 3203.)

§15306. PERSONAL FINANCIAL INTERESTS

(a) CONFLICTS OF INTEREST.—

(1) NO ROLE ALLOWED.—Except as permitted by paragraph (2), an individual who is a State member or alternate, or an officer or employee of a Commission, shall not participate personally and substantially as a member, alternate, officer, or employee of the Commission, through decision, approval, disapproval, recommendation, request for a ruling, or other determination, contract, claim, controversy, or other matter in which, to the individual's knowledge, any of the following has a financial interest:

(A) The individual.

(B) The individual's spouse, minor child, or partner.

(C) An organization (except a State or political subdivision of a State) in which the individual is serving as an officer, director, trustee, partner, or employee.

(D) Any person or organization with whom the individual is negotiating or has any arrangement concerning prospective employment.

(2) EXCEPTION.—Paragraph (1) shall not apply if the individual, in advance of the proceeding, application, request for a ruling or other determination, contract, claim controversy, or other particular matter presenting a potential conflict of interest—

(A) advises the Commission of the nature and circumstances of the matter presenting the conflict of interest;

(B) makes full disclosure of the financial interest; and

(C) receives a written decision of the Commission that the interest is not so substantial as to be considered likely to affect the integrity of the services that the Commission may expect from the individual.

(3) VIOLATION.—An individual violating this subsection shall be fined under title 18, imprisoned for not more than 1 year, or both.

(b) STATE MEMBER OR ALTERNATE.—A State member or alternate member may not receive any salary, or any contribution to, or supplementation of, salary, for services on a Commission from a source other than the State of the member or alternate.

(c) DETAILED EMPLOYEES.—

(1) IN GENERAL.—No person detailed to serve a Commission shall receive any salary, or any contribution to, or supplementation of, salary, for services provided to the Commission from any source other than the State, local, or intergovernmental department or agency from which the person was detailed to the Commission.

(2) VIOLATION.—Any person that violates this subsection shall be fined under title 18, imprisoned not more than 1 year, or both.

(d) FEDERAL COCHAIRMAN, ALTERNATE TO FEDERAL COCHAIRMAN, AND FEDERAL OFFICERS AND EMPLOYEES.—The Federal Cochairman, the alternate to the Federal Cochairman, and any Federal officer or employee detailed to duty with the Commission are not subject to this section but remain subject to sections 202 through 209 of title 18.

(e) RESCISSION.—A Commission may declare void any contract, loan, or grant of or by the Commission in relation to which the Commission determines that there has been a violation of any provision under subsection (a)(1), (b), or (c), or any of the provisions of sections 202 through 209 of title 18.

(Added Pub. L. 110–234, title XIV, §14217(a)(2), May 22, 2008, 122 Stat. 1473, and Pub. L. 110–246, §4(a), title XIV, §14217(a)(2), June 18, 2008, 122 Stat. 1664, 2235.)

§15307. TRIBAL PARTICIPATION

Governments of Indian tribes in the region of the Southwest Border Regional Commission shall be allowed to participate in matters before that Commission in the same manner and to the same extent as State agencies and instrumentalities in the region.

(Added Pub. L. 110–234, title XIV, §14217(a)(2), May 22, 2008, 122 Stat. 1474, and Pub. L. 110–246, §4(a), title XIV, §14217(a)(2), June 18, 2008, 122 Stat. 1664, 2236.)

§15308. TRANSFER OF FUNDS AMONG FEDERAL AGENCIES

(a) IN GENERAL.—Subject to subsection (c), for purposes of this subtitle, each Commission may transfer funds to and accept transfers of funds from other Federal agencies.

(b) TRANSFER OF FUNDS TO OTHER FEDERAL AGENCIES.—Funds made available to a Commission may be transferred to other Federal agencies if the funds are used consistently with the purposes for which the funds were specifically authorized and appropriated.

(c) TRANSFER OF FUNDS FROM OTHER FEDERAL AGENCIES.—Funds may be transferred to any Commission under this section if—

(1) the statutory authority for the funds provided by the Federal agency does not expressly prohibit use of funds for authorities being carried out by a Commission; and

(2) the Federal agency that provides the funds determines that the activities for which the funds are to be used are otherwise eligible for funding under such a statutory authority.

(Added Pub. L. 118–272, div. B, title II, §2243(a)(2), Jan. 4, 2025, 138 Stat. 3203.)

§15309. ANNUAL REPORT

(a) IN GENERAL.—Not later than 180 days after the last day of each fiscal year, each Commission shall submit to the President and Congress a report on the activities carried out by the Commission under this subtitle in the fiscal year.

(b) CONTENTS.—The report shall include—

(1) a description of the criteria used by the Commission to designate counties under section 15702 and a list of the counties designated in each category;

(2) an evaluation of the progress of the Commission in meeting the goals identified in the Commission's economic and infrastructure development plan under section 15303 and State economic and infrastructure development plans under section 15502; and

(3) any policy recommendations approved by the Commission.

(Added Pub. L. 110–234, title XIV, §14217(a)(2), May 22, 2008, 122 Stat. 1474, and Pub. L. 110–246, §4(a), title XIV, §14217(a)(2), June 18, 2008, 122 Stat. 1664, 2236, §15308; renumbered §15309 and amended Pub. L. 118–272, div. B, title II, §§2242(e), 2243(a)(1), Jan. 4, 2025, 138 Stat. 3203.)

CHAPTER 155—FINANCIAL ASSISTANCE

Sec.
15501. Economic and infrastructure development grants.
15502. Comprehensive economic and infrastructure development plans.
15503. Approval of applications for assistance.
15504. Program development criteria.
15505. Local development districts and organizations.
15506. Supplements to Federal grant programs.
15507. Payment of non-Federal share for certain Federal grant programs.

§15501. ECONOMIC AND INFRASTRUCTURE DEVELOPMENT GRANTS

(a) IN GENERAL.—A Commission may make grants to States and local governments, Indian tribes, and public and nonprofit organizations for projects, approved in accordance with section 15503—

(1) to develop the transportation infrastructure of its region;

(2) to develop the basic public infrastructure of its region;

(3) to develop the telecommunications infrastructure of its region;

(4) to assist its region in obtaining job skills training, skills development and employment-related education, entrepreneurship, technology, and business development;

(5) to provide assistance to severely economically distressed and underdeveloped areas of its region that lack financial resources for improving basic health care and other public services;

(6) to promote resource conservation, tourism, recreation, and preservation of open space in a manner consistent with economic development goals;

(7) to promote the development of renewable and alternative energy sources;

(8) to grow the capacity for successful community economic development in its region; and

(9) to otherwise achieve the purposes of this subtitle.

(b) ALLOCATION OF FUNDS.—A Commission shall allocate at least 40 percent of any grant amounts provided by the Commission in a fiscal year for projects described in paragraph (1), (2), (3), or (7) of subsection (a).

(c) SOURCES OF GRANTS.—Grant amounts may be provided entirely from appropriations to carry out this subtitle, in combination with amounts available under other Federal grant programs, or from any other source.

(d) MAXIMUM COMMISSION CONTRIBUTIONS.—

(1) IN GENERAL.—Subject to paragraphs (2) and (3), the Commission may contribute not more than 50 percent of a project or activity cost eligible for financial assistance under this section from amounts appropriated to carry out this subtitle.

(2) DISTRESSED COUNTIES.—The maximum Commission contribution for a project or activity to be carried out in a county for which a distressed county designation is in effect under section 15702 may be increased to 80 percent.

(3) SPECIAL RULE FOR REGIONAL PROJECTS.—A Commission may increase to 60 percent under paragraph (1) and 90 percent under paragraph (2) the maximum

Commission contribution for a project or activity if—

(A) the project or activity involves 3 or more counties or more than one State; and

(B) the Commission determines in accordance with section 15302(a) that the project or activity will bring significant interstate or multicounty benefits to a region.

(e) MAINTENANCE OF EFFORT.—Funds may be provided by a Commission for a program or project in a State under this section only if the Commission determines that the level of Federal or State financial assistance provided under a law other than this subtitle, for the same type of program or project in the same area of the State within region, will not be reduced as a result of funds made available by this subtitle.

(f) NO RELOCATION ASSISTANCE.—Financial assistance authorized by this section may not be used to assist a person or entity in relocating from one area to another, except that financial assistance may be used as otherwise authorized by this subtitle to attract businesses to the region from outside the United States.

(Added Pub. L. 110–234, title XIV, §14217(a)(2), May 22, 2008, 122 Stat. 1474, and Pub. L. 110–246, §4(a), title XIV, §14217(a)(2), June 18, 2008, 122 Stat. 1664, 2236; amended Pub. L. 115–334, title VI, §6304(b), Dec. 20, 2018, 132 Stat. 4749.)

§15502. COMPREHENSIVE ECONOMIC AND INFRASTRUCTURE DEVELOPMENT PLANS

(a) STATE PLANS.—In accordance with policies established by a Commission, each State member of the Commission shall submit a comprehensive economic and infrastructure development plan for the area of the region represented by the State member.

(b) CONTENT OF PLAN.—A State economic and infrastructure development plan shall reflect the goals, objectives, and priorities identified in any applicable economic and infrastructure development plan developed by a Commission under section 15303.

(c) CONSULTATION WITH INTERESTED LOCAL PARTIES.—In carrying out the development planning process (including the selection of programs and projects for assistance), a State shall—

(1) consult with local development districts, local units of government, and local colleges and universities; and

(2) take into consideration the goals, objectives, priorities, and recommendations of the entities described in paragraph (1).

(d) PUBLIC PARTICIPATION.—

(1) IN GENERAL.—A Commission and applicable State and local development districts shall encourage and assist, to the maximum extent practicable, public participation in the development, revision, and implementation of all plans and programs under this subtitle.

(2) GUIDELINES.—A Commission shall develop guidelines for providing public participation, including public hearings.

(Added Pub. L. 110–234, title XIV, §14217(a)(2), May 22, 2008, 122 Stat. 1476, and Pub. L. 110–246, §4(a), title XIV, §14217(a)(2), June 18, 2008, 122 Stat. 1664, 2238.)

§15503. APPROVAL OF APPLICATIONS FOR ASSISTANCE

(a) EVALUATION BY STATE MEMBER.—An application to a Commission for a grant or any other assistance for a project under this subtitle shall be made through, and evaluated for approval by, the State member of the Commission representing the applicant.

(b) CERTIFICATION.—An application to a Commission for a grant or other assistance for a project under this subtitle shall be eligible for assistance only on certification by the State member of the Commission representing the applicant that the application for the project—

(1) describes ways in which the project complies with any applicable State economic and infrastructure development plan;

(2) meets applicable criteria under section 15504;

(3) adequately ensures that the project will be properly administered, operated, and maintained; and

(4) otherwise meets the requirements for assistance under this subtitle.

(c) VOTES FOR DECISIONS.—On certification by a State member of a Commission of an application for a grant or other assistance for a specific project under this section, an affirmative vote of the Commission under section 15302 shall be required for approval of the application.

(Added Pub. L. 110–234, title XIV, §14217(a)(2), May 22, 2008, 122 Stat. 1476, and Pub. L. 110–246, §4(a), title XIV, §14217(a)(2), June 18, 2008, 122 Stat. 1664, 2238.)

§15504. PROGRAM DEVELOPMENT CRITERIA

In considering programs and projects to be provided assistance by a Commission under this subtitle, and in establishing a priority ranking of the requests for assistance provided to the Commission, the Commission shall follow procedures that ensure, to the maximum extent practicable, consideration of—

(1) the relationship of the project or class of projects to overall regional development;

(2) the per capita income and poverty and unemployment and outmigration rates in an area;

(3) the financial resources available to the applicants for assistance seeking to carry out the project, with emphasis on ensuring that projects are adequately financed to maximize the probability of successful economic development;

(4) the importance of the project or class of projects in relation to the other projects or classes of projects that may be in competition for the same funds;

(5) the prospects that the project for which assistance is sought will improve, on a continuing rather than a temporary basis, the opportunities for employment, the average level of income, or the economic development of the area to be served by the project; and

(6) the extent to which the project design provides for detailed outcome measurements by which grant expenditures and the results of the expenditures may be evaluated.

(Added Pub. L. 110–234, title XIV, §14217(a)(2), May 22, 2008, 122 Stat. 1476, and Pub. L. 110–246, §4(a), title XIV, §14217(a)(2), June 18, 2008, 122 Stat. 1664, 2238.)

§15505. LOCAL DEVELOPMENT DISTRICTS AND ORGANIZATIONS

(a) GRANTS TO LOCAL DEVELOPMENT DISTRICTS.—Subject to the requirements of this section, a Commission may make grants to a local development district to assist in the payment of development planning and administrative expenses.

(b) CONDITIONS FOR GRANTS.—

(1) MAXIMUM AMOUNT.—The amount of a grant awarded under this section may not exceed 80 percent of the administrative and planning expenses of the local development district receiving the grant.

(2) MAXIMUM PERIOD FOR STATE AGENCIES.—In the case of a State agency certified as a local development district, a grant may not be awarded to the agency under this section for more than 3 fiscal years.

(3) LOCAL SHARE.—The contributions of a local development district for administrative expenses may be in cash or in kind, fairly evaluated, including space, equipment, and services.

(c) DUTIES OF LOCAL DEVELOPMENT DISTRICTS.—A local development district shall—

(1) operate as a lead organization serving multicounty areas in the region at the local level;

(2) assist the Commission in carrying out outreach activities for local governments, community development groups, the business community, and the public;

(3) serve as a liaison between State and local governments, nonprofit organizations (including community-based groups and educational institutions), the business community, and citizens; and

(4) assist the individuals and entities described in paragraph (3) in identifying, assessing, and facilitating projects and programs to promote the economic development of the region.

(Added Pub. L. 110–234, title XIV, §14217(a)(2), May 22, 2008, 122 Stat. 1477, and Pub. L. 110–246, §4(a), title XIV, §14217(a)(2), June 18, 2008, 122 Stat. 1664, 2239.)

§15506. SUPPLEMENTS TO FEDERAL GRANT PROGRAMS

(a) FINDING.—Congress finds that certain States and local communities of the region, including local development districts, may be unable to take maximum advantage of Federal grant programs for which the States and communities are eligible because—

(1) they lack the economic resources to provide the required matching share; or

(2) there are insufficient funds available under the applicable Federal law with respect to a project to be carried out in the region.

(b) FEDERAL GRANT PROGRAM FUNDING.—A Commission, with the approval of the Federal Cochairperson, may use amounts made available to carry out this subtitle—

(1) for any part of the basic Federal contribution to projects or activities under the Federal grant programs authorized by Federal laws; and

(2) to increase the Federal contribution to projects and activities under the programs above the fixed maximum part of the cost of the projects or activities otherwise authorized by the applicable law.

(c) CERTIFICATION REQUIRED.—For a program, project, or activity for which any part of the basic Federal contribution to the project or activity under a Federal grant program is proposed to be made under subsection (b), the Federal contribution shall not be made until the responsible Federal official administering the Federal law authorizing the Federal contribution certifies that the program, project, or activity meets the applicable requirements of the Federal law and could be approved for Federal contribution under that law if amounts were available under the law for the program, project, or activity.

(d) LIMITATIONS IN OTHER LAWS INAPPLICABLE.—Amounts provided pursuant to this subtitle are available without regard to any limitations on areas eligible for assistance or authorizations for appropriation in any other law.

(e) FEDERAL SHARE.—The Federal share of the cost of a project or activity receiving assistance under this section shall not exceed 80 percent.

(f) MAXIMUM COMMISSION CONTRIBUTION.—Section 15501(d), relating to limitations on Commission contributions, shall apply to a program, project, or activity receiving assistance under this section.

(Added Pub. L. 110–234, title XIV, §14217(a)(2), May 22, 2008, 122 Stat. 1477, and Pub. L. 110–246, §4(a), title XIV, §14217(a)(2), June 18, 2008, 122 Stat. 1664, 2239.)

§15507. PAYMENT OF NON-FEDERAL SHARE FOR CERTAIN FEDERAL GRANT PROGRAMS

Amounts made available to carry out this subtitle shall be available for the payment of the non-Federal share for any project carried out under another Federal grant program—

    (1) for which a Commission is not the sole or primary funding source; and

    (2) that is consistent with the authorities of the applicable Commission.

(Added Pub. L. 118–272, div. B, title II, §2244(a), Jan. 4, 2025, 138 Stat. 3204.)

CHAPTER 157—ADMINISTRATIVE PROVISIONS

SUBCHAPTER I—GENERAL PROVISIONS

Sec.
15701. Consent of States.
15702. Distressed counties and areas.
15703. Counties eligible for assistance in more than one region.
15704. Inspector General; records.
15705. Biannual meetings of representatives of all Commissions.

SUBCHAPTER II—DESIGNATION OF REGIONS

15731. Southeast Crescent Regional Commission.
15732. Southwest Border Regional Commission.
15733. Northern Border Regional Commission.
15734. Great Lakes Authority.
15735. Mid-Atlantic Regional Commission.
15736. Southern New England Regional Commission.

SUBCHAPTER III—AUTHORIZATION OF APPROPRIATIONS

15751. Authorization of appropriations.

SUBCHAPTER I—GENERAL PROVISIONS

§15701. CONSENT OF STATES

This subtitle does not require a State to engage in or accept a program under this subtitle without its consent.

(Added Pub. L. 110–234, title XIV, §14217(a)(2), May 22, 2008, 122 Stat. 1479, and Pub. L. 110–246, §4(a), title XIV, §14217(a)(2), June 18, 2008, 122 Stat. 1664, 2241.)

§15702. DISTRESSED COUNTIES AND AREAS

(a) DESIGNATIONS.—Not later than 90 days after the date of the enactment of this section, and annually thereafter, each Commission shall make the following designations:

(1) DISTRESSED COUNTIES.—The Commission shall designate as distressed counties those counties in its region that are the most severely and persistently economically distressed and underdeveloped and have high rates of poverty, unemployment, or outmigration.

(2) TRANSITIONAL COUNTIES.—The Commission shall designate as transitional counties those counties in its region that are economically distressed and underdeveloped or have recently suffered high rates of poverty, unemployment, or outmigration.

(3) ATTAINMENT COUNTIES.—The Commission shall designate as attainment counties, those counties in its region that are not designated as distressed or transitional counties under this subsection.

(4) ISOLATED AREAS OF DISTRESS.—The Commission shall designate as isolated

areas of distress, areas located in counties designated as attainment counties under paragraph (3) that have high rates of poverty, unemployment, or outmigration.

(b) ALLOCATION.—A Commission shall allocate at least 50 percent of the appropriations made available to the Commission to carry out this subtitle for programs and projects designed to serve the needs of distressed counties and isolated areas of distress in the region.

(c) ATTAINMENT COUNTIES.—

(1) IN GENERAL.—Except as provided in paragraph (2), funds may not be provided under this subtitle for a project located in a county designated as an attainment county under subsection (a).

(2) EXCEPTIONS.—

(A) ADMINISTRATIVE EXPENSES OF LOCAL DEVELOPMENT DISTRICTS.—The funding prohibition under paragraph (1) shall not apply to grants to fund the administrative expenses of local development districts under section 15505.

(B) MULTICOUNTY AND OTHER PROJECTS.—A Commission may waive the application of the funding prohibition under paragraph (1) with respect to—

(i) a multicounty project that includes participation by an attainment county; and

(ii) any other type of project, if a Commission determines that the project could bring significant benefits to areas of the region outside an attainment county.

(3) APPLICATION.—Paragraph (2) shall not apply to—

(A) a county described in paragraph (2) or (3) of section 15735; or

(B) the Southern New England Regional Commission.

(4) ISOLATED AREAS OF DISTRESS.—For a designation of an isolated area of distress to be effective, the designation shall be supported—

(A) by the most recent Federal data available; or

(B) if no recent Federal data are available, by the most recent data available through the government of the State in which the isolated area of distress is located.

(Added Pub. L. 110–234, title XIV, §14217(a)(2), May 22, 2008, 122 Stat. 1479, and Pub. L. 110–246, §4(a), title XIV, §14217(a)(2), June 18, 2008, 122 Stat. 1664, 2241; amended Pub. L. 118–272, div. B, title II, §§2249(c), 2250(c), Jan. 4, 2025, 138 Stat. 3209, 3210.)

§15703. COUNTIES ELIGIBLE FOR ASSISTANCE IN MORE THAN ONE REGION

(a) LIMITATION.—A political subdivision of a State may not receive assistance under this subtitle in a fiscal year from more than one Commission.

(b) SELECTION OF COMMISSION.—A political subdivision included in the region of more than one Commission shall select the Commission with which it will participate by notifying, in writing, the Federal Cochairperson and the appropriate State member of that Commission.

(c) CHANGES IN SELECTIONS.—The selection of a Commission by a political subdivision shall apply in the fiscal year in which the selection is made, and shall apply in each subsequent fiscal year unless the political subdivision, at least 90 days before the first day of the fiscal year, notifies the Cochairpersons of another Commission in writing that the political subdivision will participate in that Commission and also transmits a copy of such notification to the Cochairpersons of the Commission in which the political subdivision is currently participating.

(d) INCLUSION OF APPALACHIAN REGIONAL COMMISSION.—In this section, the term "Commission" includes the Appalachian Regional Commission established under chapter 143.

(Added Pub. L. 110–234, title XIV, §14217(a)(2), May 22, 2008, 122 Stat. 1480, and Pub. L. 110–246, §4(a), title XIV, §14217(a)(2), June 18, 2008, 122 Stat. 1664, 2242.)

§15704. INSPECTOR GENERAL; RECORDS

(a) APPOINTMENT OF INSPECTOR GENERAL.—There shall be an Inspector General for the Commissions appointed in accordance with section 403(a) of title 5. All of the Commissions shall be subject to a single Inspector General.

(b) RECORDS OF A COMMISSION.—

(1) IN GENERAL.—A Commission shall maintain accurate and complete records of all its transactions and activities.

(2) AVAILABILITY.—All records of a Commission shall be available for audit and examination by the Inspector General (including authorized representatives of the Inspector General).

(c) RECORDS OF RECIPIENTS OF COMMISSION ASSISTANCE.—

(1) IN GENERAL.—A recipient of funds from a Commission under this subtitle shall maintain accurate and complete records of transactions and activities financed with the funds and report to the Commission on the transactions and activities.

(2) AVAILABILITY.—All records required under paragraph (1) shall be available for audit by the Commission and the Inspector General (including authorized representatives of the Commission and the Inspector General).

(d) ANNUAL AUDIT.—The Inspector General shall audit the activities, transactions, and records of each Commission on an annual basis.

(Added Pub. L. 110–234, title XIV, §14217(a)(2), May 22, 2008, 122 Stat. 1480, and Pub. L. 110–246, §4(a), title XIV, §14217(a)(2), June 18, 2008, 122 Stat. 1664, 2242; amended Pub. L. 117–286, §4(b)(70), Dec. 27, 2022, 136 Stat. 4350.)

§15705. BIANNUAL MEETINGS OF REPRESENTATIVES OF ALL COMMISSIONS

(a) IN GENERAL.—Representatives of each Commission, the Appalachian Regional Commission, and the Denali Commission shall meet biannually to discuss issues confronting regions suffering from chronic and contiguous distress and successful strategies for promoting regional development.

(b) CHAIR OF MEETINGS.—The chair of each meeting shall rotate among the Commissions, with the Appalachian Regional Commission to host the first meeting.

(Added Pub. L. 110–234, title XIV, §14217(a)(2), May 22, 2008, 122 Stat. 1480, and Pub. L. 110–246, §4(a), title XIV, §14217(a)(2), June 18, 2008, 122 Stat. 1664, 2242.)

SUBCHAPTER II—DESIGNATION OF REGIONS

§15731. SOUTHEAST CRESCENT REGIONAL COMMISSION

The region of the Southeast Crescent Regional Commission shall consist of all counties of the States of Virginia, North Carolina, South Carolina, Georgia, Alabama, Mississippi, and Florida not already served by the Appalachian Regional Commission or the Delta Regional Authority.

(Added Pub. L. 110–234, title XIV, §14217(a)(2), May 22, 2008, 122 Stat. 1481, and Pub. L. 110–246, §4(a), title XIV, §14217(a)(2), June 18, 2008, 122 Stat. 1664, 2243.)

§15732. SOUTHWEST BORDER REGIONAL COMMISSION

The region of the Southwest Border Regional Commission shall consist of the following political subdivisions:

(1) ARIZONA.—The counties of Cochise, Gila, Graham, Greenlee, La Paz, Maricopa, Pima, Pinal, Santa Cruz, and Yuma in the State of Arizona.

(2) CALIFORNIA.—The counties of Imperial, Los Angeles, Orange, Riverside, San Bernardino, San Diego, and Ventura in the State of California.

(3) NEW MEXICO.—The counties of Bernalillo, Catron, Chaves, Cibola, Curry, De Baca, Dona Ana, Eddy, Grant, Guadalupe, Hidalgo, Lea, Lincoln, Luna, Otero, Roosevelt, Sierra, Socorro, Torrance, and Valencia in the State of New Mexico.

(4) TEXAS.—The counties of Atascosa, Bandera, Bee, Bexar, Brewster, Brooks, Cameron, Coke, Concho, Crane, Crockett, Culberson, Dimmit, Duval, Ector, Edwards, El Paso, Frio, Gillespie, Glasscock, Guadalupe, Hidalgo, Hudspeth, Irion, Jeff Davis, Jim Hogg, Jim Wells, Karnes, Kendall, Kenedy, Kerr, Kimble, Kinney, Kleberg, La Salle, Live Oak, Loving, Mason, Maverick, McMullen, Medina, Menard, Midland, Nueces, Pecos, Presidio, Reagan, Real, Reeves, San Patricio, Shleicher, Sutton, Starr, Sterling, Terrell, Tom Green, Upton, Uvalde, Val Verde, Ward, Webb, Willacy, Wilson, Winkler, Zapata, and Zavala in the State of Texas.

(Added Pub. L. 110–234, title XIV, §14217(a)(2), May 22, 2008, 122 Stat. 1481, and Pub. L. 110–246, §4(a), title XIV, §14217(a)(2), June 18, 2008, 122 Stat. 1664, 2243; amended Pub. L. 118–272, div. B, title II, §2246, Jan. 4, 2025, 138 Stat. 3204.)

§15733. NORTHERN BORDER REGIONAL COMMISSION

The region of the Northern Border Regional Commission shall include the following counties:

(1) MAINE.—The counties of Androscoggin, Aroostook, Franklin, Hancock, Kennebec, Knox, Lincoln, Oxford, Penobscot, Piscataquis, Somerset, Waldo, and Washington in the State of Maine.

(2) NEW HAMPSHIRE.—The counties of Belknap, Carroll, Cheshire, Coos, Grafton, Merrimack, and Sullivan in the State of New Hampshire.

(3) NEW YORK.—The counties of Cayuga, Clinton, Essex, Franklin, Fulton, Genesee, Greene, Hamilton, Herkimer, Jefferson, Lewis, Livingston, Madison, Montgomery, Niagara, Oneida, Orleans, Oswego, Rensselaer, Saratoga, Schenectady, Schoharie, Seneca, St. Lawrence, Sullivan, Washington, Warren, Wayne, Wyoming, and Yates in the State of New York.

(4) VERMONT.—The counties of Addison, Bennington, Caledonia, Chittenden, Essex, Franklin, Grand Isle, Lamoille, Orange, Orleans, Rutland, Washington, Windham, and Windsor in the State of Vermont.

(Added Pub. L. 110–234, title XIV, §14217(a)(2), May 22, 2008, 122 Stat. 1481, and Pub. L. 110–246,

§4(a), title XIV, §14217(a)(2), June 18, 2008, 122 Stat. 1664, 2243; amended Pub. L. 115–334, title VI, §6304(d), Dec. 20, 2018, 132 Stat. 4752; Pub. L. 118–272, div. B, title II, §2245, Jan. 4, 2025, 138 Stat. 3204.)

§15734. GREAT LAKES AUTHORITY

The region of the Great Lakes Authority shall consist of the counties which contain, in part or in whole, the areas in the watershed of the Great Lakes and the Great Lakes System (as such terms are defined in section 118(a)(3) of the Federal Water Pollution Control Act (33 U.S.C. 1268(a)(3))), in each of the following States:

(1) Illinois.
(2) Indiana.
(3) Michigan.
(4) Minnesota.
(5) New York.
(6) Ohio.
(7) Pennsylvania.
(8) Wisconsin.

(Added Pub. L. 117–328, div. O, title IV, §401(b)(1), Dec. 29, 2022, 136 Stat. 5228; amended Pub. L. 118–272, div. B, title II, §2247, Jan. 4, 2025, 138 Stat. 3204.)

§15735. MID-ATLANTIC REGIONAL COMMISSION.

The region of the Mid-Atlantic Regional Commission shall include the following counties:

(1) DELAWARE.—Each county in the State of Delaware.
(2) MARYLAND.—Each county in the State of Maryland that is not already served by the Appalachian Regional Commission.
(3) PENNSYLVANIA.—Each county in the Commonwealth of Pennsylvania that is not already served by the Appalachian Regional Commission.

(Added Pub. L. 118–272, div. B, title II, §2249(b)(1), Jan. 4, 2025, 138 Stat. 3209.)

§15736. SOUTHERN NEW ENGLAND REGIONAL COMMISSION

The region of the Southern New England Regional Commission shall include the following counties:

(1) RHODE ISLAND.—Each county in the State of Rhode Island.
(2) CONNECTICUT.—The counties of Hartford, Middlesex, New Haven, New London, Tolland, and Windham in the State of Connecticut.
(3) MASSACHUSETTS.—Each county in the Commonwealth of Massachusetts.

(Added Pub. L. 118–272, div. B, title II, §2250(b)(1), Jan. 4, 2025, 138 Stat. 3209.)

SUBCHAPTER III—AUTHORIZATION OF APPROPRIATIONS

§15751. AUTHORIZATION OF APPROPRIATIONS

(a) IN GENERAL.—There is authorized to be appropriated to each Commission to carry out this subtitle $40,000,000 for each of fiscal years 2025 through 2029.

(b) ADMINISTRATIVE EXPENSES.—

(1) IN GENERAL.—Except as provided in paragraph (2), not more than 10 percent of the funds made available to a Commission in a fiscal year under this section may be used for administrative expenses.

(2) LIMITED FUNDING.—In a case in which less than $10,000,000 is made available to a Commission for a fiscal year under this section, paragraph (1) shall not apply.

(Added Pub. L. 110–234, title XIV, §14217(a)(2), May 22, 2008, 122 Stat. 1482, and Pub. L. 110–246, §4(a), title XIV, §14217(a)(2), June 18, 2008, 122 Stat. 1664, 2244; amended Pub. L. 113–79, title VI, §6207, Feb. 7, 2014, 128 Stat. 861; Pub. L. 115–334, title VI, §6304(e), Dec. 20, 2018, 132 Stat. 4752; Pub. L. 118–272, div. B, title II, §2241, Jan. 4, 2025, 138 Stat. 3202.)

CHAPTER 159—ADDITIONAL REGIONAL COMMISSION PROGRAMS

Sec.
15901.   State capacity building grant program.
15902.   Demonstration health projects.

§15901. STATE CAPACITY BUILDING GRANT PROGRAM

(a) DEFINITIONS.—In this section:

(1) COMMISSION STATE.—The term "Commission State" means a State that contains 1 or more eligible counties.

(2) ELIGIBLE COUNTY.—The term "eligible county" means a county described in subchapter II of chapter 157.

(3) PROGRAM.—The term "program" means a State capacity building grant program established by a Commission under subsection (b).

(b) ESTABLISHMENT.—Each Commission shall establish a State capacity building grant program to provide grants to Commission States in the area served by the Commission for the purposes described in subsection (c).

(c) PURPOSES.—The purposes of a program are to support the efforts of the Commission—

(1) to better support business retention and expansion in eligible counties;

(2) to create programs to encourage job creation and workforce development in eligible counties, including projects and activities, in coordination with other relevant Federal agencies, to strengthen the water sector workforce and facilitate the sharing of best practices;

(3) to partner with universities in distressed counties (as designated under section 15702(a)(1))—

(A) to strengthen the capacity in eligible counties to train new professionals in fields for which there is a shortage of workers;

(B) to increase local capacity in eligible counties for project management, project execution, and financial management; and

(C) to leverage funding sources for eligible counties;

(4) to prepare economic and infrastructure plans for eligible counties;

(5) to expand access to high-speed broadband in eligible counties;

(6) to provide technical assistance that results in Commission investments in transportation, water, wastewater, and other critical infrastructure;

(7) to promote workforce development in eligible counties to support resilient infrastructure projects;

(8) to develop initiatives to increase the effectiveness of local development districts in eligible counties; and

(9) to implement new or innovative economic development practices that will better position eligible counties to compete in the global economy.

(d) USE OF FUNDS.—

(1) IN GENERAL.—Funds from a grant under a program may be used to support a project, program, or related expense of the Commission State in an eligible county.

(2) LIMITATION.—Funds from a grant under a program shall not be used for—

(A) the purchase of furniture, fixtures, or equipment;

(B) the compensation of—

(i) any State member of the Commission (as described in section 15301(b)(1)(B)); or

(ii) any State alternate member of the Commission (as described in section 15301(b)(2)(B)); or

(C) the cost of supplanting existing State programs.

(e) ANNUAL WORK PLAN.—

(1) IN GENERAL.—For each fiscal year, before providing a grant under a program, each Commission State shall provide to the Commission an annual work plan that includes the proposed use of the grant.

(2) APPROVAL.—No grant under a program shall be provided to a Commission State unless the Commission has approved the annual work plan of the State.

(f) AMOUNT OF GRANT.—

(1) IN GENERAL.—The amount of a grant provided to a Commission State under a program for a fiscal year shall be based on the proportion that—

(A) the amount paid by the Commission State (including any amounts paid on behalf of the Commission State by a nonprofit organization) for administrative expenses for the applicable fiscal year (as determined under section 15304(c)); bears to

(B) the amount paid by all Commission States served by the Commission (including any amounts paid on behalf of a Commission State by a nonprofit organization) for administrative expenses for that fiscal year (as determined under that section).

(2) REQUIREMENT.—To be eligible to receive a grant under a program for a fiscal year, a Commission State (or a nonprofit organization on behalf of the Commission State) shall pay the amount of administrative expenses of the Commission State for the applicable fiscal year (as determined under section 15304(c)).

(3) APPROVAL.—For each fiscal year, a grant provided under a program shall be approved and made available as part of the approval of the annual budget of the Commission.

(g) GRANT AVAILABILITY.—Funds from a grant under a program shall be available only during the fiscal year for which the grant is provided.

(h) REPORT.—Each fiscal year, each Commission State shall submit to the relevant Commission and make publicly available a report that describes the use of the grant funds and the impact of the program in the Commission State.

(i) CONTINUATION OF PROGRAM AUTHORITY FOR NORTHERN BORDER REGIONAL COMMISSION.—With respect to the Northern Border Regional Commission, the program shall be a continuation of the program under section 6304(c) of the Agriculture Improvement Act of 2018 (40 U.S.C. 15501 note; Public Law 115–334) (as in effect on the day before the date of enactment of this section).

(Added Pub. L. 118–272, div. B, title II, §2248(a), Jan. 4, 2025, 138 Stat. 3205.)

§15902. DEMONSTRATION HEALTH PROJECTS

(a) PURPOSE.—To demonstrate the value of adequate health facilities and services to the economic development of the region, a Commission may make grants for the planning, construction, equipment, and operation of demonstration health, nutrition, and child care projects to serve distressed areas (referred to in this section as a "demonstration health project"), including hospitals, regional health diagnostic and treatment centers, and other facilities and services necessary for the purposes of this section.

(b) ELIGIBLE ENTITIES.—An entity eligible to receive a grant under this section is—

(1) an entity described in section 15501(a);

(2) an institution of higher education (as defined in section 101(a) of the Higher Education Act of 1965 (20 U.S.C. 1001(a)));

(3) a hospital (as defined in section 1861 of the Social Security Act (42 U.S.C. 1395x)); or

(4) a critical access hospital (as defined in that section).

(c) PLANNING GRANTS.—

(1) IN GENERAL.—A Commission may make grants for planning expenses necessary for the development and operation of demonstration health projects for the region served by the Commission.

(2) MAXIMUM COMMISSION CONTRIBUTION.—The maximum Commission contribution for a demonstration health project that receives a grant under paragraph (1) shall be made in accordance with section 15501(d).

(3) SOURCES OF ASSISTANCE.—A grant under paragraph (1) may be provided entirely from amounts made available to carry out this section or in combination with amounts provided under other Federal grant programs.

(4) FEDERAL SHARE FOR GRANTS UNDER OTHER FEDERAL GRANT PROGRAMS.—Notwithstanding any provision of law limiting the Federal share in other Federal grant programs, amounts made available to carry out this subsection may be used to increase the Federal share of another Federal grant up to the maximum contribution described in paragraph (2).

(d) CONSTRUCTION AND EQUIPMENT GRANTS.—

(1) IN GENERAL.—A grant under this section for construction or equipment of a demonstration health project may be used for—

(A) costs of construction;

(B) the acquisition of privately owned facilities—

(i) not operated for profit; or

(ii) previously operated for profit if the Commission finds that health services would not otherwise be provided in the area served by the facility if the acquisition is not made; and

(C) the acquisition of initial equipment.

(2) STANDARDS FOR MAKING GRANTS.—A grant under paragraph (1)—

(A) shall be approved in accordance with section 15503; and

(B) shall not be incompatible with the applicable provisions of title VI of the Public Health Service Act (42 U.S.C. 291 et seq.), the Developmental Disabilities Assistance and Bill of Rights Act of 2000 (42 U.S.C. 15001 et seq.), and other laws authorizing grants for the construction of health-related facilities, without regard to any provisions in those laws relating to appropriation authorization ceilings or to allotments among the States.

(3) MAXIMUM COMMISSION CONTRIBUTION.—The maximum Commission contribution for a demonstration health project that receives a grant under paragraph (1) shall be made in accordance with section 15501(d).

(4) SOURCES OF ASSISTANCE.—A grant under paragraph (1) may be provided entirely from amounts made available to carry out this section or in combination with amounts provided under other Federal grant programs.

(5) CONTRIBUTION TO INCREASED FEDERAL SHARE FOR OTHER FEDERAL GRANTS.—Notwithstanding any provision of law limiting the Federal share in another Federal grant program for the construction or equipment of a demonstration health project, amounts made available to carry out this subsection may be used to increase Federal grants for component facilities of a demonstration health project to a maximum of 90 percent of the cost of the facilities.

(e) OPERATION GRANTS.—

(1) IN GENERAL.—A grant under this section for the operation of a demonstration health project may be used for—

(A) the costs of operation of the facility; and

(B) initial operating costs, including the costs of attracting, training, and retaining qualified personnel.

(2) STANDARDS FOR MAKING GRANTS.—A grant for the operation of a demonstration health project shall not be made unless the facility funded by the grant is—

(A) publicly owned;

(B) owned by a public or private nonprofit organization;

(C) a private hospital described in section 501(c)(3) of the Internal Revenue Code of 1986 and exempt from taxation under section 501(a) of that Code; or

(D) a private hospital that provides a certain amount of uncompensated care, as determined by the Commission, and applies for the grant in partnership with a State, local government, or Indian Tribe.

(3) MAXIMUM COMMISSION CONTRIBUTION.—The maximum Commission contribution for a demonstration health project that receives a grant under paragraph (1) shall be made in accordance with section 15501(d).

(4) SOURCES OF ASSISTANCE.—A grant under paragraph (1) may be provided entirely from amounts made available to carry out this section or in combination with amounts provided under other Federal grant programs for the operation of health-related facilities or the provision of health and child development services, including parts A and B of title IV and title XX of the Social Security Act (42 U.S.C. 601 et seq., 621 et seq., 1397 et seq.).

(5) FEDERAL SHARE.—Notwithstanding any provision of law limiting the Federal share in the other Federal programs described in paragraph (4), amounts made available to carry out this subsection may be used to increase the Federal share of a grant under those programs up to the maximum contribution described in paragraph (3).

(f) PRIORITY HEALTH PROGRAMS.—If a Commission elects to make grants under this section, the Commission shall establish specific regional health priorities for such grants that address—

    (1) addiction treatment and access to resources helping individuals in recovery;

    (2) workforce shortages in the healthcare industry; or

    (3) access to services for screening and diagnosing chronic health issues.

(Added Pub. L. 118–272, div. B, title II, §2248(a), Jan. 4, 2025, 138 Stat. 3207.)

DENALI COMMISSION

TITLE III, DIV. C OF PUB. L. 105–277

DENALI COMMISSION ACT OF 1998

(Title III, Div. C of the Omnibus Consolidated and Emergency Supplemental Appropriations Act, 1999)

[(Public Law 105–277; 112 Stat. 2681–856; approved Oct. 21, 1998)]

TITLE III—DENALI COMMISSION

SEC. 301. [42 U.S.C. 3121 note] SHORT TITLE.

This title may be cited as the "Denali Commission Act of 1998".

SEC. 302. [42 U.S.C. 3121 note] PURPOSES.

The purposes of this title are as follows:

(1) To deliver the services of the Federal Government in the most cost-effective manner practicable by reducing administrative and overhead costs.

(2) To provide job training and other economic development services in rural communities particularly distressed communities (many of which have a rate of unemployment that exceeds 50 percent).

(3) To promote rural development, provide power generation and transmission facilities, modern communication systems, water and sewer systems and other infrastructure needs.

SEC. 303. [42 U.S.C. 3121 note] ESTABLISHMENT OF COMMISSION.

(a) ESTABLISHMENT.— There is established a commission to be known as the Denali Commission (referred to in this title as the Commission).

(b) MEMBERSHIP.—

(1) COMPOSITION.—The Commission shall be composed of 7 members, who shall be appointed by the Secretary of Commerce (referred to in this title as the Secretary), of whom—

(A) one shall be the Governor of the State of Alaska, or an individual selected from nominations submitted by the Governor, who shall serve as the State Cochairperson;

(B) one shall be the President of the University of Alaska, or an individual selected from nominations submitted by the President of the University of Alaska;

(C) one shall be the President of the Alaska Municipal League or an

135

SEC. 303. [42 U.S.C. 3121 note]
ESTABLISHMENT OF COMMISSION.

Denali Commission Act of 1998

individual selected from nominations submitted by the President of the Alaska Municipal League;

(D)   one shall be the President of the Alaska Federation of Natives or an individual selected from nominations submitted by the President of the Alaska Federation of Natives;

(E)   one shall be the Executive President of the Alaska State AFL–CIO or an individual selected from nominations submitted by the Executive President;

(F)   one shall be the President of the Associated General Contractors of Alaska or an individual selected from nominations submitted by the President of the Associated General Contractors of Alaska; and

(G)   one shall be the Federal Cochairperson, who shall be selected in accordance with the requirements of paragraph (2).

(2) FEDERAL COCHAIRPERSON.—

(A) IN GENERAL.— The President pro temporare of the Senate and the Speaker of the House of Representatives shall each submit a list of nominations for the position of the Federal Cochairperson under paragraph (1)(G), including pertinent biographical information, to the Secretary.

(B) APPOINTMENT.— The Secretary shall appoint the Federal Cochairperson from among the list of nominations submitted under subparagraph (A). The Federal Cochairperson shall serve as an employee of the Department of Commerce, and may be removed by the Secretary for cause.

(C) FEDERAL COCHAIRPERSON VOTE.— The Federal Cochairperson appointed under this paragraph shall break any tie in the voting of the Commission.

(4) DATE.— The appointments of the members of the Commission shall be made no later than January 1, 1999.

(c) PERIOD OF APPOINTMENT; VACANCIES.—

(1) TERM OF FEDERAL COCHAIRPERSON.— The Federal Cochairperson shall serve for a term of four years and may be reappointed. shall be appointed for the life of the Commission.

(2) INTERIM FEDERAL COCHAIRPERSON.— In the event of a vacancy for any reason in the position of Federal Cochairperson, the Secretary may appoint an Interim Federal Cochairperson, who shall have all the authority of the Federal Cochairperson, to serve until such time as the vacancy in the position of Federal Cochairperson is filled in accordance with subsection (b)(2)).

(3) TERM OF ALL OTHER MEMBERS.— All other members shall be appointed for the life of the Commission.

(4) VACANCIES.— Except as provided in paragraph (2), any vacancy in the Commission shall not affect its powers, but shall be filled in the same manner as the original appointment.

(d) MEETINGS.—

(1) IN GENERAL.— The Commission shall meet at the call of the Federal Cochairperson not less frequently than 2 times each year, and may, as appropriate, conduct business by telephone or other electronic means.

(2) NOTIFICATION.—Not later than 2 weeks before calling a meeting under this subsection, the Federal Cochairperson shall—

(A) notify each member of the Commission of the time, date and location of that meeting; and

(B) provide each member of the Commission with a written agenda for the meeting, including any proposals for discussion and consideration, and any appropriate background materials.

(e) QUORUM.— A majority of the members of the Commission shall constitute a quorum, but a lesser number of members may hold hearings.

(f) NO FEDERAL EMPLOYEE STATUS.— No member of the Commission, other than the Federal Cochairperson, shall be considered to be a Federal employee for any purpose.

(g) CONFLICTS OF INTEREST.—

(1) IN GENERAL.—Except as provided in paragraphs (2) and (3), no member of the Commission (referred to in this subsection as a member) shall participate personally or substantially, through recommendation, the rendering of advice, investigation, or otherwise, in any proceeding, application, request for a ruling or other determination, contract claim, controversy, or other matter in which, to the knowledge of the member, 1 or more of the following has a direct financial interest:

(A) The member.

(B) The spouse, minor child, or partner of the member.

(C) An organization described in subparagraph (B), (C), (D), (E), or (F) of subsection (b)(1) for which the member is serving as an officer, director, trustee, partner, or employee.

(D) Any individual, person, or organization with which the member is negotiating or has any arrangement concerning prospective employment.

(2) DISCLOSURE.—Paragraph (1) shall not apply if the member—

(A) immediately advises the designated agency ethics official for the Commission of the nature and circumstances of the matter presenting a potential conflict of interest;

(B) makes full disclosure of the financial interest; and

(C) before the proceeding concerning the matter presenting the conflict of interest, receives a written determination by the designated agency ethics official for the Commission that the interest is not so substantial as to be likely to affect the integrity of the services that the Commission may expect from the member. The written determination shall specify the rationale and any evidence or support for the decision, identify steps, if any, that should be taken to mitigate any conflict of interest, and be available to the public.

(3) ANNUAL DISCLOSURES.— Once each calendar year, each member shall make full disclosure of financial interests, in a manner to be determined by the

designated agency ethics official for the Commission.

(4) TRAINING.— Once each calendar year, each member shall undergo disclosure of financial interests training, as prescribed by the designated agency ethics official for the Commission.

(5) CLARIFICATION.— A member of the Commission may continue to participate personally or substantially, through decision, approval, or disapproval on the focus of applications to be considered but not on individual applications where a conflict of interest exists.

(6) VIOLATION.— Any person that violates this subsection shall be fined not more than $10,000, imprisoned for not more than 2 years, or both.

SEC. 304. [42 U.S.C. 3121 note] DUTIES OF THE COMMISSION.

(a) WORK PLAN.—

(1) IN GENERAL.— Not later than 1 year after the date of enactment of this Act and annually thereafter, the Commission shall develop a proposed work plan for Alaska that meets the requirements of paragraph (2) and submit that plan to the Federal Cochairperson for review in accordance with the requirements of subsection (b).

(2) WORK PLAN.—In developing the work plan, the Commission shall—

(A) solicit project proposals from local governments and other entities and organizations; and

(B) provide for a comprehensive work plan for rural and infrastructure development and necessary job training in the area covered under the work plan.

(3) REPORT.— Upon completion of a work plan under this subsection, the Commission shall prepare, and submit to the Secretary, the Federal Cochairperson, and the Director of the Office of Management and Budget, a report that outlines the work plan and contains recommendations for funding priorities.

(b) REVIEW BY FEDERAL COCHAIRPERSON.—

(1) IN GENERAL.— Upon receiving a work plan under this section, the Secretary, acting through the Federal Cochairperson, shall publish the work plan in the Federal Register, with notice and an opportunity for public comment. The period for public review and comment shall be the 30-day period beginning on the date of publication of that notice.

(2) CRITERIA FOR REVIEW.—In conducting a review under paragraph (1), the Secretary, acting through the Federal Cochairperson, shall—

(A) take into consideration the information, views, and comments received from interested parties through the public review and comment process specified in paragraph (1); and

(B) consult with appropriate Federal officials in Alaska including but not limited to Bureau of Indian Affairs, Economic Development Administration, and Rural Development Administration.

(3) APPROVAL.—Not later than 30 days after the end of the period specified in paragraph (1), the Secretary acting through the Federal Cochairperson, shall—

(A) approve, disapprove, or partially approve the work plan that is the subject of the review; and

(B) issue to the Commission a notice of the approval, disapproval, or partial approval that—

(i) specifies the reasons for disapproving any portion of the work plan; and

(ii) if applicable, includes recommendations for revisions to the work plan to make the plan subject to approval.

(4) REVIEW OF DISAPPROVAL OR PARTIAL APPROVAL.— If the Secretary, acting through the Federal Cochairperson, disapproves or partially approves a work plan, the Federal Cochairperson shall submit that work plan to the Commission for review and revision.

SEC. 305. [42 U.S.C. 3121 note] POWERS OF THE COMMISSION.

(a) INFORMATION FROM FEDERAL AGENCIES.— The Commission may secure directly from any Federal department or agency such information as it considers necessary to carry out the provisions of this Act. Upon request of the Federal Cochairperson of the Commission, the head of such department or agency shall furnish such information to the Commission. Agencies must provide the Commission with the requested information in a timely manner. Agencies are not required to provide the Commission any information that is exempt from disclosure by the Freedom of Information Act. Agenices may, upon request by the Commission, make services and personnel available to the Commission to carry out the duties of the Commission. To the maximum extent practicable, the Commission shall contract for completion of necesssary work utilizing local firms and labor to minimize costs.

(b) POSTAL SERVICES.— The Commission may use the United States mails in the same manner and under the same conditions as other departments and agencies of the Federal Government.

(c) GIFTS.—

(1) IN GENERAL.— Except as provided in paragraph (2), the Commission, on behalf of the United States, may accept use, and dispose of gifts or donations of services, property, or money for purposes of carrying out this Act.

(2) CONDITIONAL.—With respect to conditional gifts—

(A)(i) the Commission, on behalf of the United States, may accept conditional gifts for purposes of carrying out this Act, if approved by the Federal Cochairperson; and

(ii) the principal of and income from any such conditional gift shall be held, invested, reinvested, and used in accordance with the condition applicable to the gift; but

(B) no gift shall be accepted that is conditioned on any expenditure not to be funded from the gift or from the income generated by the gift unless the expenditure has been approved by Act of Congress.

(d) The Commission, acting through the Federal Cochairperson, is authorized to enter into contracts and cooperative agreements, award grants, enter into leases

SEC. 306. [42 U.S.C. 3121 note] COMMISSION
PERSONNEL MATTERS.

Denali Commission Act of 1998

(including the lease of office space for any term), and make payments necessary to carry out the purposes of the Commission. With respect to funds appropriated to the Commission for fiscal year 1999, the Commission, acting through the Federal Cochairperson, is authorized to enter into contracts and cooperative agreements, award grants, and make payments to implement an interim work plan for fiscal year 1999 approved by the Commission.

(e) USE OF FUNDS TOWARD NON-FEDERAL SHARE OF CERTAIN PROJECTS.— Notwithstanding any other provision of law regarding payment of a non-Federal share in connection with a grant-in-aid program, the Commission may use amounts made available to the Commission for the payment of such a non-Federal share for programs undertaken to carry out the purposes of the Commission.

SEC. 306. [42 U.S.C. 3121 note] COMMISSION PERSONNEL MATTERS.

(a) COMPENSATION OF MEMBERS.— Each member of the Commission who is not an officer or employee of the Federal Government shall be compensated at a rate equal to the daily equivalent of the annual rate of basic pay prescribed for level IV of the Executive Schedule under section 5315 of title 5, United States Code, for each day (including travel time) during the time such member is engaged in the performance of the duties of the Commission. The Federal Cochairperson shall be compensated at the annual rate prescribed for level IV of the Executive Schedule under section 5315 of title 5, United States Code. All members of the Commission who are officers or employees of the United States shall serve without compensation that is in addition to that received for their services as officers or employees of the United States.

(b) TRAVEL EXPENSES.— The members of the Commission shall be allowed travel expenses, including per diem in lieu of subsistence, at rates authorized for employees of agencies under subchapter I of chapter 57 of title 5, United States Code, while away from their homes or regular places of business in the performance of services for the Commission.

(c) STAFF.—

(1) IN GENERAL.— The Federal Cochairperson of the Commission may, without regard to the civil service laws and regulations, appoint such personnel as may be necessary to enable the Commission to perform its duties.

(2) COMPENSATION.— The Federal Cochairperson of the Commission may fix the compensation of personnel without regard to the provisions of chapter 51 and subchapter III of chapter 53 of title 5, United States Code, relating to classification of positions and General Schedule pay rates.

(d) DETAIL OF GOVERNMENT EMPLOYEES.— Any Federal Government employee may be detailed to the Commission without reimbursement, and such detail shall be without interruption or loss of civil service status or privilege.

(e) PROCUREMENT OF TEMPORARY AND INTERMITTENT SERVICES.— The Federal Cochairperson of the Commission may procure temporary and intermittent services under section 3109(b) of title 5, United States Code, at rates for individuals which do not exceed the daily equivalent of the annual rate of basic pay prescribed for level V of the Executive Schedule under section 5316 of such title.

(f) OFFICES.— The principal office of the Commission shall be located in Alaska, at a location that the Commission shall select.

(g) ADMINISTRATIVE EXPENSES AND RECORDS.— The Commission is hereby prohibited from using more than 5 percent of the amounts appropriated under the authority of this Act or transferred pursuant to section 329 of the Department of Transportation and Related Agencies Appropriations Act, 1999 (section 101(g) of division A of this Act) for administrative expenses. The Commission and its grantees shall maintain accurate and complete records which shall be available for audit and examination by the Comptroller General or his or her designee.

(h) INSPECTOR GENERAL.— Section 8G(a)(2) of the Inspector General Act of 1978 (5 U.S.C. App. 3, section 8G(a)(2)) is amended by inserting the Denali Commission, after "the Corporation for Public Broadcasting,".

SEC. 307. [42 U.S.C. 3121 note] SPECIAL FUNCTIONS.

(a) BULK FUELS.—Funds transferred to the Commission pursuant to section 329 of the Department of Transportation and Related Agencies Appropriations Act, 1999 (section 101(g) of division A of this Act) shall be available without further appropriation and until expended. The Commission, in consultation with the Commandant of the Coast Guard, shall develop a plan to provide for the repair or replacement of bulk fuel storage tanks in Alaska that are not in compliance with applicable—

(1)   Federal law, including the Oil Pollution Act of 1990 (104 Stat. 484); or

(2)   State law.

(b) DEMONSTRATION HEALTH PROJECTS.— In order to demonstrate the value of adequate health facilities and services to the economic development of the region, the Secretary of Health and Human Services is authorized to make interagency transfers to the Denali Commission to plan, construct, and equip demonstration health, nutrition, and child care projects, including hospitals, health care clinics, and mental health facilities (including drug and alcohol treatment centers) in accordance with the Work Plan referred to under section 304 of Title III-Denali Commission of Division C-Other Matters of Public Law 105–277. No grant for construction or equipment of a demonstration project shall exceed 50 percentum of such costs, unless the project is located in a severely economically distressed community, as identified in the Work Plan referred to under section 304 of Title III-Denali Commission of Division C-Other Matters of Public Law 105–277, in which case no grant shall exceed 80 percentum of such costs. To carry out this section, there is authorized to be appropriated such sums as may be necessary.

(c) SOLID WASTE.— The Secretary of Agriculture is authorized to make direct lump sum payments, including interagency transfers, which shall remain available until expended to the Denali Commission to address deficiencies in solid waste disposal sites which threaten to contaminate rural drinking water supplies.

(d) DOCKS, WATERFRONT TRANSPORTATION DEVELOPMENT, AND RELATED INFRASTRUCTURE PROJECTS.— The Secretary of Transportation is authorized to make direct lump sum payments to the Commission to construct docks, waterfront development projects, and related transportation infrastructure, provided the local community provides a ten percent non-Federal match in the form of any necessary land or planning and design funds. To carry out this section, there is authorized to be appropriated such sums as may be necessary.

SEC. 308. [42 U.S.C. 3121 note] EXEMPTION FROM CHAPTER 10 OF TITLE 5, UNITED STATES CODE.

Chapter 10 of title 5, United States Code, shall not apply to the Commission.

SEC. 309. [42 U.S.C. 3121 note] DENALI ACCESS SYSTEM PROGRAM.

(a) ESTABLISHMENT OF THE DENALI ACCESS SYSTEM PROGRAM.— Not later than 3 months after the date of enactment of the SAFETEA-LU, the Secretary of Transportation shall establish a program to pay the costs of planning, designing, engineering, and constructing road and other surface transportation infrastructure identified for the Denali access system program under this section.

(b) DENALI ACCESS SYSTEM PROGRAM ADVISORY COMMITTEE.—

(1) ESTABLISHMENT.— Not later than 3 months after the date of enactment of the SAFETEA-LU, the Denali Commission shall establish a Denali Access System Program Advisory Committee (referred to in this section as the advisory committee).

(2) MEMBERSHIP.—The advisory committee shall be composed of nine members to be appointed by the Governor of the State of Alaska as follows:

(A) The chairman of the Denali Commission.

(B) Four members who represent existing regional native corporations, native nonprofit entities, or tribal governments, including one member who is a civil engineer.

(C) Four members who represent rural Alaska regions or villages, including one member who is a civil engineer.

(3) TERMS.—

(A) IN GENERAL.— Except for the chairman of the Commission who shall remain a member of the advisory committee, members shall be appointed to serve a term of 4 years.

(B) INITIAL MEMBERS.— Except for the chairman of the Commission, of the eight initial members appointed to the advisory committee, two shall be appointed for a term of 1 year, two shall be appointed for a term of 2 years, two shall be appointed for a term of 3 years, and two shall be appointed for a term of 4 years. All subsequent appointments shall be for 4 years.

(4) RESPONSIBILITIES.—The advisory committee shall be responsible for the following activities:

(A) Advising the Commission on the surface transportation needs of Alaska Native villages and rural communities, including projects for the construction of essential access routes within remote Alaska Native villages and rural communities and for the construction of roads and facilities necessary to connect isolated rural communities to a road system.

(B) Advising the Commission on considerations for coordinatedtransportation planning among the Alaska Native villages, Alaska rural villages, the State of Alaska, and other government entities.

SEC. 309. [42 U.S.C. 3121 note] DENALI
ACCESS SYSTEM PROGRAM.

Denali Commission Act of 1998

(C) Establishing a list of transportation priorities for Alaska Native village and rural community transportation projects on an annual basis, including funding recommendations.

(D) Facilitate the Commission's work on transportation projects involving more than one region.

(5) CHAPTER 10 OF TITLE 5, UNITED STATES CODE, EXEMPTION.— The provisions of chapter 10 of title 5, United States Code, shall not apply to the advisory committee.

(c) ALLOCATION OF FUNDS.—

(1) IN GENERAL.— The Secretary of Transportation shall allocate funding authorized and made available for the Denali access system program to the Commission to carry out this section.

(2) DISTRIBUTION OF FUNDING.— In distributing funds for surface transportation projects funded under the program, the Commission shall consult the list of transportation priorities developed by the advisory committee.

(d) PREFERENCE TO ALASKA MATERIALS AND PRODUCTS.— To construct a project under this section, the Commission shall encourage, to the maximum extent practicable, the use of employees and businesses that are residents of Alaska.

(e) DESIGN STANDARDS.— Each project carried out under this section shall use technology and design standards determined by the Commission to be appropriate given the location and the functionality of the project.

(f) MAINTENANCE.— Funding for a construction project under this section may include an additional amount equal to not more than 10 percent of the total cost of construction, to be retained for future maintenance of the project. All such retained funds shall be dedicated for maintenance of the project and may not be used for other purposes.

(g) LEAD AGENCY DESIGNATION.— For purposes of projects carried out under this section, the Commission shall be designated as the lead agency for purposes of accepting Federal funds and for purposes of carrying out this project.

(h) NON-FEDERAL SHARE.— Notwithstanding any other provision of law, funds made available to carry out this section may be used to meet the non-Federal share of the cost of projects under title 23, United States Code.

(i) SURFACE TRANSPORTATION PROGRAM TRANSFERABILITY.—

(1) TRANSFERABILITY.— In any fiscal year, up to 15 percent of the amounts made available to the State of Alaska for surface transportation by section 133 of title 23, United States Code, may be transferred to the Denali access system program.

(2) NO EFFECT ON SET-ASIDE.— Paragraph (2) of section 133(d), United States Code, shall not apply to funds transferred under paragraph (1).

(j) AUTHORIZATION OF APPROPRIATIONS.—

(1) IN GENERAL.— There is authorized to be appropriated out of the Highway Trust Fund (other than the Mass Transit Account) to carry out this section $15,000,000 for each of fiscal years 2006 through 2009.

Sec. 310. [42 U.S.C. 3121 note] DENALI
ACCESS SYSTEM PROGRAM.

Denali Commission Act of 1998

(2) APPLICABILITY OF TITLE 23.— Funds made available to carry out this section shall be available for obligation in the same manner as if such funds were apportioned under chapter 1 of title 23, United States Code; except that such funds shall not be transferable and shall remain available until expended, and the Federal share of the cost of any project carried out using such funds shall be determined in accordance with section 120(b).

SEC. 310. [42 U.S.C. 3121 note] (a) The Federal Co-chairman of the Denali Commission shall appoint an economic development committee to be chaired by the president of the Alaska federation of natives which shall include the commissioner of community and economic affairs for the state of Alaska, a representative from the Alaska bankers association, the chairman of the Alaska permanent fund, a representative from the Alaska state chamber of commerce, and a representative from each region. of the regional representatives, at least two each shall be from native regional corporations, native non-profit corporations, tribes, and borough governments

(b) The Economic Development Committee is authorized to consider and approve applications from Regional Advisory Committees for grants and loans to promote economic development and promote private sector investment to reduce poverty in economically distressed rural villages. The Economic Development Committee may make mini-grants to individual applicants and may issue loans under such terms and conditions as it determines.

(c) The State Co-chairman of the Denali Commission shall appoint a Regional Advisory Committee for each region which may include representatives from local, borough, and tribal governments, the Alaska Native non-profit corporation operating in the region, local Chambers of Commerce, and representatives of the private sector. Each Regional Advisory Committee shall develop a regional economic development plan for consideration by the Economic Development Committee.

(d) The Economic Development Committee, in consultation with the First Alaskans Institute, may develop rural development performance measures linking economic growth to poverty reduction to measure the success of its program which may include economic, educational, social, and cultural indicators. The performance measures will be tested in one region for years and evaluated by the University of Alaska before being deployed statewide. Thereafter, performance in each region shall be evaluated using the performance measures, and the Economic Development Committee shall not fund projects which do not demonstrate success.

(e) Within the amounts made available annually to the Denali Commission for training, the Commission may make a grant to the First Alaskans Foundation upon submittal of an acceptable work plan to assist Alaska Natives and other rural residents in acquiring the skills and training necessary to participate fully in private sector business and economic and development opportunities through fellowships, scholarships, internships, public service programs, and other leadership initiatives.

(f) The Committee shall sponsor a statewide economic development summit in consultation with the World Bank to evaluate the best practices for economic development worldwide and how they can be incorporated into regional economic development plans.

(g) There is authorized to be appropriated such sums as may be necessary to the following agencies which shall be transferred to the Denali Commission as a direct lump sum payment to implement this section—

    (1)   Department of Commerce, Economic Development Administration,

    (2)   Department of Housing and Urban Development,

    (3)   Department of the Interior, Bureau of Indian Affairs,

    (4)   Department of Agriculture, Rural Development Administration, and

    (5)   Small Business Administration.

SEC. 311. [42 U.S.C. 3121 note] TRANSFER OF FUNDS FROM OTHER FEDERAL AGENCIES.

(a) IN GENERAL.— Subject to subsection (c), for purposes of this Act, the Commission may accept transfers of funds from other Federal agencies.

(b) TRANSFERS.— Any Federal agency authorized to carry out an activity that is within the authority of the Commission may transfer to the Commission any appropriated funds for the activity.

(c) TREATMENT.—Any funds transferred to the Commission under this subsection—

    (1)   shall remain available until expended;

    (2)   may, to the extent necessary to carry out this Act, be transferred to, and merged with, the amounts made available by appropriations Acts for the Commission by the Federal Cochairperson; and

    (3) notwithstanding any other provision of law, shall—

        (A)   be treated as if directly appropriated to the Commission and subject to applicable provisions of this Act; and

        (B)   not be subject to any requirements that applied to the funds before the transfer, including a requirement in an appropriations Act or a requirement or regulation of the Federal agency from which the funds are transferred.

SEC. 312.[7] [42 U.S.C. 3121 note] AUTHORIZATION OF APPROPRIATIONS.

(a) IN GENERAL.— There are authorized to be appropriated to the Commission to carry out the duties of the Commission consistent with the purposes of this title and pursuant to the work plan approved under section 304, $35,000,000 for each of fiscal years 2025 through 2029.

---

[7]   The placement of section 312 reflects the probable intent of Congress. The amendment made by paragraph (2) of section 5002(b) of Public Law 114–322 did not include language to transfer section 312 (as so redesignated) to appear after section 311.

(b) AVAILABILITY.— Any sums appropriated under the authorization contained in this section shall remain available until expended.

* * * * * * *

SEC. 323. [16 U.S.C. 1011a] (a) WATERSHED RESTORATION AND ENHANCEMENT AGREEMENTS.— For fiscal year 2006 and each fiscal year thereafter, to the extent funds are otherwise available, appropriations for the Forest Service may be used by the Secretary of Agriculture for the purpose of entering into cooperative agreements with

Sec. 323. [16 U.S.C. 1011a] AUTHORIZATION
OF APPROPRIATIONS.

Denali Commission Act of 1998

willing Federal, tribal, State and local governments, private and nonprofit entities and landowners for the protection, restoration and enhancement of fish and wildlife habitat, and other resources on public or private land, the reduction of risk from natural disaster where public safety is threatened, or a combination thereof or both that benefit these resources within the watershed.

(b) DIRECT AND INDIRECT WATERSHED AGREEMENTS.—The Secretary of Agriculture may enter into a watershed restoration and enhancement agreement—

(1) directly with a willing private landowner; or

(2) indirectly through an agreement with a State, local or tribal government or other public entity, educational institution, or private nonprofit organization.

(c) TERMS AND CONDITIONS.—In order for the Secretary to enter into a watershed restoration and enhancement agreement—

(1) the agreement shall—

(A) include such terms and conditions mutually agreed to by the Secretary and the landowner, state[8] or local government, or private or nonprofit entity;

---

[8]   The term "state should be capitalized in subsection (c)(1)(A).

(B) improve the viability of and otherwise benefit the fish, wildlife, and other resources on national forests lands within the watershed;

(C) authorize the provision of technical assistance by the Secretary in the planning of management activities that will further the purposes of the agreement;

(D) provide for the sharing of costs of implementing the agreement among the Federal Government, the landowner(s), and other entities, as mutually agreed on by the affected interests; and

(E) ensure that any expenditure by the Secretary pursuant to the agreement is determined by the Secretary to be in the public interest; and

(2) the Secretary may require such other terms and conditions as are necessary to protect the public investment on non-Federal lands, provided such terms and conditions are mutually agreed to by the Secretary and other landowners, State and local governments or both.

(d) APPLICABLE LAW.—Chapter 63 of title 31, United States Code, shall not apply to—

(1) a watershed restoration and enhancement agreement entered into under this section; or

(2) an agreement entered into under the first section of Public Law 94–148 (16 U.S.C. 565a–1).

(e) REPORTING REQUIREMENTS.—Not later than December 31, 1999, the Secretary shall submit a report to the Committees on Appropriations of the House and Senate, which contains—

(1) A concise description of each project, including the project purpose, location on federal and non-federal land, key activities, and all parties to the

agreement.

(2)   the[9] funding and/or other contributions provided by each party for each project agreement.

___

[9]   The first letter of subsection (e)(2) should be capitalized.

___

SEC. 329. [16 U.S.C. 535a] (a) PROHIBITION ON TIMBER PURCHASER ROAD CREDITS.— In financing any forest development road pursuant to section 4 of Public Law 88–657 (16 U.S.C. 535, commonly known as the National Forest Roads and Trails Act), the Secretary of Agriculture may not provide effective credit for road construction to any purchaser of national forest timber or other forest products or for the construction and repair of barge mooring points and barge landing sites to facilitate pumping fuel from fuel transport barges into bulk fuel storage tanks. .

(b)(1) CONSTRUCTION OF ROADS BY TIMBER PURCHASERS.— Whenever the Secretary of Agriculture makes a determination that a forest development road referred to in subsection (a) shall be constructed or paid for, in whole or in part, by a purchaser of national forest timber or other forest products, the Secretary shall include notice of the determination in the notice of sale of the timber or other forest products or for the construction and repair of barge mooring points and barge landing sites to facilitate pumping fuel from fuel transport barges into bulk fuel storage tanks. . The notice of sale shall contain, or announce the availability of, sufficient information related to the road described in the notice to permit a prospective bidder on the sale to calculate the likely cost that would be incurred by the bidder to construct or finance the construction of the road so that the bidder may reflect such cost in the bid.

(2)   If there is an increase or decrease in the cost of roads constructed by the timber purchaser, caused by variations in quantities, changes or modifications subsequent to the sale of timber made in accordance with applicable timber sale contract provisions, then an adjustment to the price paid for timber harvested by the purchaser shall be made. The adjustment shall be applied by the Secretary as soon as practicable after any such design change is implemented.

(c) SPECIAL ELECTION BY SMALL BUSINESS CONCERNS.—(1)   A notice of sale referred to in subsection (b) containing specified road construction of $50,000 or more, shall give a purchaser of national forest timber or other forest products that qualifies as a small business concern under the Small Business Act (15 U.S.C. 631 et seq.), and regulations issued thereunder, the option to elect that the Secretary of Agriculture build the roads described in the notice. The Secretary shall provide the small business concern with an estimate of the cost that would be incurred by the Secretary to construct the roads on behalf of the small business concern. The notice of sale shall also include the date on which the roads described in the notice will be completed by the Secretary if the election is made.

(2)   If the election referred to in paragraph (1) is made, the purchaser of the national forest timber or other forest products shall pay to the Secretary of Agriculture, in addition to the price paid for the timber or other forest products, an amount equal to the estimated cost of the roads which otherwise would be paid by the purchaser as provided in the notice of sale. Pending receipt of such amount, the Secretary may use receipts from the sale of national forest timber or other forest

products and such additional sums as may be appropriated for the construction of roads, such funds to be available until expended, to accomplish the requested road construction.

(d) POST CONSTRUCTION HARVESTING.— In each sale of national forest timber or other forest products referred to in this section, the Secretary of Agriculture is encouraged to authorize harvest of the timber or other forest products in a unit included in the sale as soon as road work for that unit is completed and the road work is approved by the Secretary.

(e) CONSTRUCTION STANDARD.— For any forest development road that is to be constructed or paid for by a purchaser of national forest timber or other forest products, the Secretary of Agriculture may not require the purchaser to design, construct, or maintain the road (or pay for the design, construction, or maintenance of the road) to a standard higher than the standard, consistent with applicable environmental laws and regulations, that is sufficient for the harvesting and removal of the timber or other forest products, unless the Secretary bears that part of the cost necessary to meet the higher standard.

(f) TREATMENT OF ROAD VALUE.— For any forest development road that is constructed or paid for by a purchaser of national forest timber or other forest products, the estimated cost of the road construction, including subsequent design changes, shall be considered to be money received for purposes of the payments required to be made under the sixth paragraph under the heading FOREST SERVICE in the Act of May 23, 1908 (35 Stat. 260, 16 U.S.C. 500), and section 13 of the Act of March 1, 1911 (35 Stat. 963; commonly known as the Weeks Act; 16 U.S.C. 500). To the extent that the appraised value of road construction determined under this subsection reflects funds contributed by the Secretary of Agriculture to build the road to a higher standard pursuant to subsection (e), the Secretary shall modify the appraisal of the road construction to exclude the effect of the Federal funds.

(g) EFFECTIVE DATE.—(1) This section and the requirements of this section shall take effect (and apply thereafter) upon the earlier of—

(A)   April 1, 1999; or

(B) the date that is the later of—

(i)   the effective date of regulations issued by the Secretary of Agriculture to implement this section; and

(ii)   the date on which new timber sale contract provisions designed to implement this section, that have been published for public comment, are approved by the Secretary.

(2)   Notwithstanding paragraph (1), any sale of national forest timber or other forest products for which notice of sale is provided before the effective date of this section, and any effective purchaser road credit earned pursuant to a contract resulting from such a notice of sale or otherwise earned before that effective date shall remain in effect, and shall continue to be subject to section 4 of Public Law 88–657 and section 14(i) of the National Forest Management Act of 1976 (16 U.S.C. 472a(i)), and rules issued thereunder, as in effect on the day before the date of the enactment of this Act.

[Section 347 (relating to Stewardship End Result Contracting Projects) was repealed by section 8205(b) of Public Law 113–79.]

* * * * * * *

★

ENERGY POLICY ACT OF 2005–SEC. 356

PUBLIC LAW 109–58
AS AMENDED THROUGH PUB. L. 118-159

ENERGY POLICY ACT OF 2005

[Public Law 109–58, Enacted August 8, 2005]

[As Amended Through P.L. 118–159, Enacted December 23, 2024]

SEC. 356. [42 U.S.C. 15911] DENALI COMMISSION.

(a) DEFINITION OF COMMISSION.— In this section, the term Commission means the Denali Commission established by the Denali Commission Act of 1998 (42 U.S.C. 3121 note; Public Law 105–277).

(b) ENERGY PROGRAMS.— The Commission shall use amounts made available under subsection (d) to carry out energy programs, including—

(1) energy generation and development, including—

(A) fuel cells, hydroelectric, solar, wind, wave, and tidal energy; and

(B) alternative energy sources;

(2) the construction of energy transmission, including interties;

(3) the replacement and cleanup of fuel tanks;

(4) the construction of fuel transportation networks and related facilities;

(5) power cost equalization programs; and

(6) projects using coal as a fuel, including coal gasification projects.

(c) OPEN MEETINGS.—

(1) IN GENERAL.— Except as provided in paragraph (2), a meeting of the Commission shall be open to the public if—

(A) the Commission members take action on behalf of the Commission; or

(B) the deliberations of the Commission determine, or result in the joint conduct or disposition of, official Commission business.

(2) EXCEPTIONS.— Paragraph (1) shall not apply to any portion of a Commission meeting for which the Commission, in public session, votes to close the meeting for the reasons described in paragraph (2), (4), (5), or (6) of subsection (c) of section 552b of title 5, United States Code.

(3) PUBLIC NOTICE.—

(A) IN GENERAL.— At least 1 week before a meeting of the Commission, the Commission shall make a public announcement of the meeting that describes—

(i)   the time, place, and subject matter of the meeting;

(ii)   whether the meeting is to be open or closed to the public; and

(iii)   the name and telephone number of an appropriate person to respond to requests for information about the meeting.

(B) ADDITIONAL NOTICE.—   The Commission shall make a public announcement of any change to the information made available under subparagraph (A) at the earliest practicable time.

(4) MINUTES.—   The Commission shall keep, and make available to the public, a transcript, electronic recording, or minutes from each Commission meeting, except for portions of the meeting closed under paragraph (2).

(d) AUTHORIZATION OF APPROPRIATIONS.—   There is authorized to be appropriated to the Commission not more than $55,000,000 for each of fiscal years 2006 through 2015 to carry out subsection (b).

★

DEPARTMENT OF TRANSPORTATION AND RELATED AGENCIES APPROPRIATIONS ACT, 1999–SEC. 329

43 U.S.C. §1653NT

Section 329 of the Department of Transportation and Related Agencies Appropriations Act, 1999

TITLE 43—PUBLIC LANDS

CHAPTER 34—TRANS-ALASKA PIPELINE

* * * * * * *

Sec.

1653.   Liability for damages.

* * * * * * *

§1653. LIABILITY FOR DAMAGES

(Pub. L. 93–153, title II, §204, Nov. 16, 1973, 87 Stat. 586; Pub. L. 101–380, title VIII, §§8101, 8102(a)(1), (4), (b)–(e), Aug. 18, 1990, 104 Stat. 565–567.)

* * * * * * *

BULK FUEL STORAGE TANKS

Pub. L. 105–277, div. A, §101(g) [title III, §329(a), (b)], Oct. 21, 1998, 112 Stat. 2681–439, 2681–470, as amended by Pub. L. 114–113, div. D, title IV, §403, Dec. 18, 2015, 129 Stat. 2422, provided that:

"(a) TRANSFER OF FUNDS.—Notwithstanding any other provision "of law, the remainder of the balance in the Trans-Alaska Pipeline Liability Fund that is transferred and deposited into the Oil Spill Liability Trust Fund under section 8102(a)(2)(B)(ii) of the Oil Pollution Act of 1990 (43 U.S.C. 1653 note) after June 16, 1998 shall be used in accordance with this section.

"(b) USE OF INTEREST ONLY.—The interest produced from the investment of the Trans-Alaska Pipeline Liability Fund balance that is transferred and deposited into the Oil Spill Liability Trust Fund under section 8102(a)(2)(B)(ii) of the Oil Pollution Act of 1990 [Pub. L. 101–380] (43 U.S.C. 1653 note) after June 16, 1998 shall be transferred annually by the National Pollution Funds Center to the Denali Commission for a program, to be developed in consultation with the Coast Guard, to repair or replace bulk fuel storage tanks in Alaska which are not in compliance with federal law, including the Oil Pollution Act of 1990 [33 U.S.C. 2701 et seq.], or State law or for the construction and repair of barge mooring points and barge landing sites to facilitate pumping fuel from fuel transport barges into bulk fuel storage tanks.. [sic]"

[For transfer of authorities, functions, personnel, and assets of the Coast Guard, including the authorities and functions of the Secretary of Transportation relating thereto, to the Department of Homeland Security, and for treatment of related references, see sections 468(b), 551(d), 552(d), and 557 of Title 6, Domestic Security, and the Department of Homeland Security Reorganization Plan of November 25, 2002, as modified, set out as a note under section 542 of Title 6.]

DELTA REGIONAL AUTHORITY

SUBTITLE F OF THE CONSOLIDATED FARM AND RURAL DEVELOPMENT ACT

SUBTITLE F OF PUBLIC LAW 87–128
AS AMENDED THROUGH PUB. L. 118-272

DELTA REGIONAL AUTHORITY

Subtitle F of the Consolidated Farm and Rural Credit Development Act

[(Public Law 87–128; 75 Stat. 294)]

[As Amended Through P.L. 118–272, Enacted January 4, 2025]

TABLE OF CONTENTS[1]

---

[1] This table of contents is not part of the Act but is included for user convenience. The numbers in brackets refer to section numbers in title 7, United States Code.

---

* * * * * * *

Subtitle F—Delta Regional Authority

Sec. 382A.   Definitions.
Sec. 382B.   Delta Regional Authority.
Sec. 382C.   Economic and community development grants.
Sec. 382D.   Supplements to Federal grant programs.
Sec. 382E.   Local development districts; certification and administrative expenses.
Sec. 382F.   Distressed counties and areas and nondistressed counties.
Sec. 382G.   Development planning process.
Sec. 382H.   Program development criteria.
Sec. 382I.   Approval of development plans and projects.
Sec. 382J.   Consent of States.
Sec. 382K.   Records.
Sec. 382L.   Annual report.
Sec. 382M.   Authorization of appropriations.
Sec. 382N.   Termination of authority.

* * * * * * *

SUBTITLE F—DELTA REGIONAL AUTHORITY

SEC. 382A. [7 U.S.C. 2009aa] DEFINITIONS.

In this subtitle:

(1) AUTHORITY.— The term Authority means the Delta Regional Authority established by section 382B.

161

(2) REGION.— The term region means the Lower Mississippi (as defined in section 4 of the Delta Development Act (42 U.S.C. 3121 note; Public Law 100–460)).

(3) FEDERAL GRANT PROGRAM.—The term Federal grant program means a Federal grant program to provide assistance in—

(A) acquiring or developing land;

(B) constructing or equipping a highway, road, bridge, or facility; or

(C) carrying out other economic development activities.

(4) Notwithstanding any other provision of law, the State of Alabama shall be a full member of the Delta Regional Authority and shall be entitled to all rights and privileges that said membership affords to all other participating States in the Delta Regional Authority.

SEC. 382B. [7 U.S.C. 2009aa–1] DELTA REGIONAL AUTHORITY.

(a) ESTABLISHMENT.—

(1) IN GENERAL.— There is established the Delta Regional Authority.

(2) COMPOSITION.—The Authority shall be composed of—

(A) a Federal member, to be appointed by the President, with the advice and consent of the Senate; and

(B) the Governor (or a designee of the Governor) of each State in the region that elects to participate in the Authority.

(3) COCHAIRPERSONS.—The Authority shall be headed by—

(A) the Federal member, who shall serve—

(i) as the Federal cochairperson; and

(ii) as a liaison between the Federal Government and the Authority; and

(B) a State cochairperson, who—

(i) shall be a Governor of a participating State in the region; and

(ii) shall be elected by the State members for a term of not less than 1 year.

(b) ALTERNATE MEMBERS.—

(1) STATE ALTERNATES.—The State member of a participating State may have a single alternate, who shall be—

(A) a resident of that State; and

(B) appointed by the Governor of the State.

(2) ALTERNATE FEDERAL COCHAIRPERSON.— The President shall appoint an alternate Federal cochairperson.

(3) QUORUM.— A State alternate shall not be counted toward the establishment of a quorum of the Authority in any instance in which a quorum of the State members is required to be present.

(4) DELEGATION OF POWER.—No power or responsibility of the Authority

specified in paragraphs (2) and (3) of subsection (c), and no voting right of any Authority member, shall be delegated to any person—

    (A)   who is not an Authority member; or

    (B)   who is not entitled to vote in Authority meetings.

(c) VOTING.—

    (1) IN GENERAL.—

        (A) TEMPORARY METHOD.— During the period beginning on the date of enactment of this subparagraph and ending on December 31, 2008, a decision by the Authority shall require the affirmative vote of the Federal cochairperson and a majority of the State members (not including any member representing a State that is delinquent under subsection (g)(2)(C)) to be effective.

        (B) PERMANENT METHOD.— Effective beginning on January 1, 2009, a decision by the Authority shall require a majority vote of the Authority (not including any member representing a State that is delinquent under subsection (g)(2)(C)) to be effective.

    (2) QUORUM.—A quorum of State members shall be required to be present for the Authority to make any policy decision, including—

        (A)   a modification or revision of an Authority policy decision;

        (B)   approval of a State or regional development plan; and

        (C)   any allocation of funds among the States.

    (3) PROJECT AND GRANT PROPOSALS.—The approval of project and grant proposals shall be—

        (A)   a responsibility of the Authority; and

        (B) conducted in accordance with section 382I.

        VOTING BY ALTERNATE MEMBERS.— An alternate member shall vote in the case of the absence, death, disability, removal, or resignation of the Federal or State representative for which the alternate member is an alternate.

(d) DUTIES.—The Authority shall—

    (1)   develop, on a continuing basis, comprehensive and coordinated plans and programs to establish priorities and approve grants for the economic development of the region, giving due consideration to other Federal, State, and local planning and development activities in the region;

    (2)   not later than 220 days after the date of enactment of this subtitle, establish priorities in a development plan for the region (including 5-year regional outcome targets);

    (3)   assess the needs and assets of the region based on available research, demonstrations, investigations, assessments, and evaluations of the region prepared by Federal, State, and local agencies, universities, local development districts, and other nonprofit groups;

    (4)   formulate and recommend to the Governors and legislatures of States

that participate in the Authority forms of interstate cooperation;

(5) work with State and local agencies in developing appropriate model legislation;

(6)(A) enhance the capacity of, and provide support for, local development districts in the region; or

(B) if no local development district exists in an area in a participating State in the region, foster the creation of a local development district;

(7) encourage private investment in industrial, commercial, and other economic development projects in the region; and

(8) cooperate with and assist State governments with economic development programs of participating States.

(e) ADMINISTRATION.—In carrying out subsection (d), the Authority may—

(1) hold such hearings, sit and act at such times and places, take such testimony, receive such evidence, and print or otherwise reproduce and distribute a description of the proceedings and reports on actions by the Authority as the Authority considers appropriate;

(2) authorize, through the Federal or State cochairperson or any other member of the Authority designated by the Authority, the administration of oaths if the Authority determines that testimony should be taken or evidence received under oath;

(3) request from any Federal, State, or local department or agency such information as may be available to or procurable by the department or agency that may be of use to the Authority in carrying out duties of the Authority;

(4) adopt, amend, and repeal bylaws, rules, and regulations governing the conduct of Authority business and the performance of Authority duties;

(5) request the head of any Federal department or agency to detail to the Authority such personnel as the Authority requires to carry out duties of the Authority, each such detail to be without loss of seniority, pay, or other employee status;

(6) request the head of any State department or agency or local government to detail to the Authority such personnel as the Authority requires to carry out duties of the Authority, each such detail to be without loss of seniority, pay, or other employee status;

(7) provide for coverage of Authority employees in a suitable retirement and employee benefit system by—

(A) making arrangements or entering into contracts with any participating State government; or

(B) otherwise providing retirement and other employee benefit coverage;

(8) accept, use, and dispose of gifts or donations of services or real, personal, tangible, or intangible property;

(9) enter into and perform such contracts, leases, cooperative agreements, or other transactions as are necessary to carry out Authority duties, including any

contracts, leases, or cooperative agreements with—

(A) any department, agency, or instrumentality of the United States;

(B) any State (including a political subdivision, agency, or instrumentality of the State); or

(C) any person, firm, association, or corporation;

(10) establish and maintain a central office and field offices at such locations as the Authority may select; and

(11) collect fees for the Delta Doctors program of the Authority and retain and expend those fees.

(f) FEDERAL AGENCY COOPERATION.—A Federal agency shall—

(1) cooperate with the Authority; and

(2) provide, on request of the Federal cochairperson, appropriate assistance in carrying out this subtitle, in accordance with applicable Federal laws (including regulations).

(g) ADMINISTRATIVE EXPENSES.—

(1) IN GENERAL.—Administrative expenses of the Authority (except for the expenses of the Federal cochairperson, including expenses of the alternate and staff of the Federal cochairperson, which shall be paid solely by the Federal Government) shall be paid—

(A) by the Federal Government, in an amount equal to 50 percent of the administrative expenses; and

(B) by the States in the region participating in the Authority, in an amount equal to 50 percent of the administrative expenses.

(2) STATE SHARE.—

(A) IN GENERAL.— The share of administrative expenses of the Authority to be paid by each State shall be determined by the Authority.

(B) NO FEDERAL PARTICIPATION.— The Federal cochairperson shall not participate or vote in any decision under subparagraph (A).

(C) DELINQUENT STATES.—If a State is delinquent in payment of the State's share of administrative expenses of the Authority under this subsection—

(i) no assistance under this subtitle shall be furnished to the State (including assistance to a political subdivision or a resident of the State); and

(ii) no member of the Authority from the State shall participate or vote in any action by the Authority.

(h) COMPENSATION.—

(1) FEDERAL COCHAIRPERSON.— The Federal cochairperson shall be compensated by the Federal Government at level III of the Executive Schedule in subchapter II of chapter 53 of title 5, United States Code.

(2) ALTERNATE FEDERAL COCHAIRPERSON.—The alternate Federal cochairperson—

(A)   shall be compensated by the Federal Government at level V of the Executive Schedule described in paragraph (1); and

(B)   when not actively serving as an alternate for the Federal cochairperson, shall perform such functions and duties as are delegated by the Federal cochairperson.

(3) STATE MEMBERS AND ALTERNATES.—

(A) IN GENERAL.— A State shall compensate each member and alternate representing the State on the Authority at the rate established by law of the State.

(B) NO ADDITIONAL COMPENSATION.— No State member or alternate member shall receive any salary, or any contribution to or supplementation of salary from any source other than the State for services provided by the member or alternate to the Authority.

(4) DETAILED EMPLOYEES.—

(A) IN GENERAL.—No person detailed to serve the Authority under subsection (e)(6) shall receive any salary or any contribution to or supplementation of salary for services provided to the Authority from—

(i)   any source other than the State, local, or intergovernmental department or agency from which the person was detailed; or

(ii)   the Authority.

(B) VIOLATION.— Any person that violates this paragraph shall be fined not more than $5,000, imprisoned not more than 1 year, or both.

(C) APPLICABLE LAW.— The Federal cochairperson, the alternate Federal cochairperson, and any Federal officer or employee detailed to duty on the Authority under subsection (e)(5) shall not be subject to subparagraph (A), but shall remain subject to sections 202 through 209 of title 18, United States Code.

(5) ADDITIONAL PERSONNEL.—

(A) COMPENSATION.—

(i) IN GENERAL.— The Authority may appoint and fix the compensation of an executive director and such other personnel as are necessary to enable the Authority to carry out the duties of the Authority.

(ii) EXCEPTION.— Compensation under clause (i) shall not exceed the maximum rate for the Senior Executive Service under section 5382 of title 5, United States Code, including any applicable locality-based comparability payment that may be authorized under section 5304(h)(2)(C) of that title.

(B) EXECUTIVE DIRECTOR.—The executive director shall be responsible for—

(i)   the carrying out of the administrative duties of the Authority;

(ii)   direction of the Authority staff;

(iii)   assuming the duties of the Federal cochairperson and the alternate Federal cochairperson for purposes of continuation of normal operations in the event that both positions are vacant; and

(iv) such other duties as the Authority may assign.

(C) NO FEDERAL EMPLOYEE STATUS.— No member, alternate, officer, or employee of the Authority (except the Federal cochairperson of the Authority, the alternate and staff for the Federal cochairperson, and any Federal employee detailed to the Authority under subsection (e)(5)) shall be considered to be a Federal employee for any purpose.

(i) CONFLICTS OF INTEREST.—

(1) IN GENERAL.—Except as provided under paragraph (2), no State member, alternate, officer, or employee of the Authority shall participate personally and substantially as a member, alternate, officer, or employee of the Authority, through decision, approval, disapproval, recommendation, the rendering of advice, investigation, or otherwise, in any proceeding, application, request for a ruling or other determination, contract, claim, controversy, or other matter in which, to knowledge of the member, alternate, officer, or employee—

(A) the member, alternate, officer, or employee;

(B) the spouse, minor child, partner, or organization (other than a State or political subdivision of the State) of the member, alternate, officer, or employee, in which the member, alternate, officer, or employee is serving as officer, director, trustee, partner, or employee; or

(C) any person or organization with whom the member, alternate, officer, or employee is negotiating or has any arrangement concerning prospective employment;

has a financial interest.

(2) DISCLOSURE.—Paragraph (1) shall not apply if the State member, alternate, officer, or employee—

(A) immediately advises the Authority of the nature and circumstances of the proceeding, application, request for a ruling or other determination, contract, claim, controversy, or other particular matter presenting a potential conflict of interest;

(B) makes full disclosure of the financial interest; and

(C) before the proceeding concerning the matter presenting the conflict of interest, receives a written determination by the Authority that the interest is not so substantial as to be likely to affect the integrity of the services that the Authority may expect from the State member, alternate, officer, or employee.

(3) VIOLATION.— Any person that violates this subsection shall be fined not more than $10,000, imprisoned not more than 2 years, or both.

(j) VALIDITY OF CONTRACTS, LOANS, AND GRANTS.— The Authority may declare void any contract, loan, or grant of or by the Authority in relation to which the Authority determines that there has been a violation of any provision under subsection (h)(4), subsection (i), or sections 202 through 209 of title 18, United States Code.

SEC. 382C. [7 U.S.C. 2009aa–2] ECONOMIC AND COMMUNITY DEVELOPMENT GRANTS.

(a) IN GENERAL.—The Authority may approve grants to States, Indian Tribes, and public and nonprofit entities for projects, approved in accordance with section 382I—

(1) to develop the transportation infrastructure of the region for the purpose of facilitating economic development in the region (except that grants for this purpose may only be made to a State, Tribal, or local government);

(2) to assist the region in obtaining the job training, employment-related education, and business development (with an emphasis on entrepreneurship) that are needed to build and maintain strong local economies;

(3) to provide assistance to severely distressed and underdeveloped areas that lack financial resources for improving basic public services;

(4) to provide assistance to severely distressed and underdeveloped areas that lack financial resources for equipping industrial parks and related facilities; and

(5) to otherwise achieve the purposes of this subtitle.

(b) FUNDING.—

(1) IN GENERAL.—Funds for grants under subsection (a) may be provided—

(A) entirely from appropriations to carry out this section;

(B) in combination with funds available under another Federal or Federal grant program; or

(C) from any other source.

(2) PRIORITY OF FUNDING.—To best build the foundations for long-term economic development and to complement other Federal and State resources in the region, Federal funds available under this subtitle shall be focused on the activities in the following order or priority:

(A) Basic public infrastructure in distressed counties and isolated areas of distress.

(B) Transportation infrastructure for the purpose of facilitating economic development in the region.

(C) Business development, with emphasis on entrepreneurship.

(D) Job training or employment-related education, with emphasis on use of existing public educational institutions located in the region.

SEC. 382D. [7 U.S.C. 2009aa–3] SUPPLEMENTS TO FEDERAL GRANT PROGRAMS.

(a) FINDING.—Congress finds that certain States and local communities of the region, including local development districts, may be unable to take maximum advantage of Federal grant programs for which the States and communities are eligible because—

(1) the States or communities lack the economic resources to provide the required matching share; or

(2) there are insufficient funds available under the applicable Federal law authorizing the Federal grant program to meet pressing needs of the region.

(b) FEDERAL GRANT PROGRAM FUNDING.—Notwithstanding any provision of law limiting the Federal share, the areas eligible for assistance, or the authorizations of appropriations of any Federal grant program, and in accordance with subsection (c), the Authority, with the approval of the Federal cochairperson and with respect to a project to be carried out in the region—

(1) may increase the Federal share of the costs of a project under the Federal grant program to not more than 90 percent (except as provided in section 382F(b)); and

(2) shall use amounts made available to carry out this subtitle to pay the increased Federal share.

(c) CERTIFICATIONS.—

(1) IN GENERAL.—In the case of any project for which all or any portion of the basic Federal share of the costs of the project is proposed to be paid under this section, no Federal contribution shall be made until the Federal official administering the Federal law that authorizes the Federal grant program certifies that the project—

(A) meets (except as provided in subsection (b)) the applicable requirements of the applicable Federal grant program; and

(B) could be approved for Federal contribution under the Federal grant program if funds were available under the law for the project.

(2) CERTIFICATION BY AUTHORITY.—

(A) IN GENERAL.—The certifications and determinations required to be made by the Authority for approval of projects under this Act in accordance with section 382I—

(i) shall be controlling; and

(ii) shall be accepted by the Federal agencies.

(B) ACCEPTANCE BY FEDERAL COCHAIRPERSON.— In the case of any project described in paragraph (1), any finding, report, certification, or documentation required to be submitted with respect to the project to the head of the department, agency, or instrumentality of the Federal Government responsible for the administration of the Federal grant program under which the project is carried out shall be accepted by the Federal cochairperson.

SEC. 382E. [7 U.S.C. 2009aa–4] LOCAL DEVELOPMENT DISTRICTS; CERTIFICATION AND ADMINISTRATIVE EXPENSES.

(a) DEFINITION OF LOCAL DEVELOPMENT DISTRICT.—In this section, the term local development district means an entity that—

(1) is—

(A) a planning district in existence on the date of enactment of this subtitle that is recognized by the Economic Development Administration of the Department of Commerce; or

(B) where an entity described in subparagraph (A) does not exist—

(i) organized and operated in a manner that ensures broad-based community participation and an effective opportunity for other nonprofit groups to contribute to the development and implementation of programs in the region;

(ii)   governed by a policy board with at least a simple majority of members consisting of elected officials or employees of a general purpose unit of local government who have been appointed to represent the government;

(iii) certified to the Authority as having a charter or authority that includes the economic development of counties or parts of counties or other political subdivisions within the region—

(I)   by the Governor of each State in which the entity is located; or

(II)   by the State officer designated by the appropriate State law to make the certification; and

(iv)(I)   a nonprofit incorporated body organized or chartered under the law of the State in which the entity is located;

(II)   a nonprofit agency or instrumentality of a State or local government;

(III)   a public organization established before the date of enactment of this subtitle under State law for creation of multi-jurisdictional, area-wide planning organizations; or

(IV)   a nonprofit association or combination of bodies, agencies, and instrumentalities described in subclauses (I) through (III); and

(2) has not, as certified by the Federal cochairperson—

(A)   inappropriately used Federal grant funds from any Federal source; or

(B)   appointed an officer who, during the period in which another entity inappropriately used Federal grant funds from any Federal source, was an officer of the other entity.

(b) GRANTS TO LOCAL DEVELOPMENT DISTRICTS.—

(1) IN GENERAL.— The Authority shall make grants for administrative expenses under this section.

(2) CONDITIONS FOR GRANTS.—

(A) MAXIMUM AMOUNT.— The amount of any grant awarded under paragraph (1) shall not exceed 80 percent of the administrative expenses of the local development district receiving the grant.

(B) MAXIMUM PERIOD.— No grant described in paragraph (1) shall be awarded to a State agency certified as a local development district for a period greater than 3 years.

(C) LOCAL SHARE.— The contributions of a local development district for administrative expenses may be in cash or in kind, fairly evaluated, including space, equipment, and services.

(c) DUTIES OF LOCAL DEVELOPMENT DISTRICTS.—A local development district shall—

(1) operate as a lead organization serving multicounty areas in the region at the local level; and

(2) serve as a liaison between State and local governments, nonprofit organizations (including community-based groups and educational institutions), the business community, and citizens that—

(A) are involved in multijurisdictional planning;

(B) provide technical assistance to local jurisdictions and potential grantees; and

(C) provide leadership and civic development assistance.

SEC. 382F. [7 U.S.C. 2009aa–5] DISTRESSED COUNTIES AND AREAS AND NONDISTRESSED COUNTIES.

(a) DESIGNATIONS.—Not later than 90 days after the date of enactment of this subtitle, and annually thereafter, the Authority, in accordance with such criteria as the Authority may establish, shall designate—

(1) as distressed counties, counties in the region that are the most severely and persistently distressed and underdeveloped and have high rates of poverty or unemployment;

(2) as nondistressed counties, counties in the region that are not designated as distressed counties under paragraph (1); and

(3) as isolated areas of distress, areas located in nondistressed counties (as designated under paragraph (2)) that have high rates of poverty or unemployment.

(b) DISTRESSED COUNTIES.—

(1) IN GENERAL.— The Authority shall allocate at least 75 percent of the appropriations made available under section 382M for programs and projects designed to serve the needs of distressed counties and isolated areas of distress in the region.

(2) FUNDING LIMITATIONS.— The funding limitations under section 382D(b) shall not apply to a project providing transportation or basic public services to residents of one or more distressed counties or isolated areas of distress in the region.

(c) NONDISTRESSED COUNTIES.—

(1) IN GENERAL.— Except as provided in this subsection, no funds shall be provided under this subtitle for a project located in a county designated as a nondistressed county under subsection (a)(2).

(2) EXCEPTIONS.—

(A) IN GENERAL.— The funding prohibition under paragraph (1) shall not apply to grants to fund the administrative expenses of local development districts under section 382E(b).

(B) MULTICOUNTY PROJECTS.—The Authority may waive the application of the funding prohibition under paragraph (1) to—

SEC. 382G. [7 U.S.C. 2009aa–6]
DEVELOPMENT PLANNING PROCESS.

Delta Regional Authority

        (i)   a multicounty project that includes participation by a nondistressed county; or

        (ii)   any other type of project;

if the Authority determines that the project could bring significant benefits to areas of the region outside a nondistressed county.

    (C) ISOLATED AREAS OF DISTRESS.—For a designation of an isolated area of distress for assistance to be effective, the designation shall be supported—

        (i)   by the most recent Federal data available; or

        (ii)   if no recent Federal data are available, by the most recent data available through the government of the State in which the isolated area of distress is located.

    (d) TRANSPORTATION AND BASIC PUBLIC INFRASTRUCTURE.— The Authority shall allocate at least 50 percent of any funds made available under section 382M for transportation and basic public infrastructure projects authorized under paragraphs (1) and (3) of section 382C(a).

SEC. 382G. [7 U.S.C. 2009aa–6] DEVELOPMENT PLANNING PROCESS.

    (a) STATE DEVELOPMENT PLAN.— In accordance with policies established by the Authority, each State member shall submit a development plan for the area of the region represented by the State member.

    (b) CONTENT OF PLAN.— A State development plan submitted under subsection (a) shall reflect the goals, objectives, and priorities identified in the regional development plan developed under section 382B(d)(2).

    (c) CONSULTATION WITH INTERESTED LOCAL PARTIES.—In carrying out the development planning process (including the selection of programs and projects for assistance), a State may—

    (1) consult with—

        (A)   local development districts; and

        (B)   local units of government; and

    (2)   take into consideration the goals, objectives, priorities, and recommendations of the entities described in paragraph (1).

    (d) PUBLIC PARTICIPATION.—

    (1) IN GENERAL.— The Authority and applicable State and local development districts shall encourage and assist, to the maximum extent practicable, public participation in the development, revision, and implementation of all plans and programs under this subtitle.

    (2) REGULATIONS.— The Authority shall develop guidelines for providing public participation described in paragraph (1), including public hearings.

SEC. 382H. [7 U.S.C. 2009aa–7] PROGRAM DEVELOPMENT CRITERIA.

    (a) IN GENERAL.—In considering programs and projects to be provided assistance under this subtitle, and in establishing a priority ranking of the requests for assistance provided by the Authority, the Authority shall follow procedures that ensure, to the maximum extent practicable, consideration of—

(1)   the relationship of the project or class of projects to overall regional development;

(2)   the per capita income and poverty and unemployment rates in an area;

(3)   the financial resources available to the applicants for assistance seeking to carry out the project, with emphasis on ensuring that projects are adequately financed to maximize the probability of successful economic development;

(4)   the importance of the project or class of projects in relation to other projects or classes of projects that may be in competition for the same funds;

(5)   the prospects that the project for which assistance is sought will improve, on a continuing rather than a temporary basis, the opportunities for employment, the average level of income, or the economic development of the area served by the project; and

(6)   the extent to which the project design provides for detailed outcome measurements by which grant expenditures and the results of the expenditures may be evaluated.

(b) NO RELOCATION ASSISTANCE.— No financial assistance authorized by this subtitle shall be used to assist a person or entity in relocating from one area to another, except that financial assistance may be used as otherwise authorized by this title to attract businesses from outside the region to the region.

(c) REDUCTION OF FUNDS.— Funds may be provided for a program or project in a State under this subtitle only if the Authority determines that the level of Federal or State financial assistance provided under a law other than this subtitle, for the same type of program or project in the same area of the State within the region, will not be reduced as a result of funds made available by this subtitle.

SEC. 382I. [7 U.S.C. 2009aa–8] APPROVAL OF DEVELOPMENT PLANS AND PROJECTS.

(a) IN GENERAL.— A State or regional development plan or any multistate subregional plan that is proposed for development under this subtitle shall be reviewed and approved by the Authority.

(b) EVALUATION BY STATE MEMBER.— An application for a grant or any other assistance for a project under this subtitle shall be made through and evaluated for approval by the State member of the Authority representing the applicant.

(c) CERTIFICATION.—An application for a grant or other assistance for a project shall be approved only on certification by the State member that the application for the project—

(1)   describes ways in which the project complies with any applicable State development plan;

(2)   meets applicable criteria under section 382H;

(3)   provides adequate assurance that the proposed project will be properly administered, operated, and maintained; and

(4)   otherwise meets the requirements of this subtitle.

(d) APPROVAL OF GRANT APPLICATIONS.— On certification by a State member of the Authority of an application for a grant or other assistance for a specific project under this section, an affirmative vote of the Authority under section 382B(c) shall be required for approval of the application.

SEC. 382J. [7 U.S.C. 2009aa–9] CONSENT OF STATES.

Nothing in this subtitle requires any State to engage in or accept any program under this subtitle without the consent of the State.

SEC. 382K. [7 U.S.C. 2009aa–10] RECORDS.

(a) RECORDS OF THE AUTHORITY.—

(1) IN GENERAL.— The Authority shall maintain accurate and complete records of all transactions and activities of the Authority.

(2) AVAILABILITY.— All records of the Authority shall be available for audit and examination by the Comptroller General of the United States and the Inspector General of the Department of Agriculture (including authorized representatives of the Comptroller General and the Inspector General of the Department of Agriculture).

(b) RECORDS OF RECIPIENTS OF FEDERAL ASSISTANCE.—

(1) IN GENERAL.— A recipient of Federal funds under this subtitle shall, as required by the Authority, maintain accurate and complete records of transactions and activities financed with Federal funds and report on the transactions and activities to the Authority.

(2) AVAILABILITY.— All records required under paragraph (1) shall be available for audit by the Comptroller General of the United States, the Inspector General of the Department of Agriculture, and the Authority (including authorized representatives of the Comptroller General, the Inspector General of the Department of Agriculture, and the Authority).

SEC. 382L. [7 U.S.C. 2009aa–11] ANNUAL REPORT.

Not later than 180 days after the end of each fiscal year, the Authority shall submit to the President and to Congress a report describing the activities carried out under this subtitle.

SEC. 382M. [7 U.S.C. 2009aa–12] AUTHORIZATION OF APPROPRIATIONS.

(a) IN GENERAL.— There is authorized to be appropriated to the Authority to carry out this subtitle $40,000,000 for each of fiscal years 2025 through 2029, to remain available until expended.

(b) ADMINISTRATIVE EXPENSES.— Not more than 5 percent of the amount appropriated under subsection (a) for a fiscal year shall be used for administrative expenses of the Authority.

★

Great Northern Plains Regional Authority
Subtitle G of the Consolidated Farm and Rural Development Act

Subtitle G of Public Law 87–128
As amended through Pub. L. 118-272

Subtitle G of the Consolidated Farm and Rural Development Act

[(Public Law 87–128; 75 Stat. 294)]

[As Amended Through P.L. 118–272, Enacted January 4, 2025]

TABLE OF CONTENTS[1]

---

[1] This table of contents is not part of the Act but is included for user convenience. The numbers in brackets refer to section numbers in title 7, United States Code.

---

* * * * * * *

Subtitle G—Northern Great Plains Regional Authority

Sec. 383A. Definitions.
Sec. 383B. Northern Great Plains Regional Authority.
Sec. 383D. Economic and community development grants.
Sec. 383E. Supplements to Federal grant programs.
Sec. 383F. Multistate and local development districts and organizations and Northern Great Plains Inc.
Sec. 383G. Distressed counties and areas and nondistressed counties.
Sec. 383H. Development planning process.
Sec. 383I. Program development criteria.
Sec. 383J. Approval of development plans and projects.
Sec. 383K. Consent of States.
Sec. 383L. Records.
Sec. 383M. Annual report.
Sec. 383N. Authorization of appropriations.
Sec. 383O. Termination of authority.

* * * * * * *

Subtitle G—NORTHERN GREAT PLAINS REGIONAL AUTHORITY

SEC. 383A. [7 U.S.C. 2009bb] DEFINITIONS.

In this subtitle:

(1) AUTHORITY.— The term Authority means the Northern Great Plains Regional Authority established by section 383B.

(2) FEDERAL GRANT PROGRAM.—The term Federal grant program means a Federal grant program to provide assistance in—

(A) implementing the recommendations of the Northern Great Plains Rural Development Commission established by the Northern Great Plains Rural Development Act (7 U.S.C. 2661 note; Public Law 103–318);

(B) acquiring or developing land;

(C) constructing or equipping a highway, road, bridge, or facility;

(D) carrying out other economic development activities; or

(E) conducting research activities related to the activities described in subparagraphs (A) through (D).

(3) INDIAN TRIBE.— The term Indian tribe has the meaning given the term in section 4 of the Indian Self-Determination and Education Assistance Act (25 U.S.C. 450b).

(4) REGION.— The term region means the States of Iowa, Minnesota, Missouri (other than counties included in the Delta Regional Authority), Nebraska, North Dakota, and South Dakota.

SEC. 383B. [7 U.S.C. 2009bb–1] NORTHERN GREAT PLAINS REGIONAL AUTHORITY.

(a) ESTABLISHMENT.—

(1) IN GENERAL.— There is established the Northern Great Plains Regional Authority.

(2) COMPOSITION.—The Authority shall be composed of—

(A) a Federal member, to be appointed by the President, by and with the advice and consent of the Senate;

(B) the Governor (or a designee of the Governor) of each State in the region that elects to participate in the Authority; and

(C) a member of an Indian tribe, who shall be a chairperson of an Indian tribe in the region or a designee of such a chairperson, to be appointed by the President, by and with the advice and consent of the Senate.

(3) COCHAIRPERSONS.—The Authority shall be headed by—

(A) the Federal member, who shall serve—

(i) as the Federal cochairperson; and

(ii) as a liaison between the Federal Government and the Authority;

(B) a State cochairperson, who—

(i) shall be a Governor of a participating State in the region; and

(ii) shall be elected by the State members for a term of not less than 1 year; and

(C) the member of an Indian tribe, who shall serve—

(i) as the tribal cochairperson; and

SEC. 383B. [7 U.S.C. 2009bb–1] NORTHERN
GREAT PLAINS REGIONAL AUTHORITY.

Northern Great Plains Regional Authority

(ii)   as a liaison between the governments of Indian tribes in the region and the Authority.

(4) FAILURE TO CONFIRM.—

(A) FEDERAL MEMBER.— Notwithstanding any other provision of this section, if a Federal member described in paragraph (2)(A) has not been confirmed by the Senate by not later than 180 days after the date of enactment of this paragraph, the Authority may organize and operate without the Federal member.

(B) INDIAN CHAIRPERSON.— In the case of the Indian Chairperson, if no Indian Chairperson is confirmed by the Senate, the regional authority shall consult and coordinate with the leaders of Indian tribes in the region concerning the activities of the Authority, as appropriate.

(b) ALTERNATE MEMBERS.—

(1) ALTERNATE FEDERAL COCHAIRPERSON.— The President shall appoint an alternate Federal cochairperson.

(2) STATE ALTERNATES.—

(A) IN GENERAL.—The State member of a participating State may have a single alternate, who shall be—

(i)   a resident of that State; and

(ii)   appointed by the Governor of the State.

(B) QUORUM.— A State alternate member shall not be counted toward the establishment of a quorum of the members of the Authority in any case in which a quorum of the State members is required to be present.

(3) ALTERNATE TRIBAL COCHAIRPERSON.— The President shall appoint an alternate tribal cochairperson, by and with the advice and consent of the Senate.

(4) DELEGATION OF POWER.—No power or responsibility of the Authority specified in paragraphs (2) and (3) of subsection (c), and no voting right of any member of the Authority, shall be delegated to any person who is not—

(A)   a member of the Authority; or

(B)   entitled to vote in Authority meetings.

(c) VOTING.—

(1) IN GENERAL.— A decision by the Authority shall require a majority vote of the Authority (not including any member representing a State that is delinquent under subsection (g)(2)(D)) to be effective.

(2) QUORUM.—A quorum of State members shall be required to be present for the Authority to make any policy decision, including—

(A)   a modification or revision of an Authority policy decision;

(B)   approval of a State or regional development plan; and

(C)   any allocation of funds among the States.

(3) PROJECT AND GRANT PROPOSALS.—The approval of project and grant proposals shall be—

(A)   a responsibility of the Authority; and

SEC. 383B. [7 U.S.C. 2009bb–1] NORTHERN
GREAT PLAINS REGIONAL AUTHORITY.

Northern Great Plains Regional Authority

(B)   conducted in accordance with section 383J.

(4) VOTING BY ALTERNATE MEMBERS.— An alternate member shall vote in the case of the absence, death, disability, removal, or resignation of the Federal, State, or Indian tribe member for whom the alternate member is an alternate.

(d) DUTIES.—The Authority shall—

(1)   develop, on a continuing basis, comprehensive and coordinated plans and programs for multistate cooperation to advance the economic and social well-being of the region and to approve grants for the economic development of the region, giving due consideration to other Federal, State, tribal, and local planning and development activities in the region;

(2)   not later than 220 days after the date of enactment of this subtitle, establish priorities in a development plan for the region (including 5-year regional outcome targets);

(3)   assess the needs and assets of the region based on available research, demonstrations, investigations, assessments, and evaluations of the region prepared by Federal, State, tribal, and local agencies, universities, regional and local development districts or organizations, regional boards established under subtitle I, and other nonprofit groups;

(4) formulate and recommend to the Governors and legislatures of States that participate in the Authority forms of interstate cooperation for—

(i)   renewable energy development and transmission;

(ii)   transportation planning and economic development;

(iii)   information technology;

(iv)   movement of freight and individuals within the region;

(v)   federally-funded research at institutions of higher education; and

(vi)   conservation land management;

(5)   work with State, tribal, and local agencies in developing appropriate model legislation;

(6)   enhance the capacity of, and provide support for, multistate development and research organizations, local development organizations and districts, and resource conservation districts in the region;

(7)   encourage private investment in industrial, commercial, renewable energy, and other economic development projects in the region; and

(8)   cooperate with and assist State governments with economic development programs of participating States.

(e) ADMINISTRATION.—In carrying out subsection (d), the Authority may—

(1)   hold such hearings, sit and act at such times and places, take such testimony, receive such evidence, and print or otherwise reproduce and distribute a description of the proceedings and reports on actions by the Authority as the Authority considers appropriate;

(2)   authorize, through the Federal, State, or tribal cochairperson or any other

SEC. 383B. [7 U.S.C. 2009bb–1] NORTHERN
GREAT PLAINS REGIONAL AUTHORITY.

Northern Great Plains Regional Authority

member of the Authority designated by the Authority, the administration of oaths if the Authority determines that testimony should be taken or evidence received under oath;

(3)   request from any Federal, State, tribal, or local agency such information as may be available to or procurable by the agency that may be of use to the Authority in carrying out the duties of the Authority;

(4)   adopt, amend, and repeal bylaws and rules governing the conduct of business and the performance of duties of the Authority;

(5)   request the head of any Federal agency to detail to the Authority such personnel as the Authority requires to carry out duties of the Authority, each such detail to be without loss of seniority, pay, or other employee status;

(6)   request the head of any State agency, tribal government, or local government to detail to the Authority such personnel as the Authority requires to carry out duties of the Authority, each such detail to be without loss of seniority, pay, or other employee status;

(7) provide for coverage of Authority employees in a suitable retirement and employee benefit system by—

(A)   making arrangements or entering into contracts with any participating State government or tribal government; or

(B)   otherwise providing retirement and other employee benefit coverage;

(8)   accept, use, and dispose of gifts or donations of services or real, personal, tangible, or intangible property;

(9) enter into and perform such contracts, leases, cooperative agreements, or other transactions as are necessary to carry out Authority duties, including any contracts, leases, or cooperative agreements with—

(A)   any department, agency, or instrumentality of the United States;

(B)   any State (including a political subdivision, agency, or instrumentality of the State);

(C)   any Indian tribe in the region; or

(D)   any person, firm, association, or corporation; and

(10)   establish and maintain a central office and field offices at such locations as the Authority may select.

(f) FEDERAL AGENCY COOPERATION.—A Federal agency shall—

(1)   cooperate with the Authority; and

(2)   provide, on request of a cochairperson, appropriate assistance in carrying out this subtitle, in accordance with applicable Federal laws (including regulations).

(g) ADMINISTRATIVE EXPENSES.—

(1) FEDERAL SHARE.—The Federal share of the administrative expenses of the Authority shall be—

(A)   for each of fiscal years 2008 and 2009, 100 percent;

SEC. 383B. [7 U.S.C. 2009bb–1] NORTHERN
GREAT PLAINS REGIONAL AUTHORITY.

Northern Great Plains Regional Authority

    (B)   for fiscal year 2010, 75 percent; and

    (C)   for fiscal year 2011 and each fiscal year thereafter, 50 percent.

  (2) NON-FEDERAL SHARE.—

    (A) IN GENERAL.— The non-Federal share of the administrative expenses of the Authority shall be paid by non-Federal sources in the States that participate in the Authority.

    (B) SHARE PAID BY EACH STATE.— The share of administrative expenses of the Authority to be paid by non-Federal sources in each State shall be determined by the Authority.

    (C) NO FEDERAL PARTICIPATION.— The Federal cochairperson shall not participate or vote in any decision under subparagraph (B).

    (D) DELINQUENT STATES.—If a State is delinquent in payment of the State's share of administrative expenses of the Authority under this subsection—

      (i)   no assistance under this subtitle shall be provided to the State (including assistance to a political subdivision or a resident of the State); and

      (ii)   no member of the Authority from the State shall participate or vote in any action by the Authority.

(h) COMPENSATION.—

  (1) FEDERAL AND TRIBAL COCHAIRPERSONS.— The Federal cochairperson and the tribal cochairperson shall be compensated by the Federal Government at the annual rate of basic pay prescribed for level III of the Executive Schedule in subchapter II of chapter 53 of title 5, United States Code.

  (2) ALTERNATE FEDERAL AND TRIBAL COCHAIRPERSONS.—The alternate Federal cochairperson and the alternate tribal cochairperson—

    (A)   shall be compensated by the Federal Government at the annual rate of basic pay prescribed for level V of the Executive Schedule described in paragraph (1); and

    (B)   when not actively serving as an alternate, shall perform such functions and duties as are delegated by the Federal cochairperson or the tribal cochairperson, respectively.

  (3) STATE MEMBERS AND ALTERNATES.—

    (A) IN GENERAL.— A State shall compensate each member and alternate representing the State on the Authority at the rate established by State law.

    (B) NO ADDITIONAL COMPENSATION.— No State member or alternate member shall receive any salary, or any contribution to or supplementation of salary from any source other than the State for services provided by the member or alternate member to the Authority.

  (4) DETAILED EMPLOYEES.—

    (A) IN GENERAL.—No person detailed to serve the Authority under subsection (e)(6) shall receive any salary or any contribution to or supplementation of salary for services provided to the Authority from—

SEC. 383B. [7 U.S.C. 2009bb–1] NORTHERN
GREAT PLAINS REGIONAL AUTHORITY.

Northern Great Plains Regional Authority

(i)   any source other than the State, tribal, local, or
intergovernmental agency from which the person was detailed; or

(ii)   the Authority.

(B) VIOLATION.— Any person that violates this paragraph shall be fined
not more than $5,000, imprisoned not more than 1 year, or both.

(C) APPLICABLE LAW.— The Federal cochairperson, the alternate
Federal cochairperson, and any Federal officer or employee detailed to duty
on the Authority under subsection (e)(5) shall not be subject to subparagraph
(A), but shall remain subject to sections 202 through 209 of title 18, United
States Code.

(5) ADDITIONAL PERSONNEL.—

(A) COMPENSATION.—

(i) IN GENERAL.— The Authority may appoint and fix the
compensation of an executive director and such other personnel as are
necessary to enable the Authority to carry out the duties of the
Authority.

(ii) EXCEPTION.— Compensation under clause (i) shall not exceed
the maximum rate for the Senior Executive Service under section 5382
of title 5, United States Code, including any applicable locality-based
comparability payment that may be authorized under section
5304(h)(2)(C) of that title.

(B) EXECUTIVE DIRECTOR.—The executive director shall be responsible
for—

(i)   the carrying out of the administrative duties of the Authority;

(ii)   direction of the Authority staff; and

(iii)   such other duties as the Authority may assign.

(C) NO FEDERAL EMPLOYEE STATUS.— No member, alternate, officer, or
employee of the Authority (except the Federal cochairperson of the Authority,
the alternate and staff for the Federal cochairperson, and any Federal
employee detailed to the Authority under subsection (e)(5)) shall be
considered to be a Federal employee for any purpose.

(i) CONFLICTS OF INTEREST.—

(1) IN GENERAL.—Except as provided under paragraph (2), no State member,
Indian tribe member, State alternate, officer, or employee of the Authority shall
participate personally and substantially as a member, alternate, officer, or employee
of the Authority, through decision, approval, disapproval, recommendation, the
rendering of advice, investigation, or otherwise, in any proceeding, application,
request for a ruling or other determination, contract, claim, controversy, or other
matter in which, to knowledge of the member, alternate, officer, or employee—

(A)   the member, alternate, officer, or employee;

(B)   the spouse, minor child, partner, or organization (other than a
State or political subdivision of the State or the Indian tribe) of the member,
alternate, officer, or employee, in which the member, alternate, officer, or

employee is serving as officer, director, trustee, partner, or employee; or

(C)   any person or organization with whom the member, alternate, officer, or employee is negotiating or has any arrangement concerning prospective employment;

has a financial interest.

(2) DISCLOSURE.—Paragraph (1) shall not apply if the State member, Indian tribe member, alternate, officer, or employee—

(A)   immediately advises the Authority of the nature and circumstances of the proceeding, application, request for a ruling or other determination, contract, claim, controversy, or other particular matter presenting a potential conflict of interest;

(B)   makes full disclosure of the financial interest; and

(C)   before the proceeding concerning the matter presenting the conflict of interest, receives a written determination by the Authority that the interest is not so substantial as to be likely to affect the integrity of the services that the Authority may expect from the State member, Indian tribe member, alternate, officer, or employee.

(3) VIOLATION.—   Any person that violates this subsection shall be fined not more than $10,000, imprisoned not more than 2 years, or both.

(j) VALIDITY OF CONTRACTS, LOANS, AND GRANTS.—   The Authority may declare void any contract, loan, or grant of or by the Authority in relation to which the Authority determines that there has been a violation of any provision under subsection (h)(4) or subsection (i) of this subtitle, or sections 202 through 209 of title 18, United States Code.

SEC. 383C. [7 U.S.C. 2009bb–1a] INTERSTATE COOPERATION FOR ECONOMIC OPPORTUNITY AND EFFICIENCY.

(a) IN GENERAL.—The Authority shall provide assistance to States in developing regional plans to address multistate economic issues, including plans—

(1)   to develop a regional transmission system for movement of renewable energy to markets outside the region;

(2)   to address regional transportation concerns, including the establishment of a Northern Great Plains Regional Transportation Working Group;

(3)   to encourage and support interstate collaboration on federally-funded research that is in the national interest; and

(4)   to establish a Regional Working Group on Agriculture Development and Transportation.

(b) ECONOMIC ISSUES.—The multistate economic issues referred to in subsection (a) shall include—

(1)   renewable energy development and transmission;

(2)   transportation planning and economic development;

(3)   information technology;

(4)   movement of freight and individuals within the region;

(5)   federally-funded research at institutions of higher education; and

(6)   conservation land management.

SEC. 383D. [7 U.S.C. 2009bb–2] ECONOMIC AND COMMUNITY DEVELOPMENT GRANTS.

(a) IN GENERAL.—The Authority may approve grants to States, Indian tribes, local governments, and public and nonprofit organizations for projects, approved in accordance with section 383J—

(1)   to assist the region in obtaining the job training, employment-related education, and business development (with an emphasis on entrepreneurship) that are needed to build and maintain strong local economies;

(2)   to develop the transportation, renewable energy transmission, and telecommunication infrastructure of the region for the purpose of facilitating economic development in the region (except that grants for this purpose may be made only to States, Indian tribes, local governments, and nonprofit organizations);

(3)   to provide assistance to severely distressed and underdeveloped areas that lack financial resources for improving basic public services;

(4)   to provide assistance to severely distressed and underdeveloped areas that lack financial resources for equipping industrial parks and related facilities; and

(5)   to otherwise achieve the purposes of this subtitle.

(b) FUNDING.—

(1) IN GENERAL.—Funds for grants under subsection (a) may be provided—

(A)   entirely from appropriations to carry out this section;

(B)   in combination with funds available under another Federal grant program; or

(C)   from any other source.

(2) PRIORITY OF FUNDING.—To best build the foundations for long-term economic development and to complement other Federal, State, and tribal resources in the region, Federal funds available under this subtitle shall be focused on the following activities:

(A)   Basic public infrastructure in distressed counties and isolated areas of distress.

(B)   Transportation and telecommunication infrastructure for the purpose of facilitating economic development in the region.

(C)   Business development, with emphasis on entrepreneurship.

(D)   Job training or employment-related education, with emphasis on use of existing public educational institutions located in the region.

SEC. 383E. [7 U.S.C. 2009bb–3] SUPPLEMENTS TO FEDERAL GRANT PROGRAMS.

(a) FINDING.—Congress finds that certain States and local communities of the region may be unable to take maximum advantage of Federal grant programs for which the States and communities are eligible because—

(1)   they lack the economic resources to provide the required matching share; or

(2)   there are insufficient funds available under the applicable Federal law authorizing the Federal grant program to meet pressing needs of the region.

(b) FEDERAL GRANT PROGRAM FUNDING.—Notwithstanding any provision of law limiting the Federal share, the areas eligible for assistance, or the authorizations of appropriations, under any Federal grant program, and in accordance with subsection (c), the Authority, with the approval of the Federal cochairperson and with respect to a project to be carried out in the region—

(1)   may increase the Federal share of the costs of a project under any Federal grant program to not more than 90 percent (except as provided in section 383G(b)); and

(2)   shall use amounts made available to carry out this subtitle to pay the increased Federal share.

(c) CERTIFICATIONS.—

(1) IN GENERAL.—In the case of any project for which all or any portion of the basic Federal share of the costs of the project is proposed to be paid under this section, no Federal contribution shall be made until the Federal official administering the Federal law that authorizes the Federal grant program certifies that the project—

(A)   meets (except as provided in subsection (b)) the applicable requirements of the applicable Federal grant program; and

(B)   could be approved for Federal contribution under the Federal grant program if funds were available under the law for the project.

(2) CERTIFICATION BY AUTHORITY.—

(A) IN GENERAL.—The certifications and determinations required to be made by the Authority for approval of projects under this Act in accordance with section 383J—

(i)   shall be controlling; and

(ii)   shall be accepted by the Federal agencies.

(B) ACCEPTANCE BY FEDERAL COCHAIRPERSON.— In the case of any project described in paragraph (1), any finding, report, certification, or documentation required to be submitted with respect to the project to the head of the department, agency, or instrumentality of the Federal Government responsible for the administration of the Federal grant program under which the project is carried out shall be accepted by the Federal cochairperson.

SEC. 383F. [7 U.S.C. 2009bb–4] MULTISTATE AND LOCAL DEVELOPMENT DISTRICTS AND ORGANIZATIONS AND NORTHERN GREAT PLAINS INC.

(a) DEFINITION OF MULTISTATE AND LOCAL DEVELOPMENT DISTRICT OR ORGANIZATION.—In this section, the term multistate and local development district or organization means an entity—

(1) that—

(A)   is a planning district in existence on the date of enactment of this subtitle that is recognized by the Economic Development Administration of the Department of Commerce; or

(B) is—

(i)   organized and operated in a manner that ensures broad-based community participation and an effective opportunity for other nonprofit groups to contribute to the development and implementation of programs in the region;

(ii)   a nonprofit incorporated body organized or chartered under the law of the State in which the entity is located;

(iii)   a nonprofit agency or instrumentality of a State or local government;

(iv)   a public organization established before the date of enactment of this subtitle under State law for creation of multijurisdictional, area-wide planning organizations;

(v)   a nonprofit agency or instrumentality of a State that was established for the purpose of assisting with multistate cooperation; or

(vi)   a nonprofit association or combination of bodies, agencies, and instrumentalities described in clauses (ii) through (v); and

(2) that has not, as certified by the Authority (in consultation with the Federal cochairperson or Secretary, as appropriate)—

(A)   inappropriately used Federal grant funds from any Federal source; or

(B)   appointed an officer who, during the period in which another entity inappropriately used Federal grant funds from any Federal source, was an officer of the other entity.

(b) Grants to Multistate, Local, or Regional Development Districts and Organizations.—

(1) In general.— The Authority may make grants for administrative expenses under this section to multistate, local, and regional development districts and organizations.

(2) Conditions for grants.—

(A) Maximum amount.— The amount of any grant awarded under paragraph (1) shall not exceed 80 percent of the administrative expenses of the multistate, local, or regional development district or organization receiving the grant.

(B) Maximum period.— No grant described in paragraph (1) shall be awarded for a period greater than 3 years.

(3) Local share.— The contributions of a multistate, local, or regional development district or organization for administrative expenses may be in cash or in kind, fairly evaluated, including space, equipment, and services.

(c) Duties.—

(1) In general.— Except as provided in paragraph (2), a local development

district shall operate as a lead organization serving multicounty areas in the region at the local level.

(2) DESIGNATION.— The Federal cochairperson may designate an Indian tribe or multijurisdictional organization to serve as a lead organization in such cases as the Federal cochairperson or Secretary, as appropriate, determines appropriate.

(d) NORTHERN GREAT PLAINS INC.—Northern Great Plains Inc., a nonprofit corporation incorporated in the State of Minnesota to implement the recommendations of the Northern Great Plains Rural Development Commission established by the Northern Great Plains Rural Development Act (7 U.S.C. 2661 note; Public Law 103–318)—

(1) shall serve as an independent, primary resource for the Authority on issues of concern to the region;

(2) shall advise the Authority on development of international trade;

(3) may provide research, education, training, and other support to the Authority; and

(4) may carry out other activities on its own behalf or on behalf of other entities.

SEC. 383G. [7 U.S.C. 2009bb–5] DISTRESSED COUNTIES AND AREAS AND NONDISTRESSED COUNTIES.

(a) DESIGNATIONS.—Not later than 90 days after the date of enactment of this subtitle, and annually thereafter, the Authority, in accordance with such criteria as the Authority may establish, shall designate—

(1) as distressed counties, counties in the region that are the most severely and persistently distressed and underdeveloped and have high rates of poverty, unemployment, or outmigration;

(2) as nondistressed counties, counties in the region that are not designated as distressed counties under paragraph (1); and

(3) as isolated areas of distress, areas located in nondistressed counties (as designated under paragraph (2)) that have high rates of poverty, unemployment, or outmigration.

(b) DISTRESSED COUNTIES.—

(1) IN GENERAL.— The Authority shall allocate at least 50 percent of the appropriations made available under section 383N for programs and projects designed to serve the needs of distressed counties and isolated areas of distress in the region.

(2) FUNDING LIMITATIONS.— The funding limitations under section 383E(b) shall not apply to a project to provide transportation or telecommunication or basic public services to residents of 1 or more distressed counties or isolated areas of distress in the region.

(c) TRANSPORTATION TELECOMMUNICATION, RENEWABLE ENERGY, AND BASIC PUBLIC INFRASTRUCTURE.— The Authority shall allocate at least 50 percent of any funds made available under section 383N for transportation, telecommunication, renewable energy, and basic public infrastructure projects authorized under paragraphs

SEC. 383H. [7 U.S.C. 2009bb–6]
DEVELOPMENT PLANNING PROCESS.

Northern Great Plains Regional Authority

(1) and (3) of section 383D(a).

SEC. 383H. [7 U.S.C. 2009bb–6] DEVELOPMENT PLANNING PROCESS.

(a) STATE DEVELOPMENT PLAN.— In accordance with policies established by the Authority, each State member shall submit a development plan for the area of the region represented by the State member.

(b) CONTENT OF PLAN.— A State development plan submitted under subsection (a) shall reflect the goals, objectives, and priorities identified in the regional development plan developed under section 383B(d)(2).

(c) CONSULTATION WITH INTERESTED LOCAL PARTIES.—In carrying out the development planning process (including the selection of programs and projects for assistance), a State may—

(1) consult with—

(A) multistate, regional, and local development districts and organizations; and

(B) local units of government; and

(2) take into consideration the goals, objectives, priorities, and recommendations of the entities described in paragraph (1).

(d) PUBLIC PARTICIPATION.—

(1) IN GENERAL.— The Authority and applicable multistate, regional, and local development districts and organizations shall encourage and assist, to the maximum extent practicable, public participation in the development, revision, and implementation of all plans and programs under this subtitle.

(2) REGULATIONS.— The Authority shall develop guidelines for providing public participation described in paragraph (1), including public hearings.

SEC. 383I. [7 U.S.C. 2009bb–7] PROGRAM DEVELOPMENT CRITERIA.

(a) IN GENERAL.—In considering programs and projects to be provided assistance under this subtitle, and in establishing a priority ranking of the requests for assistance provided to the Authority, the Authority shall follow procedures that ensure, to the maximum extent practicable, consideration of—

(1) the relationship of the project or class of projects to overall multistate or regional development;

(2) the per capita income and poverty and unemployment and outmigration rates in an area;

(3) the financial resources available to the applicants for assistance seeking to carry out the project, with emphasis on ensuring that projects are adequately financed to maximize the probability of successful economic development;

(4) the importance of the project or class of projects in relation to other projects or classes of projects that may be in competition for the same funds;

(5) the prospects that the project for which assistance is sought will improve, on a continuing rather than a temporary basis, the opportunities for employment, the average level of income, or the economic development of the area to be served

by the project; and

(6) the extent to which the project design provides for detailed outcome measurements by which grant expenditures and the results of the expenditures may be evaluated.

(b) No RELOCATION ASSISTANCE.— No financial assistance authorized by this subtitle shall be used to assist a person or entity in relocating from one area to another, except that financial assistance may be used as otherwise authorized by this title to attract businesses from outside the region to the region.

(c) MAINTENANCE OF EFFORT.— Funds may be provided for a program or project in a State under this subtitle only if the Authority determines that the level of Federal or State financial assistance provided under a law other than this subtitle, for the same type of program or project in the same area of the State within the region, will not be reduced as a result of funds made available by this subtitle.

SEC. 383J. [7 U.S.C. 2009bb–8] APPROVAL OF DEVELOPMENT PLANS AND PROJECTS.

(a) IN GENERAL.— A State or regional development plan or any multistate subregional plan that is proposed for development under this subtitle shall be reviewed by the Authority.

(b) EVALUATION BY STATE MEMBER.— An application for a grant or any other assistance for a project under this subtitle shall be made through and evaluated for approval by the State member of the Authority representing the applicant.

(c) CERTIFICATION.—An application for a grant or other assistance for a project shall be approved only on certification by the State member that the application for the project—

(1) describes ways in which the project complies with any applicable State development plan;

(2) meets applicable criteria under section 383I;

(3) provides adequate assurance that the proposed project will be properly administered, operated, and maintained; and

(4) otherwise meets the requirements of this subtitle.

(d) VOTES FOR DECISIONS.— On certification by a State member of the Authority of an application for a grant or other assistance for a specific project under this section, an affirmative vote of the Authority under section 383B(c) shall be required for approval of the application.

SEC. 383K. [7 U.S.C. 2009bb–9] CONSENT OF STATES.

Nothing in this subtitle requires any State to engage in or accept any program under this subtitle without the consent of the State.

SEC. 383L. [7 U.S.C. 2009bb–10] RECORDS.

(a) RECORDS OF THE AUTHORITY.—

(1) IN GENERAL.— The Authority shall maintain accurate and complete records of all transactions and activities of the Authority.

(2) AVAILABILITY.— All records of the Authority shall be available for audit

and examination by the Comptroller General of the United States and the Inspector General of the Department of Agriculture (including authorized representatives of the Comptroller General and the Inspector General of the Department of Agriculture).

(b) RECORDS OF RECIPIENTS OF FEDERAL ASSISTANCE. —

(1) IN GENERAL.— A recipient of Federal funds under this subtitle shall, as required by the Authority, maintain accurate and complete records of transactions and activities financed with Federal funds and report to the Authority on the transactions and activities to the Authority.

(2) AVAILABILITY.— All records required under paragraph (1) shall be available for audit by the Comptroller General of the United States, the Inspector General of the Department of Agriculture, and the Authority (including authorized representatives of the Comptroller General, the Inspector General of the Department of Agriculture, and the Authority).

(c) ANNUAL AUDIT.— The Inspector General of the Department of Agriculture shall audit the activities, transactions, and records of the Authority on an annual basis for any fiscal year for which funds are appropriated.

SEC. 383M. [7 U.S.C. 2009bb–11] ANNUAL REPORT.

Not later than 180 days after the end of each fiscal year, the Authority shall submit to the President and to Congress a report describing the activities carried out under this subtitle.

SEC. 383N. [7 U.S.C. 2009bb–12] AUTHORIZATION OF APPROPRIATIONS.

(a) IN GENERAL.— There is authorized to be appropriated to the Authority to carry out this subtitle $40,000,000 for each of fiscal years 2025 through 2029, to remain available until expended.

(b) ADMINISTRATIVE EXPENSES.— Not more than 5 percent of the amount appropriated under subsection (a) for a fiscal year shall be used for administrative expenses of the Authority.

(c) MINIMUM STATE SHARE OF GRANTS.—Notwithstanding any other provision of this subtitle, for any fiscal year, the aggregate amount of grants received by a State and all persons or entities in the State under this subtitle shall be not less than ⅓ of the product obtained by multiplying—

(1) the aggregate amount of grants under this subtitle for the fiscal year; and

(2) the ratio that—

(A) the population of the State (as determined by the Secretary of Commerce based on the most recent decennial census for which data are available); bears to

(B) the population of the region (as so determined).

★

FEDERAL CAPITAL INVESTMENT PROGRAM INFORMATION ACT OF 1984

TITLE 31 U.S.C. SEC. 1105(E)

TITLE 31—MONEY AND FINANCE

This title was enacted by Pub. L. 97–258, §1, Sept. 13, 1982, 96 Stat. 877

CHAPTER 11—THE BUDGET AND FISCAL, BUDGET, AND PROGRAM INFORMATION

§1101. Definitions

Short Title of 1984 Amendment

Pub. L. 98–501, title II, §201, Oct. 19, 1984, 98 Stat. 2324, provided that: "This title [amending section 1105 of this title and enacting provisions set out as a note under section 1105 of this title] may be cited as the 'Federal Capital Investment Program Information Act of 1984'."

(Pub. L. 97–258, Sept. 13, 1982, 96 Stat. 907.)

* * * * * * *

§1105. Budget contents and submission to Congress

* * * * * * *

(e)(1) The President shall submit with materials related to each budget transmitted under subsection (a) on or after January 1, 1985, an analysis for the ensuing fiscal year that shall identify requested appropriations or new obligational authority and outlays for each major program that may be classified as a public civilian capital investment program and for each major program that may be classified as a military capital investment program, and shall contain summaries of the total amount of such appropriations or new obligational authority and outlays for public civilian capital investment programs and summaries of the total amount of such appropriations or new obligational authority and outlays for military capital investment programs. In addition, the analysis under this paragraph shall contain— * * *

[See next section for text of Secction 1105(e) of Title 31, United States Code.]

Amendments

1984—Subsec. (e). Pub. L. 98–501 added subsec. (e).

* * * * * * *

FEDERAL CAPITAL INVESTMENT PROGRAM; CONGRESSIONAL STATEMENT OF PURPOSES

Pub. L. 98–501, title II, §202, Oct. 19, 1984, 98 Stat. 2324, provided that: "The purposes of this title [amending this section and enacting provisions set out as notes under this section and section 1101 of this title] are—

"(1) to provide budget projections for major Federal capital investment programs;

"(2) to provide a summary of the most recent needs assessment analyses for these programs;

"(3) to provide information on the sensitivity of the needs estimates to major policy issues and technical and economic variables;

"(4) to assist the planning capabilities of State and local governments on the assessment of major capital investment programs; and

"(5) to improve legislative oversight over Federal capital investment programs."

TITLE 31 U.S.C. SEC. 1105(E)

TITLE 31—MONEY AND FINANCE

This title was enacted by Pub. L. 97–258, §1, Sept. 13, 1982, 96 Stat. 877

Subtitle	Sec.

* * * * * * *

II. The Budget Process	1101

* * * * * * *

SUBTITLE II—THE BUDGET PROCESS

Chap.		Sec.
11.	The Budget and Fiscal, Budget, and Program Information	1101

* * * * * * *

CHAPTER 11—THE BUDGET AND FISCAL, BUDGET, AND PROGRAM INFORMATION

Sec.

* * * * * * *

1105.	Budget contents and submission to Congress.

* * * * * * *

§1105. BUDGET CONTENTS AND SUBMISSION TO CONGRESS

* * * * * * *

(e)(1) The President shall submit with materials related to each budget transmitted under subsection (a) on or after January 1, 1985, an analysis for the ensuing fiscal year that shall identify requested appropriations or new obligational authority and outlays for each major program that may be classified as a public civilian capital investment program and for each major program that may be classified as a military capital investment program, and shall contain summaries of the total amount of such appropriations or new obligational authority and outlays for public civilian capital investment programs and summaries of the total amount of such appropriations or new obligational authority and outlays for military capital investment programs. In addition, the analysis under this paragraph shall contain—

(A) an estimate of the current service levels of public civilian capital investment and of military capital investment and alternative high and low levels of such investments over a period of ten years in current dollars and over a period of five years in constant dollars;

(B) the most recent assessment analysis and summary, in a standard format, of public civilian capital investment needs in each major program area over a period of ten years;

(C) an identification and analysis of the principal policy issues that affect estimated public civilian capital investment needs for each major program; and

(D) an identification and analysis of factors that affect estimated public civilian capital investment needs for each major program, including but not limited to the following factors:

(i) economic assumptions;

(ii) engineering standards;

(iii) estimates of spending for operation and maintenance;

(iv) estimates of expenditures for similar investments by State and local governments; and

(v) estimates of demand for public services derived from such capital investments and estimates of the service capacity of such investments.

To the extent that any analysis required by this paragraph relates to any program for which Federal financial assistance is distributed under a formula prescribed by law, such analysis shall be organized by State and within each State by major metropolitan area if data are available.

(2) For purposes of this subsection, any appropriation, new obligational authority, or outlay shall be classified as a public civilian capital investment to the extent that such appropriation, authority, or outlay will be used for the construction, acquisition, or rehabilitation of any physical asset that is capable of being used to produce services or other benefits for a number of years and is not classified as a military capital investment under paragraph (3). Such assets shall include (but not be limited to)—

(A) roadways or bridges,

(B) airports or airway facilities,

(C) mass transportation systems,

(D) wastewater treatment or related facilities,

(E) water resources projects,

(F) hospitals,

(G) resource recovery facilities,

(H) public buildings,

(I) space or communications facilities,

(J) railroads, and

(K) federally assisted housing.

(3) For purposes of this subsection, any appropriation, new obligational authority, or outlay shall be classified as a military capital investment to the extent that such appropriation, authority, or outlay will be used for the construction, acquisition, or

rehabilitation of any physical asset that is capable of being used to produce services or other benefits for purposes of national defense and security for a number of years. Such assets shall include military bases, posts, installations, and facilities.

(4) Criteria and guidelines for use in the identification of public civilian and military capital investments, for distinguishing between public civilian and military capital investments, and for distinguishing between major and nonmajor capital investment programs shall be issued by the Director of the Office of Management and Budget after consultation with the Comptroller General and the Congressional Budget Office. The analysis submitted under this subsection shall be accompanied by an explanation of such criteria and guidelines.

(5) For purposes of this subsection—

(A) the term "construction" includes the design, planning, and erection of new structures and facilities, the expansion of existing structures and facilities, the reconstruction of a project at an existing site or adjacent to an existing site, and the installation of initial and replacement equipment for such structures and facilities;

(B) the term "acquisition" includes the addition of land, sites, equipment, structures, facilities, or rolling stock by purchase, lease-purchase, trade, or donation; and

(C) the term "rehabilitation" includes the alteration of or correction of deficiencies in an existing structure or facility so as to extend the useful life or improve the effectiveness of the structure or facility, the modernization or replacement of equipment at an existing structure or facility, and the modernization of, or replacement of parts for, rolling stock.

* * * * * * *

(Pub. L. 97–258, Sept. 13, 1982, 96 Stat. 908; Pub. L. 97–452, §1(2), Jan. 12, 1983, 96 Stat. 2467; Pub. L. 98–501, title II, §203, Oct. 19, 1984, 98 Stat. 2324; Pub. L. 99–177, title II, §241, Dec. 12, 1985, 99 Stat. 1063; Pub. L. 100–119, title I, §106(f), Sept. 29, 1987, 101 Stat. 781; Pub. L. 100–418, title V, §5301, Aug. 23, 1988, 102 Stat. 1462; Pub. L. 100–504, title I, §108, Oct. 18, 1988, 102 Stat. 2529; Pub. L. 100–690, title I, §1006, Nov. 18, 1988, 102 Stat. 4187; Pub. L. 101–508, title XIII, §13112(c), Nov. 5, 1990, 104 Stat. 1388–608; Pub. L. 101–576, title II, §203(b), Nov. 15, 1990, 104 Stat. 2841; Pub. L. 103–62, §4(a), Aug. 3, 1993, 107 Stat. 286; Pub. L. 103–272, §4(f)(1)(E), July 5, 1994, 108 Stat. 1362; Pub. L. 103–322, title XXXI, §310001(e), Sept. 13, 1994, 108 Stat. 2103; Pub. L. 103–355, title II, §2454(a), Oct. 13, 1994, 108 Stat. 3326; Pub. L. 104–287, §4(1), Oct. 11, 1996, 110 Stat. 3388; Pub. L. 105–33, title X, §10209(b), Aug. 5, 1997, 111 Stat. 711; Pub. L. 105–277, div. C, title VII, §713(c), Oct. 21, 1998, 112 Stat. 2681–693; Pub. L. 106–58, title VI, §638(f), Sept. 29, 1999, 113 Stat. 475; Pub. L. 106–422, §2(c), Nov. 1, 2000, 114 Stat. 1874; Pub. L. 107–189, §4(a), June 14, 2002, 116 Stat. 699; Pub. L. 107–217, §3(h)(3), Aug. 21, 2002, 116 Stat. 1299; Pub. L. 107–296, title VIII, §889(a), Nov. 25, 2002, 116 Stat. 2250; Pub. L. 108–173, title VIII, §802(a), Dec. 8, 2003, 117 Stat. 2360; Pub. L. 108–178, §4(f)(1), Dec. 15, 2003, 117 Stat. 2641; Pub. L. 110–343, div. A, title II, §203(a), Oct. 3, 2008, 122 Stat. 3801; Pub. L. 110–409, §7(d)(2), Oct. 14, 2008, 122 Stat. 4313; Pub. L. 111–81, §2, Oct. 22, 2009, 123 Stat. 2137; Pub. L. 111–291, title IV, §§411(h), 415, Dec. 8, 2010, 124 Stat. 3116, 3121; Pub. L. 111–352, §11(a), Jan. 4, 2011, 124 Stat. 3881; Pub. L. 113–235, div. I, title II, §244(d), Dec. 16, 2014, 128 Stat. 2569; Pub. L. 114–315, title VI, §601(b), Dec. 16, 2016, 130 Stat. 1569; Pub. L. 115–31, div. E, title VI, §630(a), May 5, 2017, 131 Stat. 375; Pub. L. 117–40, §2(b), Sept. 24, 2021, 135 Stat. 338; Pub. L. 117–286, §4(b)(50), Dec. 27, 2022, 136 Stat. 4348; Pub. L. 118–172, §2(b), Dec. 23, 2024, 138 Stat. 2595.)

DELTA REGIONAL AUTHORITY ACT OF 2000 TITLE V OF THE COMMODITY FUTURES MODERNIZATION ACT OF 2000

PUBLIC LAW 106554
AS AMENDED THROUGH PUB. L. 117-339

DELTA REGIONAL AUTHORITY ACT OF 2000

Title V of the Commodity Futures Modernization Act of 2000

[Appendix D & E of PL 106–554; Enacted December 21, 2000]

[As Amended Through P.L. 117–339, Enacted January 5, 2023]

SECTION 1. [7 U.S.C. 1 note] SHORT TITLE; TABLE OF CONTENTS.

(a) SHORT TITLE.— This Act may be cited as the "Commodity Futures Modernization Act of 2000".

* * * * * * *

* * * * * * *

TITLE V—LOWER MISSISSIPPI RIVER REGION[3]

---

[3]   This is part of appendix D.

SEC. 501. [7 U.S.C. 1921 note] SHORT TITLE.

This title may be cited as the "Delta Regional Authority Act of 2000".

SEC. 502. [7 U.S.C. 2009aa note] FINDINGS AND PURPOSES.

(a) FINDINGS.—Congress finds that—

(1)   the lower Mississippi River region (referred to in this title as the region), though rich in natural and human resources, lags behind the rest of the United States in economic growth and prosperity;

(2)   the region suffers from a greater proportion of measurable poverty and unemployment than any other region of the United States;

(3)   the greatest hope for economic growth and revitalization in the region lies in the development of transportation infrastructure, creation of jobs, expansion of businesses, and development of entrepreneurial local economies;

(4)   the economic progress of the region requires an adequate transportation and physical infrastructure, a skilled and trained workforce, and greater opportunities for enterprise development and entrepreneurship;

(5)   a concerted and coordinated effort among Federal, State, and local agencies, the private sector, and nonprofit groups is needed if the region is to

achieve its full potential for economic development;

(6)   economic development planning on a regional or multicounty basis offers the best prospect for achieving the maximum benefit from public and private investments; and

(7)   improving the economy of the region requires a special emphasis on areas of the region that are most economically distressed.

(b) PURPOSES.—The purposes of this title are—

(1) to promote and encourage the economic development of the region—

(A)   to ensure that the communities and people in the region have the opportunity for economic development; and

(B)   to ensure that the economy of the region reaches economic parity with that of the rest of the United States;

(2)   to establish a formal framework for joint Federal-State collaboration in meeting and focusing national attention on the economic development needs of the region;

(3)   to assist the region in obtaining the transportation and basic infrastructure, skills training, and opportunities for economic development that are essential for strong local economies;

(4)   to foster coordination among all levels of government, the private sector, and nonprofit groups in crafting common regional strategies that will lead to broader economic growth;

(5)   to strengthen efforts that emphasize regional approaches to economic development and planning;

(6)   to encourage the participation of interested citizens, public officials, agencies, and others in developing and implementing local and regional plans for broad-based economic and community development; and

(7)   to focus special attention on areas of the region that suffer from the greatest economic distress.

SEC. 503. DELTA REGIONAL AUTHORITY. [Amends the Consolidated Farm and Rural Development Act (7 U.S.C. 1921 et seq.) by adding at the end a new subtitle F, which appears elsewhere in this compilation.]

SEC. 504. AREA COVERED BY LOWER MISSISSIPPI DELTA DEVELOPMENT COMMISSION.[4]

---

[4]   The amendment by section 153(b) of Public Law 106–554 (114 Stat. 2763A–252) which attempts to insert a new paragraph (4) at the end of section 382A of the Delta Regional Authority Act of 2000, probably should have been made to such section of the Consolidated Farm and Rural Development Act.

(a) IN GENERAL.—[Amends section 4(2)(D) of the Delta Development Act (42 U.S.C. 3121 note; 102 Stat. 2246).]

(b) CONFORMING AMENDMENT.—[Amends the matter under the heading salaries and expenses under the heading Farmers Home Administration in title II of Public Law 100–460 (102 Stat. 2246).]

* * * * * * *

SEC. 542. [42 U.S.C. 1395W–4 Note] TREATMENT OF CERTAIN PHYSICIAN PATHOLOGY SERVICES UNDER MEDICARE.

(a) IN GENERAL.— When an independent laboratory furnishes the technical component of a physician pathology service to a fee-for-service medicare beneficiary who is an inpatient or outpatient of a covered hospital, the Secretary of Health and Human Services shall treat such component as a service for which payment shall be made to the laboratory under section 1848 of the Social Security Act (42 U.S.C. 1395w-4) and not as an inpatient hospital service for which payment is made to the hospital under section 1886(d) of such Act (42 U.S.C. 1395ww(d)) or as an outpatient hospital service for which payment is made to the hospital under section 1833(t) of such Act (42 U.S.C. 1395l(t)).

(b) DEFINITIONS.—For purposes of this section:

(1) COVERED HOSPITAL.— The term covered hospital means, with respect to an inpatient or an outpatient, a hospital that had an arrangement with an independent laboratory that was in effect as of July 22, 1999, under which a laboratory furnished the technical component of physician pathology services to fee- for-service medicare beneficiaries who were hospital inpatients or outpatients, respectively, and submitted claims for payment for such component to a medicare carrier (that has a contract with the Secretary under section 1842 of the Social Security Act, 42 U.S.C. 1395u) and not to such hospital.

(2) FEE-FOR-SERVICE MEDICARE BENEFICIARY.—The term fee-for-service medicare beneficiary means an individual who—

(A) is entitled to benefits under part A, or enrolled under part B, or both, of such title; and

(B) is not enrolled in any of the following:

(i) A Medicare+Choice plan under part C of such title.

(ii) A plan offered by an eligible organization under section 1876 of such Act (42 U.S.C. 1395mm).

(iii) A program of all-inclusive care for the elderly (PACE) under section 1894 of such Act (42 U.S.C. 1395eee).

(iv) A social health maintenance organization (SHMO) demonstration project established under section 4018(b) of the Omnibus Budget Reconciliation Act of 1987 (Public Law 100-203).

(c) EFFECTIVE DATE.— This section shall apply to services furnished during the 2-year period beginning on January 1, 2001, and for services furnished during 2005, 2006, 2007, 2008, 2009, 2010, 2011, and the first six months of 2012.

(d) GAO REPORT.—

(1) STUDY.— The Comptroller General of the United States shall conduct a study of the effects of the previous provisions of this section on hospitals and laboratories and access of fee-for-service medicare beneficiaries to the technical component of physician pathology services.

(2) REPORT.— Not later than April 1, 2002, the Comptroller General shall

submit to Congress a report on such study. The report shall include recommendations about whether such provisions should be extended after the end of the period specified in subsection (c) for either or both inpatient and outpatient hospital services, and whether the provisions should be extended to other hospitals.

★

ECONOMIC DEVELOPMENT REAUTHORIZATION ACT OF 2024
DIV. B, TITLE II, SUBTITLE B OF THE THOMAS R. CARPER WATER RESOURCES DEVELOPMENT ACT OF 2024

PUBLIC LAW118-272

ECONOMIC DEVELOPMENT REAUTHORIZATION ACT OF 2024

Div. B, Title II, Subtitle B of the Thomas R. Carper Water Resources Development Act of 2024

[(Public Law 118–272)]

[This law has not been amended]

AN ACT To provide for improvements to the rivers and harbors of the United States, to provide for the conservation and development of water and related resources, and for other purposes.

Be it enacted by the Senate and House of Representatives of the United States of America in Congress assembled,

* * * * * * *

DIVISION B— OTHER MATTERS

* * * * * * *

TITLE II— ECONOMIC DEVELOPMENT REAUTHORIZATION ACT OF 2024

SEC. 2201. [42 U.S.C. 3121 note] SHORT TITLE.
This title may be cited as the "Economic Development Reauthorization Act of 2024".

* * * * * * *

Subtitle B— REGIONAL ECONOMIC AND INFRASTRUCTURE DEVELOPMENT

SEC. 2241. REGIONAL COMMISSION AUTHORIZATIONS.
Section 15751 of title 40, United States Code, is amended by striking subsection (a) and inserting the following:

"(a) IN GENERAL.— There is authorized to be appropriated to each Commission to carry out this subtitle $40,000,000 for each of fiscal years 2025 through 2029.".

SEC. 2242. REGIONAL COMMISSION MODIFICATIONS.

(a) MEMBERSHIP OF COMMISSIONS.— Section 15301 of title 40, United States Code, is amended—

(1) in subsection (b)(2)(C)—

(A)   by striking An alternate member and inserting the following:

"(i) IN GENERAL.—   An alternate member"; and

(B)   by adding at the end the following:

"(ii) STATE ALTERNATES.—   If the alternate State member is unable to vote in accordance with clause (i), the alternate State member may delegate voting authority to a designee, subject to the condition that the executive director shall be notified, in writing, of the designation not less than 1 week before the applicable vote is to take place."; and

(2)   in subsection (f), by striking a Federal employee and inserting an employee.

(b) DECISIONS OF COMMISSIONS.— Section 15302 of title 40, United States Code, is amended—

(1)   in subsection (a), by inserting or alternate State members, including designees after State members; and

(2)   by striking subsection (c) and inserting the following:

"(c) QUORUMS.—

"(1) IN GENERAL.—   Subject to paragraph (2), a Commission shall determine what constitutes a quorum for meetings of the Commission.

"(2) REQUIREMENTS.—   Any quorum for meetings of a Commission shall include—

"(A)   the Federal Cochairperson or the alternate Federal Cochairperson; and

"(B)   a majority of State members or alternate State members, including designees (exclusive of members representing States delinquent under section 15304(c)(3)(C)).".

(c) ADMINISTRATIVE POWERS AND EXPENSES OF COMMISSIONS.— Section 15304(a) of title 40, United States Code, is amended—

(1)   in paragraph (5), by inserting , which may be done without a requirement for the Commission to reimburse the agency or local government after status;

(2)   by redesignating paragraphs (8) and (9) as paragraphs (9) and (10), respectively;

(3)   by inserting after paragraph (7) the following:

"(8)   collect fees for services provided and retain and expend such fees;"; and

(4)   in paragraph (10) (as so redesignated), by striking maintain a government relations office in the District of Columbia and.

(d) MEETINGS OF COMMISSIONS.— Section 15305(b) of title 40, United States Code, is amended by striking with the Federal Cochairperson and all that follows through the period at the end and inserting the following: "with—

"(1)   the Federal Cochairperson; and

"(2)   at least a majority of the State members or alternate State members (including designees) present in-person or via electronic means.".

(e) ANNUAL REPORTS.— Section 15308(a) of title 40, United States Code, is amended by striking 90 and inserting 180.

SEC. 2243. TRANSFER OF FUNDS AMONG FEDERAL AGENCIES.

(a) IN GENERAL.— Chapter 153 of subtitle V of title 40, United States Code, is amended—

(1)   by redesignating section 15308 as section 15309; and

(2)   by inserting after section 15307 the following:

"SEC. 15308. [40 U.S.C. 15308] TRANSFER OF FUNDS AMONG FEDERAL AGENCIES

"(a) IN GENERAL.— Subject to subsection (c), for purposes of this subtitle, each Commission may transfer funds to and accept transfers of funds from other Federal agencies.

"(b) TRANSFER OF FUNDS TO OTHER FEDERAL AGENCIES.— Funds made available to a Commission may be transferred to other Federal agencies if the funds are used consistently with the purposes for which the funds were specifically authorized and appropriated.

"(c) TRANSFER OF FUNDS FROM OTHER FEDERAL AGENCIES.— Funds may be transferred to any Commission under this section if—

"(1)   the statutory authority for the funds provided by the Federal agency does not expressly prohibit use of funds for authorities being carried out by a Commission; and

"(2)   the Federal agency that provides the funds determines that the activities for which the funds are to be used are otherwise eligible for funding under such a statutory authority." .

(b) CLERICAL AMENDMENT.— The analysis for chapter 153 of subtitle V of title 40, United States Code, is amended by striking the item relating to section 15308 and inserting the following:

| "15308. | Transfer of funds among Federal agencies. |
| "15309. | Annual reports." |

SEC. 2244. FINANCIAL ASSISTANCE.

(a) IN GENERAL.— Chapter 155 of subtitle V of title 40, United States Code, is amended by adding at the end the following:

"SEC. 15507. [40 U.S.C. 15507] PAYMENT OF NON-FEDERAL SHARE FOR CERTAIN FEDERAL GRANT PROGRAMS

"Amounts made available to carry out this subtitle shall be available for the payment of the non-Federal share for any project carried out under another Federal grant program—

"(1) for which a Commission is not the sole or primary funding source; and

"(2) that is consistent with the authorities of the applicable Commission.".

(b) CLERICAL AMENDMENT.— The analysis for chapter 155 of subtitle V of title 40, United States Code, is amended by adding at the end the following:

"15507.   Payment of non-Federal share for certain Federal grant programs.".

SEC. 2245. NORTHERN BORDER REGIONAL COMMISSION AREA.

Section 15733 of title 40, United States Code, is amended—

(1) in paragraph (1), by inserting Lincoln, after Knox,;

(2) in paragraph (2), by inserting Merrimack, after Grafton,; and

(3) in paragraph (3)—

(A) by inserting Schoharie, after Schenectady,; and

(B) by inserting Wyoming, after Wayne,.

SEC. 2246. SOUTHWEST BORDER REGIONAL COMMISSION AREA.

Section 15732 of title 40, United States Code, is amended—

(1) in paragraph (3)—

(A) by inserting Bernalillo, before Catron,;

(B) by inserting Cibola, Curry, De Baca, after Chaves,;

(C) by inserting Guadalupe, after Grant,;

(D) by inserting Lea, after Hidalgo,;

(E) by inserting Roosevelt, after Otero,; and

(F) by striking and Socorro and inserting Socorro, Torrance, and Valencia; and

(2) in paragraph (4)—

(A) by inserting Guadalupe, after Glasscock,; and

(B) by striking Tom Green Upton, and inserting Tom Green, Upton,.

SEC. 2247. GREAT LAKES AUTHORITY AREA.

Section 15734 of title 40, United States Code, is amended, in the matter preceding paragraph (1), by inserting the counties which contain, in part or in whole, the after consist of.

SEC. 2248. ADDITIONAL REGIONAL COMMISSION PROGRAMS.

(a) IN GENERAL.— Subtitle V of title 40, United States Code, is amended by adding at the end the following:

"CHAPTER 159— ADDITIONAL REGIONAL COMMISSION PROGRAMS

"15901. State capacity building grant program.
"15902. Demonstration health projects.

"SEC. 15901. [40 U.S.C. 15901] STATE CAPACITY BUILDING GRANT PROGRAM

"(a) DEFINITIONS.— In this section:

"(1) COMMISSION STATE.— The term 'Commission State' means a State that contains 1 or more eligible counties.

"(2) ELIGIBLE COUNTY.— The term 'eligible county' means a county described in subchapter II of chapter 157.

"(3) PROGRAM.— The term 'program' means a State capacity building grant program established by a Commission under subsection (b).

"(b) ESTABLISHMENT.— Each Commission shall establish a State capacity building grant program to provide grants to Commission States in the area served by the Commission for the purposes described in subsection (c).

"(c) PURPOSES.— The purposes of a program are to support the efforts of the Commission—

"(1) to better support business retention and expansion in eligible counties;

"(2) to create programs to encourage job creation and workforce development in eligible counties, including projects and activities, in coordination with other relevant Federal agencies, to strengthen the water sector workforce and facilitate the sharing of best practices;

"(3) to partner with universities in distressed counties (as designated under section 15702(a)(1))—

"(A) to strengthen the capacity in eligible counties to train new professionals in fields for which there is a shortage of workers;

"(B) to increase local capacity in eligible counties for project management, project execution, and financial management; and

"(C) to leverage funding sources for eligible counties;

"(4) to prepare economic and infrastructure plans for eligible counties;

"(5)   to expand access to high-speed broadband in eligible counties;

"(6) · to provide technical assistance that results in Commission investments in transportation, water, wastewater, and other critical infrastructure;

"(7)   to promote workforce development in eligible counties to support resilient infrastructure projects;

"(8)   to develop initiatives to increase the effectiveness of local development districts in eligible counties; and

"(9)   to implement new or innovative economic development practices that will better position eligible counties to compete in the global economy.

"(d) USE OF FUNDS.—

"(1) IN GENERAL.—   Funds from a grant under a program may be used to support a project, program, or related expense of the Commission State in an eligible county.

"(2) LIMITATION.— Funds from a grant under a program shall not be used for—

"(A)   the purchase of furniture, fixtures, or equipment;

"(B) the compensation of—

"(i)   any State member of the Commission (as described in section 15301(b)(1)(B)); or

"(ii)   any State alternate member of the Commission (as described in section 15301(b)(2)(B)); or

"(C)   the cost of supplanting existing State programs.

"(e) ANNUAL WORK PLAN.—

"(1) IN GENERAL.—   For each fiscal year, before providing a grant under a program, each Commission State shall provide to the Commission an annual work plan that includes the proposed use of the grant.

"(2) APPROVAL.—   No grant under a program shall be provided to a Commission State unless the Commission has approved the annual work plan of the State.

"(f) AMOUNT OF GRANT.—

"(1) IN GENERAL.— The amount of a grant provided to a Commission State under a program for a fiscal year shall be based on the proportion that—

"(A)   the amount paid by the Commission State (including any amounts paid on behalf of the Commission State by a nonprofit organization) for administrative expenses for the applicable fiscal year (as determined under section 15304(c)); bears to

"(B)   the amount paid by all Commission States served by the Commission (including any amounts paid on behalf of a Commission State by a nonprofit organization) for administrative expenses for that fiscal year (as determined under that section).

"(2) REQUIREMENT.— To be eligible to receive a grant under a program for a fiscal year, a Commission State (or a nonprofit organization on behalf of the Commission State) shall pay the amount of administrative expenses of the Commission State for the applicable fiscal year (as determined under section 15304(c)).

"(3) APPROVAL.— For each fiscal year, a grant provided under a program shall be approved and made available as part of the approval of the annual budget of the Commission.

"(g) GRANT AVAILABILITY.— Funds from a grant under a program shall be available only during the fiscal year for which the grant is provided.

"(h) REPORT.— Each fiscal year, each Commission State shall submit to the relevant Commission and make publicly available a report that describes the use of the grant funds and the impact of the program in the Commission State.

"(i) CONTINUATION OF PROGRAM AUTHORITY FOR NORTHERN BORDER REGIONAL COMMISSION.— With respect to the Northern Border Regional Commission, the program shall be a continuation of the program under section 6304(c) of the Agriculture Improvement Act of 2018 (40 U.S.C. 15501 note; Public Law 115-334) (as in effect on the day before the date of enactment of this section).

"SEC. 15902. [40 U.S.C. 15902] DEMONSTRATION HEALTH PROJECTS

"(a) PURPOSE.— To demonstrate the value of adequate health facilities and services to the economic development of the region, a Commission may make grants for the planning, construction, equipment, and operation of demonstration health, nutrition, and child care projects to serve distressed areas (referred to in this section as a 'demonstration health project'), including hospitals, regional health diagnostic and treatment centers, and other facilities and services necessary for the purposes of this section.

"(b) ELIGIBLE ENTITIES.— An entity eligible to receive a grant under this section is—

"(1)   an entity described in section 15501(a);

"(2)   an institution of higher education (as defined in section 101(a) of the Higher Education Act of 1965 (20 U.S.C. 1001(a)));

"(3)   a hospital (as defined in section 1861 of the Social Security Act (42 U.S.C. 1395x)); or

"(4)   a critical access hospital (as defined in that section).

"(c) PLANNING GRANTS.—

"(1) IN GENERAL.— A Commission may make grants for planning expenses necessary for the development and operation of demonstration health projects for the region served by the Commission.

"(2) MAXIMUM COMMISSION CONTRIBUTION.— The maximum Commission contribution for a demonstration health project that receives a grant under paragraph (1) shall be made in accordance with section

15501(d).

"(3) SOURCES OF ASSISTANCE.— A grant under paragraph (1) may be provided entirely from amounts made available to carry out this section or in combination with amounts provided under other Federal grant programs.

"(4) FEDERAL SHARE FOR GRANTS UNDER OTHER FEDERAL GRANT PROGRAMS.— Notwithstanding any provision of law limiting the Federal share in other Federal grant programs, amounts made available to carry out this subsection may be used to increase the Federal share of another Federal grant up to the maximum contribution described in paragraph (2).

"(d) CONSTRUCTION AND EQUIPMENT GRANTS.—

"(1) IN GENERAL.— A grant under this section for construction or equipment of a demonstration health project may be used for—

"(A)   costs of construction;

"(B) the acquisition of privately owned facilities—

"(i)   not operated for profit; or

"(ii)   previously operated for profit if the Commission finds that health services would not otherwise be provided in the area served by the facility if the acquisition is not made; and

"(C)   the acquisition of initial equipment.

"(2) STANDARDS FOR MAKING GRANTS.— A grant under paragraph (1)—

"(A)   shall be approved in accordance with section 15503; and

"(B)   shall not be incompatible with the applicable provisions of title VI of the Public Health Service Act (42 U.S.C. 291 et seq.), the Developmental Disabilities Assistance and Bill of Rights Act of 2000 (42 U.S.C. 15001 et seq.), and other laws authorizing grants for the construction of health- related facilities, without regard to any provisions in those laws relating to appropriation authorization ceilings or to allotments among the States.

"(3) MAXIMUM COMMISSION CONTRIBUTION.— The maximum Commission contribution for a demonstration health project that receives a grant under paragraph (1) shall be made in accordance with section 15501(d).

"(4) SOURCES OF ASSISTANCE.— A grant under paragraph (1) may be provided entirely from amounts made available to carry out this section or in combination with amounts provided under other Federal grant programs.

"(5) CONTRIBUTION TO INCREASED FEDERAL SHARE FOR OTHER FEDERAL GRANTS.— Notwithstanding any provision of law limiting the Federal share in another Federal grant program for the construction or equipment of a demonstration health project, amounts made available to carry out this subsection may be used to increase Federal grants for component facilities of a demonstration health project to a maximum of 90 percent of the cost of the facilities.

"(e) OPERATION GRANTS.—

"(1) IN GENERAL.— A grant under this section for the operation of a demonstration health project may be used for—

"(A)   the costs of operation of the facility; and

"(B)   initial operating costs, including the costs of attracting, training, and retaining qualified personnel.

"(2) STANDARDS FOR MAKING GRANTS.— A grant for the operation of a demonstration health project shall not be made unless the facility funded by the grant is—

"(A)   publicly owned;

"(B)   owned by a public or private nonprofit organization;

"(C)   a private hospital described in section 501(c)(3) of the Internal Revenue Code of 1986 and exempt from taxation under section 501(a) of that Code; or

"(D)   a private hospital that provides a certain amount of uncompensated care, as determined by the Commission, and applies for the grant in partnership with a State, local government, or Indian Tribe.

"(3) MAXIMUM COMMISSION CONTRIBUTION.— The maximum Commission contribution for a demonstration health project that receives a grant under paragraph (1) shall be made in accordance with section 15501(d).

"(4) SOURCES OF ASSISTANCE.— A grant under paragraph (1) may be provided entirely from amounts made available to carry out this section or in combination with amounts provided under other Federal grant programs for the operation of health-related facilities or the provision of health and child development services, including parts A and B of title IV and title XX of the Social Security Act (42 U.S.C. 601 et seq., 621 et seq., 1397 et seq.).

"(5) FEDERAL SHARE.— Notwithstanding any provision of law limiting the Federal share in the other Federal programs described in paragraph (4), amounts made available to carry out this subsection may be used to increase the Federal share of a grant under those programs up to the maximum contribution described in paragraph (3).

"(f) PRIORITY HEALTH PROGRAMS.— If a Commission elects to make grants under this section, the Commission shall establish specific regional health priorities for such grants that address—

"(1)   addiction treatment and access to resources helping individuals in recovery;

"(2)   workforce shortages in the healthcare industry; or

"(3)   access to services for screening and diagnosing chronic health issues.".

(b) REPEAL.— Section 6304(c) of the Agriculture Improvement Act of 2018 (40 U.S.C. 15501 note; Public Law 115-334) is repealed.

(c) CLERICAL AMENDMENT.— The table of chapters for subtitle V of title 40, United States Code, is amended by inserting after the item relating to chapter 157 the following:

"**159.** **Additional Regional Commission Programs**".

SEC. 2249. ESTABLISHMENT OF MID-ATLANTIC REGIONAL COMMISSION.

(a) ESTABLISHMENT.— Section 15301(a) of title 40, United States Code, is amended by adding at the end the following:

"(5) The Mid-Atlantic Regional Commission.".

(b) DESIGNATION OF REGION.—

(1) IN GENERAL.— Subchapter II of chapter 157 of title 40, United States Code, is amended by adding at the end the following:

"**SEC. 15735. [40 U.S.C. 15735] MID-ATLANTIC REGIONAL COMMISSION**

"The region of the Mid-Atlantic Regional Commission shall include the following counties:

"(1) DELAWARE.— Each county in the State of Delaware.

"(2) MARYLAND.— Each county in the State of Maryland that is not already served by the Appalachian Regional Commission.

"(3) PENNSYLVANIA.— Each county in the Commonwealth of Pennsylvania that is not already served by the Appalachian Regional Commission.".

(2) CLERICAL AMENDMENT.— The analysis for subchapter II of chapter 157 of title 40, United States Code, is amended by adding at the end the following:

"15735. Mid-Atlantic Regional Commission.".

(c) APPLICATION.— Section 15702(c) of title 40, United States Code, is amended—

(1) by redesignating paragraph (3) as paragraph (4); and

(2) by inserting after paragraph (2) the following:

"(3) APPLICATION.— Paragraph (2) shall not apply to a county described in paragraph (2) or (3) of section 15735.".

SEC. 2250. ESTABLISHMENT OF SOUTHERN NEW ENGLAND REGIONAL COMMISSION.

(a) ESTABLISHMENT.— Section 15301(a) of title 40, United States Code (as amended by section 2249(a)), is amended by adding at the end the following:

"(6) The Southern New England Regional Commission.".

(b) DESIGNATION OF REGION.—

(1) IN GENERAL.— Subchapter II of chapter 157 of title 40, United States Code (as amended by section 2249(b)(1)), is amended by adding at the end the following:

"SEC. 15736. [40 U.S.C. 15736] SOUTHERN NEW ENGLAND REGIONAL COMMISSION

"The region of the Southern New England Regional Commission shall include the following counties:

"(1) RHODE ISLAND.— Each county in the State of Rhode Island.

"(2) CONNECTICUT.— The counties of Hartford, Middlesex, New Haven, New London, Tolland, and Windham in the State of Connecticut.

"(3) MASSACHUSETTS.— Each county in the Commonwealth of Massachusetts.".

(2) CLERICAL AMENDMENT.— The analysis for subchapter II of chapter 157 of title 40, United States Code (as amended by section 2249(b)(2)), is amended by adding at the end the following:

"15736.   Southern New England Regional Commission.".

(c) APPLICATION.— Section 15702(c)(3) of title 40, United States Code (as amended by section 2249(c)), is amended—

(1) by striking the period at the end and inserting ; or;

(2) by striking to a county and inserting the following: "to—

"(A) a county"; and

(3) by adding at the end the following:

"(B) the Southern New England Regional Commission.".

SEC. 2251. DENALI COMMISSION REAUTHORIZATION.

(a) REAUTHORIZATION.— Section 312(a) of the Denali Commission Act of 1998 (42 U.S.C. 3121 note; Public Law 105-277) is amended by striking $15,000,000 for each of fiscal years 2017 through 2021 and inserting $35,000,000 for each of fiscal years 2025 through 2029.

(b) POWERS OF THE COMMISSION.— Section 305 of the Denali Commission Act of 1998 (42 U.S.C. 3121 note; Public Law 105-277) is amended—

(1) in subsection (d), in the first sentence, by inserting enter into leases (including the lease of office space for any term), after award grants,; and

(2) by adding at the end the following:

"(e) USE OF FUNDS TOWARD NON-FEDERAL SHARE OF CERTAIN PROJECTS.— Notwithstanding any other provision of law regarding payment of a non-Federal share in connection with a grant-in-aid program, the Commission may use amounts made available to the Commission for the payment of such a non-Federal share for programs undertaken to carry out the purposes of the Commission.".

(c) SPECIAL FUNCTIONS OF THE COMMISSION.— Section 307 of the Denali Commission Act of 1998 (42 U.S.C. 4321 note; Public Law 105-277) is amended—

(1) by striking subsection (a);

(2) by redesignating subsections (b) through (e) as subsections (a) through (d), respectively; and

(3) in subsection (c) (as so redesignated), by inserting , including interagency transfers, after payments.

(d) CONFORMING AMENDMENT.— Section 309(c)(1) of the Denali Commission Act of 1998 (42 U.S.C. 4321 note; Public Law 105-277) is amended by inserting of Transportation after Secretary.

SEC. 2252. [42 U.S.C. 3121 note] DENALI HOUSING FUND.

(a) DEFINITIONS.— In this section:

(1) ELIGIBLE ENTITY.— The term eligible entity means—

(A) a nonprofit organization;

(B) a limited dividend organization;

(C) a cooperative organization;

(D) an Indian Tribe (as defined in section 4 of the Indian Self-Determination and Education Assistance Act (25 U.S.C. 5304)); and

(E) a public entity, such as a municipality, county, district, authority, or other political subdivision of a State.

(2) FEDERAL COCHAIR.— The term Federal Cochair means the Federal Cochairperson of the Denali Commission.

(3) FUND.— The term Fund means the Denali Housing Fund established under subsection (b)(1).

(4) LOW-INCOME.— The term low-income, with respect to a household means that the household income is less than 150 percent of the Federal poverty level for the State of Alaska.

(5) MODERATE-INCOME.— The term moderate-income, with respect to a household, means that the household income is less than 250 percent of the Federal poverty level for the State of Alaska.

(6) SECRETARY.— The term Secretary means the Secretary of Agriculture.

(b) DENALI HOUSING FUND.—

(1) ESTABLISHMENT.— There shall be established in the Treasury of the United States the Denali Housing Fund, to be administered by the Federal

Cochair.

(2) SOURCE AND USE OF AMOUNTS IN FUND.—

(A) IN GENERAL.— Amounts allocated to the Federal Cochair for the purpose of carrying out this section shall be deposited in the Fund.

(B) USES.— The Federal Cochair shall use the Fund as a revolving fund to carry out the purposes of this section.

(C) INVESTMENT.— The Federal Cochair may invest amounts in the Fund that are not necessary for operational expenses in bonds or other obligations, the principal and interest of which are guaranteed by the Federal Government.

(D) GENERAL EXPENSES.— The Federal Cochair may charge the general expenses of carrying out this section to the Fund.

(3) AUTHORIZATION OF APPROPRIATIONS.— There is authorized to be appropriated to the Fund $5,000,000 for each of fiscal years 2025 through 2029.

(c) PURPOSES.— The purposes of this section are—

(1) to encourage and facilitate the construction or rehabilitation of housing to meet the needs of low-income households and moderate-income households; and

(2) to provide housing for public employees.

(d) LOANS AND GRANTS.—

(1) IN GENERAL.— The Federal Cochair may provide grants and loans from the Fund to eligible entities under such terms and conditions the Federal Cochair may prescribe.

(2) PURPOSE.— The purpose of a grant or loan under paragraph (1) shall be for planning and obtaining federally insured mortgage financing or other financial assistance for housing construction or rehabilitation projects for low-income and moderate-income households in rural Alaska villages.

(e) PROVIDING AMOUNTS TO STATES FOR GRANTS AND LOANS.— The Federal Cochair may provide amounts to the State of Alaska, or political subdivisions thereof, for making the grants and loans described in subsection (d).

(f) LOANS.—

(1) LIMITATION ON AVAILABLE AMOUNTS.— A loan under subsection (d) for the cost of planning and obtaining financing (including the cost of preliminary surveys and analyses of market needs, preliminary site engineering and architectural fees, site options, application and mortgage commitment fees, legal fees, and construction loan fees and discounts) of a project described in that subsection may be for not more than 90 percent of that cost.

(2) INTEREST.— A loan under subsection (d) shall be made without interest, except that a loan made to an eligible entity established for profit shall bear interest at the prevailing market rate authorized for an insured or guaranteed loan for that type of project.

(3) PAYMENT.—

(A) IN GENERAL.— The Federal Cochair shall require payment of a loan made under this section under terms and conditions the Secretary may require by not later than the date of completion of the project.

(B) CANCELLATION.— For a loan other than a loan to an eligible entity established for profit, the Secretary may cancel any part of the debt with respect to a loan made under subsection (d) if the Secretary determines that a permanent loan to finance the project cannot be obtained in an amount adequate for repayment of a loan made under subsection (d).

(g) GRANTS.—

(1) IN GENERAL.— A grant under this section for expenses incidental to planning and obtaining financing for a project described in this section that the Federal Cochair considers unrecoverable from the proceeds of a permanent loan made to finance the project—

(A) may not be made to an eligible entity established for profit; and

(B) may not exceed 90 percent of those expenses.

(2) SITE DEVELOPMENT COSTS AND OFFSITE IMPROVEMENTS.—

(A) IN GENERAL.— The Federal Cochair may make grants and commitments for grants under terms and conditions the Federal Cochair may require to eligible entities for reasonable site development costs and necessary offsite improvements, such as sewer and water line extensions, if the grant or commitment—

(i) is essential to ensuring that housing is constructed on the site in the future; and

(ii) otherwise meets the requirements for assistance under this section.

(B) MAXIMUM AMOUNTS.— The amount of a grant under this paragraph may not—

(i) with respect to the construction of housing, exceed 40 percent of the cost of the construction; and

(ii) with respect to the rehabilitation of housing, exceed 10 percent of the reasonable value of the rehabilitation, as determined by the Federal Cochair.

(h) INFORMATION, ADVICE, AND TECHNICAL ASSISTANCE.— The Federal Cochair may provide, or contract with public or private organizations to provide, information, advice, and technical assistance with respect to the construction, rehabilitation, and operation by nonprofit organizations of housing for low-income or moderate-income households, or for public employees, in rural Alaska villages under this section.

SEC. 2253. DELTA REGIONAL AUTHORITY REAUTHORIZATION.

(a) AUTHORIZATION OF APPROPRIATIONS.— Section 382M(a) of the Consolidated Farm and Rural Development Act (7 U.S.C. 2009aa-12(a)) is amended by striking $30,000,000 for each of fiscal years 2019 through 2023 and inserting $40,000,000 for each of fiscal years 2025 through 2029.

(b) TERMINATION OF AUTHORITY.— Section 382N of the Consolidated Farm and Rural Development Act (7 U.S.C. 2009aa-13) is repealed.

(c) FEES.— Section 382B(e) of the Consolidated Farm and Rural Development Act (7 U.S.C. 2009aa-1(e)) is amended—

    (1) in paragraph (9)(C), by striking and at the end;

    (2) in paragraph (10), by striking the period at the end and inserting ; and; and

    (3) by adding at the end the following:

      "(11) collect fees for the Delta Doctors program of the Authority and retain and expend those fees.".

(d) SUCCESSION.— Section 382B(h)(5)(B) of the Consolidated Farm and Rural Development Act (7 U.S.C. 2009aa-1(h)(5)(B)) is amended—

    (1) in clause (ii), by striking and at the end;

    (2) by redesignating clause (iii) as clause (iv); and

    (3) by inserting after clause (ii) the following:

      "(iii) assuming the duties of the Federal cochairperson and the alternate Federal cochairperson for purposes of continuation of normal operations in the event that both positions are vacant; and".

(e) INDIAN TRIBES.— Section 382C(a) of the Consolidated Farm and Rural Development Act (7 U.S.C. 2009aa-2(a)) is amended—

    (1) in the matter preceding paragraph (1), by inserting , Indian Tribes, after States; and

    (2) in paragraph (1), by inserting , Tribal, after State.

(f) CLARIFICATION.— Section 4(2)(D) of the Delta Development Act (42 U.S.C. 3121 note; Public Law 100-460) is amended by inserting Sabine, Vernon, Terrebonne, after Webster,.

SEC. 2254. NORTHERN GREAT PLAINS REGIONAL AUTHORITY REAUTHORIZATION.

(a) AUTHORIZATION OF APPROPRIATIONS.— Section 383N(a) of the Consolidated Farm and Rural Development Act (7 U.S.C. 2009bb-12(a)) is amended by striking $30,000,000 for each of fiscal years 2008 through 2018 and inserting $40,000,000 for each of fiscal years 2025 through 2029.

(b) TERMINATION OF AUTHORITY.— Section 383O of the Consolidated Farm and Rural Development Act (7 U.S.C. 2009bb-13) is repealed.

★

Title 42 U.S.C., Chapter 28– Public Works and Economic Development

Economic Development Administration Reauthorization Act of 2004 - Sec. 605

Appalachian Regional Development

Regional Economic and Infrastructure Development

Denali Commission

Energy Policy Act of 2005–Sec. 356

Department of Transportation and Related Agencies Appropriations Act, 1999–Sec. 329

Delta Regional Authority

Great Northern Plains Regional Authority

Federal Capital Investment Program Information Act of 1984)

Title 31 U.S.C. Sec. 1105(e)

Delta Regional Authority Act of 2000

Economic Development Reauthorization Act of 2024

www.ingramcontent.com/pod-product-compliance
Lightning Source LLC
Chambersburg PA
CBHW061024220326
41597CB00019BB/3248